Human Well-Being Research and Policy Making

Series Editor

M. Joseph Sirgy , Department of Marketing, Virginia Polytechnic Institute &
State University, Blacksburg, VA, USA

This series includes policy-focused books on the role of the public and private sectors in advancing quality of life and well-being. It creates a dialogue between well-being scholars and public policy makers. Well-being theory, research and practice are essentially interdisciplinary in nature and embrace contributions from all disciplines within the social sciences. With the exception of leading economists, the policy relevant contributions of social scientists are widely scattered and lack the coherence and integration needed to more effectively inform the actions of policy makers. Contributions in the series focus on one more of the following four aspects of well-being and public policy:

- Discussions of the public policy and well-being focused on particular nations and worldwide regions
- Discussions of the public policy and well-being in specialized sectors of policy making such as health, education, work, social welfare, housing, transportation, use of leisure time
- Discussions of public policy and well-being associated with particular population groups such as women, children and youth, the aged, persons with disabilities and vulnerable populations
- Special topics in well-being and public policy such as technology and well-being, terrorism and well-being, infrastructure and well-being.

This series was initiated, in part, through funds provided by the Halloran Philanthropies of West Conshohocken, Pennsylvania, USA. The commitment of the Halloran Philanthropies is to "inspire, innovate and accelerate sustainable social interventions that promote human well-being." The series editors and Springer acknowledge Harry Halloran, Tony Carr and Audrey Selian for their contributions in helping to make the series a reality.

Stephanie Rossouw • Talita Greyling

Resistance to COVID-19 Vaccination

Drivers, Impact on Human Wellbeing, and Policy Implications

 Springer

Stephanie Rossouw
School of Social Science and Humanities
Auckland University of Technology
Auckland, New Zealand

Talita Greyling
School of Economics, College of Business
and Economics
University of Johannesburg
Centurion, South Africa

ISSN 2522-5367 ISSN 2522-5375 (electronic)
Human Well-Being Research and Policy Making
ISBN 978-3-031-56528-1 ISBN 978-3-031-56529-8 (eBook)
https://doi.org/10.1007/978-3-031-56529-8

This Springer imprint is published by the registered company Springer Nature Switzerland AG
The registered company address is: Gewerbestrasse 11, 6330 Cham, Switzerland

If disposing of this product, please recycle the paper.

Contents

Chapter 1
Introduction

Abstract The introductory chapter overviews the multifaceted challenges surrounding COVID-19 vaccination campaigns worldwide. Drawing upon Sherlock Holmes' dictum that the most extraordinary incidents merit thorough examination, the chapter signals what is to follow in subsequent chapters: complex emotional responses, widespread mistrust, and dissemination of misinformation that have characterised the COVID-19 vaccine rollout. It highlights the compounding effects of pandemic-related regulations on mental health and the emergence of vaccine hesitancy, exacerbated by concerns over novel vaccine technologies and reported adverse effects. Moreover, it addresses misconceptions regarding excess mortality and the vaccine's role, emphasising the urgency for governments to combat both the virus and growing resistance to vaccination. Relying on data from the World Health Organization, the chapter underscores the need for effective strategies to overcome vaccine hesitancy and inequality of vaccine distribution between nations. It argues for transparent communication, rigorous safety protocols, and policy interventions to rebuild public trust and ensure equitable vaccine access. The chapter also outlines the book's significance in providing insights into vaccine resistance's social, psychological, and policy dimensions, its implications for public health, and its relevance beyond the COVID-19 pandemic. Through multi-country analyses and practical frameworks, the book aims to equip policymakers with evidence-based strategies for addressing vaccine hesitancy and fostering community engagement in global health crises.

Keywords COVID-19 · Vaccine hesitancy · Mistrust · Side-effects · Excess mortality

> "The more outré and grotesque an incident is, the more carefully it deserves to be examined."
> – Sherlock Holmes

In an attempt to curb the spread of COVID-19, minimise the loss of life and take the pressure off the national health systems, governments worldwide started their vaccine rollout campaigns late in December 2020. The rapid deployment of the

S. Rossouw, T. Greyling, *Resistance to COVID-19 Vaccination*, Human
Well-Being Research and Policy Making,
https://doi.org/10.1007/978-3-031-56529-8_1

COVID-19 vaccine was justified since governments argued that receiving the vaccine was the best possible solution to open up economies and prevent loss of life. However, this rapid rollout of the COVID-19 vaccine created different emotional responses across the globe.

Compounding the problem was the mistrust in governments' abilities to procure and administer the rollout of vaccines and the spread of fake news by anti-vaxxers (for example, see Sharma et al., 2021; Bonnevie et al., 2021). Spreading fear and anxiety is a significant problem because we know from the existing literature that vaccine efficacy depends not only on the vaccine but also on the characteristics of the vaccinated (Glaser et al., 1992; Madison et al., 2021). Unfortunately, COVID-19 pandemic regulations such as lockdowns increased depression, loneliness, and stress levels, increasing the efficacy problem (Madison et al., 2021).

Additionally, there is widespread scepticism in pharmaceutical companies such as Pfizer, as the concept and mechanisms of its COVID-19 vaccine, using mRNA technology, are rather distinct from classic vaccines using better-known platforms. Furthermore, accepting future COVID-19 vaccines has been significantly impacted by reported adverse effects previously deemed 'very rare'. For example, a study by Oster et al. (2022) found that the crude reporting rates of myocarditis within 7 days following COVID-19 vaccination surpassed the anticipated rates across age and sex. Alarming, it was the younger male cohorts who received their second dose who suffered the most from myocarditis, aged between 12 and 24 years.

Moreover, research indicating potential connections between COVID-19 policies and excess mortality[1] death rates has meant that many people incorrectly believe that the COVID-19 vaccine was a significant contributing factor. While it is true that the COVID-19 period of 2020–2021 has seen 14.91 million excess deaths, of which 9.49 million more deaths are not directly attributable to COVID-19, it is not possible to discern how many deaths are directly related to the vaccine versus indirectly related to COVID-19, due to other causes and diseases, resulting from the wider impact of the pandemic on health systems and society (World Health Organization (WHO), 2022).

Currently, governments face a dual problem. On the one hand, they continue to fight a virus that mutates and spreads, causing new waves of infections to appear worldwide, posing an ongoing threat to public health and the global economy. On the other hand, they confront this growing resistance to vaccination (for all the reasons mentioned above), which could prove catastrophic when facing future pandemics. The latest data from the World Health Organization, as shown in Fig. 1.1, clearly indicate the emergence of a concerning trend, reflecting a general perception that people are no longer taking COVID-19 seriously.

Figure 1.1 shows that the number of people receiving COVID-19 booster shots has reached a plateau in all but high-income countries, underscoring a potential complacency in the ongoing battle against the coronavirus. We further see the

---

[1] Excess mortality is defined as the difference between the total number of deaths that have occurred and the number of deaths that would have been expected in the absence of the pandemic i.e., a no-COVID-19 scenario (World Health Organization (WHO), 2022).

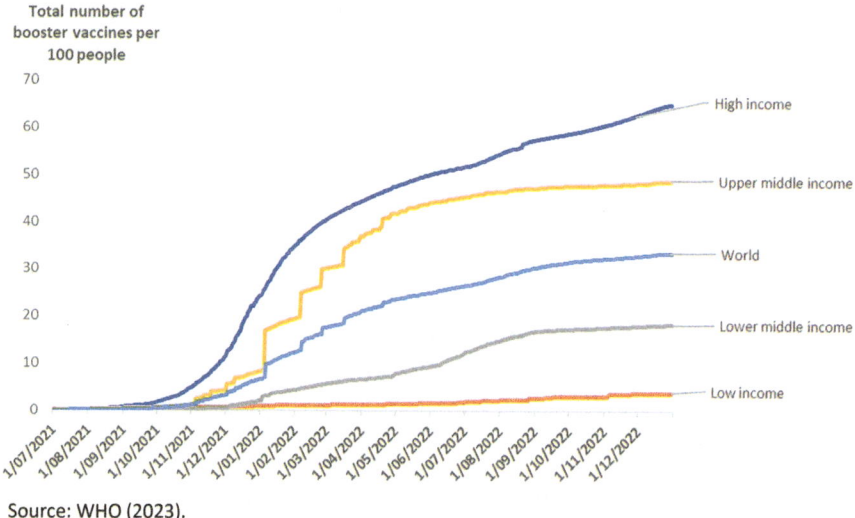

Source: WHO (2023).

Fig. 1.1 Persons received a booster or additional dose per 100 population. *Source*: World Health Organization (WHO) (2023)

significant disparity between high and upper-middle-income countries versus lower-middle and low-income countries. While initial vaccination campaigns showed remarkable global solidarity, the decreasing rate of booster uptake suggests a growing disconnect between the urgency of continued vaccination efforts and public sentiment. Therefore, the need for governments to find effective strategies to overcome vaccine hesitancy is more pressing than ever.

As this book will show, governments have a critical role in reestablishing trust in their capability to procure and distribute vaccines efficiently. Additionally, governments must ensure that their communication is transparent since it is of paramount importance in combating the widespread dissemination of vaccine-related misinformation. Furthermore, governments must be upfront about vaccine adverse effects and ensure the dissemination of accurate information to allow people to make informed decisions related to their healthcare. In parallel, pharmaceutical companies must actively work to regain the public's trust. They must convince the public that they adhere to rigorous safety protocols during vaccine trials, commit to transparency regarding potential adverse effects, and strictly avoid any perceived involvement in controversial gain-of-function research.

Moreover, the different country experiences detailed in this book regarding non-pharmaceutical and pharmaceutical interventions dealing with COVID-19 can provide valuable lessons and insights for crafting effective policies and public health strategies.

Therefore, this book is essential to understand and address these issues for the following reasons. First, vaccine hesitancy and resistance are not simple issues; instead, there are underlying complexities encompassing social, psychological, cultural and emotional factors. Our multi-country analyses in Chaps. 4, 5 and 7–10 will provide valuable insights into the complexities of the resistance to COVID-19 vaccination. Second, vaccine hesitancy can have dire public health consequences because it endangers the lives of those who remain unvaccinated and hinders the progress toward achieving herd immunity. Our analyses in Chaps. 11 and 13 address the impact of vaccine resistance on human well-being and relationships, highlighting the potential dangers when there is negative vaccine discourse. Third, the policy implications of vaccine resistance are immense. Governments, healthcare professionals, pharmaceutical companies, and public health organisations need evidence-based insights to develop effective strategies for combatting hesitancy and resistance. Chapter 12 and 14 provide information to policymakers that can aid in crafting vaccination campaigns and public health policies sensitive to different populations' nuances.

Fourth, beyond the 2020/2021 COVID-19 pandemic, understanding vaccine resistance can provide valuable lessons for future public health challenges. The insights gained from our multi-country analyses in Chaps. 9 and 10 can be applied to other vaccination campaigns and health initiatives, ensuring we are better prepared for the next pandemic. Lastly, listening to communities' concerns is vitally important to overcome vaccine resistance. We provide frameworks and practical examples of how governments can listen to communities in real-time in Chaps. 6, 9 and 14, giving governments significant future predictive powers regarding global pandemics.

References

Bonnevie, E., Gallegos-Jeffrey, A., Goldbarg, J., Byrd, B., & Smyser, J. (2021). Quantifying the rise of vaccine opposition on twitter during the COVID-19 pandemic. *Journal of Communication in Healthcare, 14*(1), 12–19.

Glaser, R., Kiecolt-Glaser, J. K., Bonneau, R. H., Malarkey, W., Kennedy, S., & Hughes, J. (1992). Stress-induced modulation of the immune response to recombinant hepatitis B vaccine. *Psychosomatic Medicine, 54*(1), 22–29.

Madison, A. A., Shrout, M. R., Renna, M. E., & Kiecolt-Glaser, J. K. (2021). Psychological and behavioral predictors of vaccine efficacy: Considerations for COVID-19. *Perspectives on Psychological Science, 16*(2), 191–203.

Oster, M. E., Shay, D. K., Su, J. R., et al. (2022). Myocarditis cases reported after mRNA-based COVID-19 vaccination in the US from December 2020 to august 2021. *JAMA, 327*(4), 331–340.

Sharma, K., Zhang, Y., & Liu, Y. (2021). COVID-19 vaccines: Characterising misinformation campaigns and vaccine hesitancy on Twitter. *arXiv*: 2106.0842.

World Health Organization (WHO). (2022). Global excess deaths associated with COVID-19, January 2020–December 2021. https://www.who.int/data/stories/global-excess-deaths-associated-with-covid-19-january-2020-december-2021. Accessed 16.11.23.

World Health Organization (WHO). (2023). WHO Coronavirus (COVID-19) Dashboard. https://covid19.who.int/?mapFilter=vaccinations. Accessed 16.11.23.

Part I
Understanding the COVID-19 pandemic

The book unfolds progressively, with chapters moving from the general to the particular. Part I commences by focusing on the history of pandemics and their impact on society. From there, we introduce the audience to the origins and epidemiology of COVID-19 and outline how the authorisation of COVID-19 vaccines by many countries, a decision based on imperfect information, sowed seeds of mistrust in governments. We retroactively explore revelations regarding the shortcomings of pharmaceutical companies in ensuring the efficacy of the COVID-19 vaccine, a factor that could impact future vaccine acceptance. Additionally, we inform readers about alternative pharmaceutical interventions designed to alleviate COVID-19 symptoms and potentially prevent hospitalisation.

Subsequently, Part I illustrates the evolution of COVID-19 and policies implemented to curb the spread of the virus across the Northern and Southern hemispheres by discussing individual country case studies. We include country case studies from Europe, Australasia and Africa, therefore giving attention to regions of the world (Africa) that remain outside the current reach of effective prevention and treatment approaches to COVID-19. The various policies, such as lockdowns and the rollout of the COVID-19 vaccine, followed by each country during the COVID-19 pandemic, are discussed, highlighting key differences.

Part I
Understanding the COVID-19 pandemic

Chapter 2
History of Pandemics

Abstract This chapter discusses pandemics' historical context and impacts, focusing on case studies including the 1918 Influenza pandemic, H1N1, and Severe Acute Respiratory Syndrome (SARS). We provide a timeline of significant pandemics since the late 1800s and highlight key events and estimated death tolls. Through detailed analyses of our three case studies, we explore the spread and the impact on people's health and the economic consequences of each pandemic.

The 1918 Influenza pandemic, characterised by three waves, is an example of a devastating global health crisis. Despite the absence of pharmaceutical interventions, the pandemic eventually subsided, showcasing the resilience of the human immune system. SARS, discovered in 2003, highlighted issues of transparency and coordination in disease response, impacting global economies through decreased consumer demand and reduced confidence.

The emergence of H1N1 in 2009 led to the first global flu pandemic in four decades. Government responses, such as social distancing measures, were crucial in controlling the outbreak. Additionally, the chapter delves into the macroeconomic implications of flu outbreaks, explaining how they affect various economic indicators and sectors.

Lessons from these pandemics underscore the importance of government transparency, effective coordination, and international cooperation in disease response. Furthermore, the chapter emphasises the intricate relationship between health crises, economic growth, and human capital development. This comprehensive analysis provides valuable insights into navigating future health crises and their economic consequences.

Keywords Influenza · H1N1 · SARS · Public policy · Macroeconomics

2.1   Introduction

This chapter starts with a brief historical timeline of previous pandemics and presents case studies of the 1918 Influenza pandemic, H1N1 and SARS virus. Through these three case studies, we will explore the impact on health, well-being and the economy and discuss public policy that arose from addressing these pandemics. The chapter ends with a discussion of the macroeconomics of flu and how we generally view the temporary effects of a health disruption on the economy.

2.2   History of Previous Pandemics

Pandemics[1] have played a role in shaping human history throughout the ages. The nexus between epidemiologic, demographic and risk transition processes shapes morbidity and mortality profile changes. Moreover, globalisation and environmental influences, with consequential climatic repercussions, have intensified these changes. Table 2.1 provides a historical timeline of significant pandemics worldwide from the late 1800s. As can be seen, the only pandemic still ongoing is HIV/AIDS, whose death toll is starting to catch up with that of the Spanish flu (1918 Influenza flu).

Let's focus on this chapter's three case studies: the 1918 Influenza pandemic, H1N1 and the SARS virus.

2.2.1   The 1918 Influenza Pandemic

In 1918, a new influenza type A subtype, H1N1 virus (Fig. 2.1), emerged, lasting between 1 and 2 years. The spread of the virus was set ablaze by conditions such as overcrowding, and to date, there is no consensus on the origin of the virus. Be it as

Table 2.1 Timeline and estimated death toll of pandemics since the late 1800s

Name	Time Period	Type/Pre-human host	Estimated death toll
Yellow fever	Late 1800s	Virus/Mosquitoes	100,000–150,000 (US)
Russian flu	1889–1890	H2N2 (avian origin)	1 million
Spanish flu	1918–1919	H1N1 virus/pigs	40–50 million
Asian flu	1957–1958	H2N2 virus	1.One million
Hong Kong flu	1968–1970	H3N2 virus	1 million
HIV/AIDS	1981-present	Virus/chimpanzees	25–35 million
SARS	2002–2003	Coronavirus/bats, civets	770
Swine flu	2009–2010	H1N1 virus/pigs	284,400
Ebola	2014–2016	Ebolavirus/ wild animals	11,000

Source: Brodeur et al. (2020)

---

[1] The worldwide spread of a new disease.

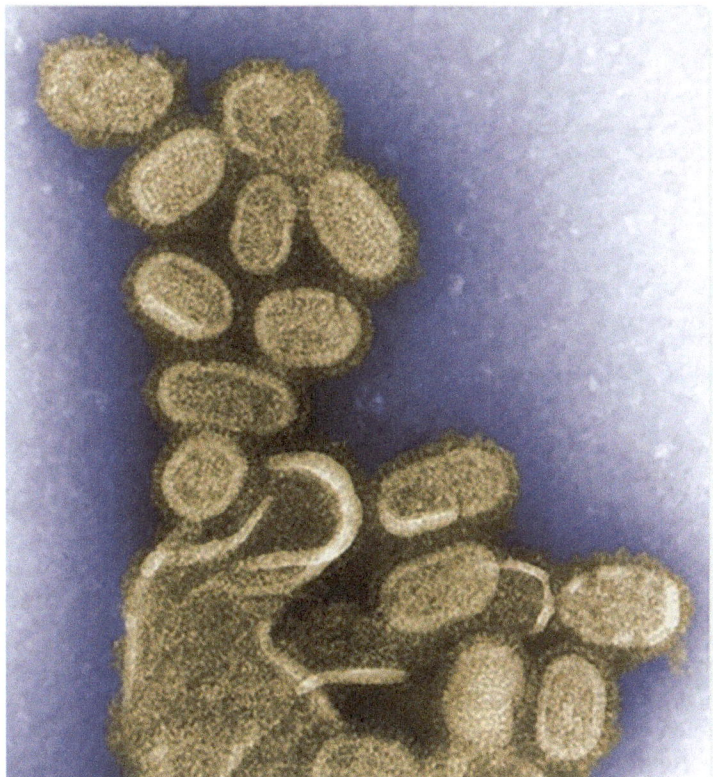

Source: Centers for Disease Control and Prevention (2013). In the public domain.

Fig. 2.1 A colourised image of the 1918 type A subtype H1N1 virus. *Source*: Centers for Disease Control and Prevention (2013). In the public domain

it may, the virus, which was transmitted from person to person through airborne respiratory secretions, spread exponentially to the entire world in less than 6 months (Patterson & Pyle, 1991).

The pandemic occurred in three waves. The first wave (see Fig. 2.2) started in early March 1918, during World War I (1914–1918), with the earliest recorded outbreak among army recruits at Camp Funston, Kansas, US (Patterson & Pyle, 1991). The virus spread quickly through Western Europe, and by July 1918, it had spread to Poland. Outbreaks of the flu occurred in nearly every inhabited part of the world except in Russia and Sub-Saharan Africa (SSA). The virus managed to reach distant islands in the South Pacific, including New Zealand and Samoa. The first wave of influenza was comparatively mild, and mortality rates were low.

The second wave came during the European summer, recognising a more lethal type of disease, and this form fully emerged in August 1918 (Britannica, 2023). The first reports were from Brest in France, a major Atlantic port and landing point for American troops, on 22 August (Patterson & Pyle, 1991). This time, it didn't spare either SSA or Russia. Pneumonia often manifests rapidly, with death usually coming 2 days after the initial flu symptoms surfaced. For example, at Camp Devens,

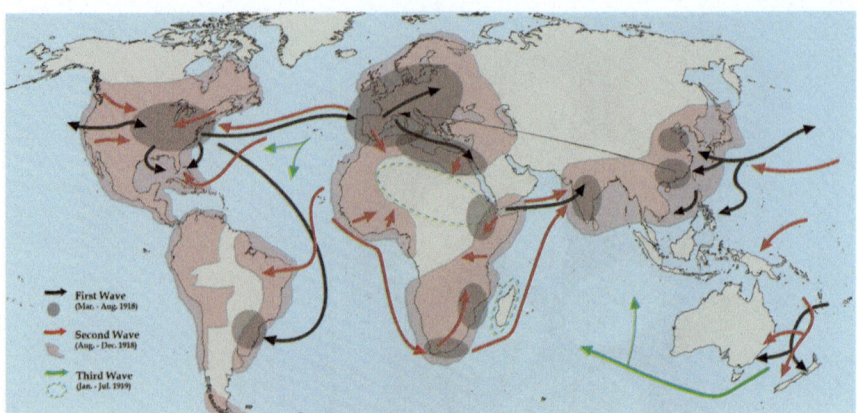

Fig. 2.2 Worldwide diffusion of influenza: first wave. *Source*: Africa Center for Strategic Studies (2020) based on Patterson and Pyle (1991). In the public domain

Massachusetts, US, 6 days after the first influenza case, a staggering 6674 cases were reported (Britannica, 2023). The third wave of the pandemic unfolded in the winter of 1919, and by spring, the virus completely subsided. In the two latter waves, nearly half of the fatalities were among 20–40-year-olds, an unusual mortality age pattern for influenza.

How did the virus spread? First, it spread from ports, then from city to city along the main transportation routes and through global troop movement during the war. The vulnerability of healthy young adults and the lack of vaccines and treatments created a major public health crisis, with the second wave causing at least 30 million deaths worldwide and making it among the most devastating pandemics in human history (Jordan, 1927; Vaughan 1921; Patterson & Pyle, 1991).

During 1918 and 1919, no effective medications or antibiotics existed to treat the infections that people got as complications of the flu. There were also no mechanical ventilation machines or intensive care units, nor were any nationwide preventative measures introduced. How did the pandemic end? According to Barry (2005), those who contracted the virus developed an immunity to the novel strand of influenza over time, and life returned to normal by the early 1920s.

2.2.2   Severe Acute Respiratory Syndrome

Health professionals first discovered Severe Acute Respiratory Syndrome (SARS) (Fig. 2.3) in Asia in February 2003. By March 2003, the World Health Organization (WHO) issued a global alert for a severe form of pneumonia of unknown origin in

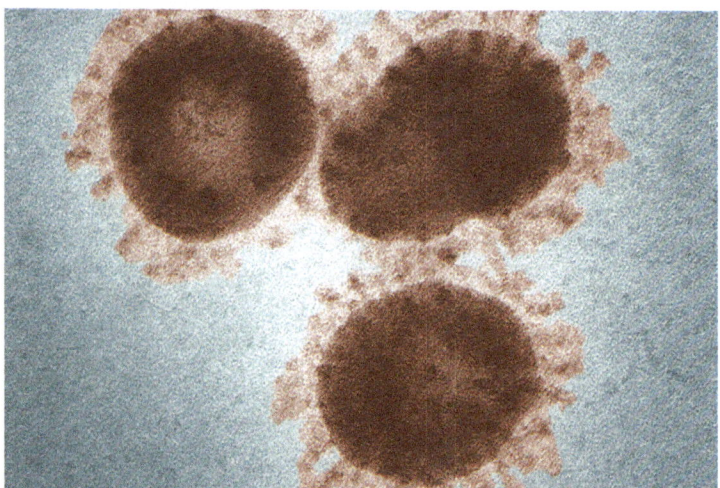

Source: Centers for Disease Control and Prevention (2013). In the public domain.

Fig. 2.3 SARS-associated coronavirus. *Source*: Centers for Disease Control and Prevention (2013). In the public domain

persons from China, Vietnam, and Hong Kong (Centers for Disease Control and Prevention, 2013).

In the 8 months after its first outbreak in China in Guangdong province on 1 November 2002, the SARS disease spread to 30 economies in North America, South America, Europe, and Asia, infecting 8437 people and causing 813 deaths worldwide (see Fig. 2.4; Lee & McKibbin, 2012). This pandemic largely spared Africa. In July 2003, the WHO announced that the global SARS outbreak was contained (Centers for Disease Control and Prevention, 2013).

The SARS outbreak highlighted several sociopolitical problems in Chinese society, including a lack of transparency, dissemination of inaccurate information, and insufficient coordination between central and local authorities. The Chinese government's response to the epidemic was fragmented and obscure. Only on 11 February 2003 did the Chinese Ministry of Health inform the WHO of an acute respiratory syndrome outbreak for the first time (Lee & McKibbin, 2012). As discussed in Chap. 3, the COVID-19 pandemic highlighted the same issues.

SARS influenced the global economy in three ways. First, fear of SARS led to a substantial decrease in consumer demand, especially for sectors such as travel and retail, since people avoided social interactions due to the fast contagion rate. The decrease in consumption had a more pronounced effect on regions such as Beijing and Hong Kong, which had more service industries and higher population densities. Second, confidence in the future decreased due to uncertainty related to future epidemics—this significantly impacted economies, particularly China, a primary foreign investment recipient. Third, the cost of disease prevention undoubtedly increased because of SARS, especially for sectors such as travel, retail and service industries. This cost was not substantial as long as the disease was transmitted only by close human contact. Still, the global cost would have been enormous if experts had discovered transmission through other channels, like international cargo (Lee & McKibbin, 2012).

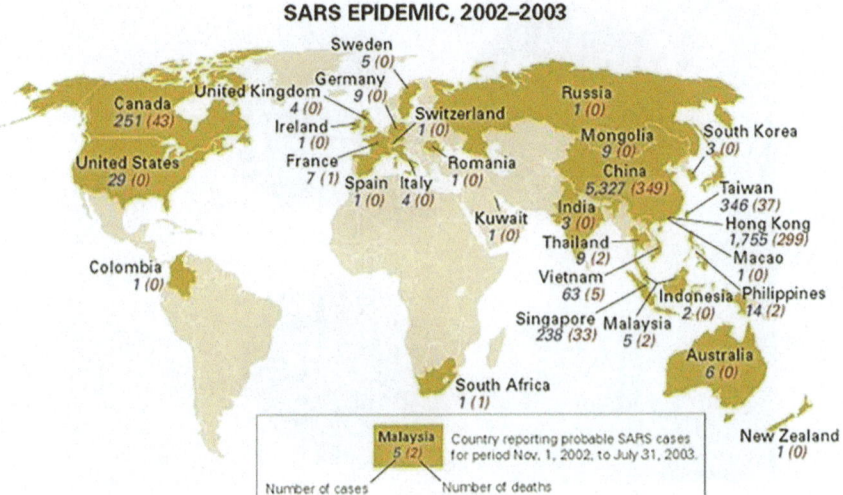

Fig. 2.4 Spread of SARS March to July 2003. *Source*: Britannica (2024). In the public domain

2.2.3   H1N1 (Swine Flu)

In 2009, a new H1N1 influenza virus emerged (Fig. 2.5), causing the first global flu pandemic in 40 years. Swine flu was a highly contagious acute respiratory disease of pigs caused by one of several influenza A viruses. Researchers have identified three predominant flu virus subtypes in pigs: H1N1, H1H2, and H3N2. The Mexican virus, belonging to the H1N1 family, derives its name from its two surface proteins. Notably, mortality rates in pigs tend to be low, ranging between 1 and 4%. Human infection with swine flu has been detected sporadically since the late 1950s, typically among individuals working closely with pigs, but secondary cases after human-to-human transmission have been infrequent. Coombes (2009) found the A/ H1N1 virus contained a unique combination of genes from pig, bird, and human flu viruses.

In La Gloria, Veracruz, Mexico, in February 2009, it is thought that the first significant outbreak associated with this strain occurred. According to Córdova-Villalobos et al. (2009), the Mexican government issued an epidemiologic alert on 17 April and declared a "state of sanitary contingency" on 23 April 2009. This declaration intensified preventive and control measures, leading to the cancellation of all education activities. On 27 April, the country implemented social distancing measures. Following the social distancing regulations, they implemented the next phase of measures, including cancelling all events held indoors or outdoors and all activities related to the federal public administration, except those deemed necessary to ensure appropriate, timely, and continuous service provision.

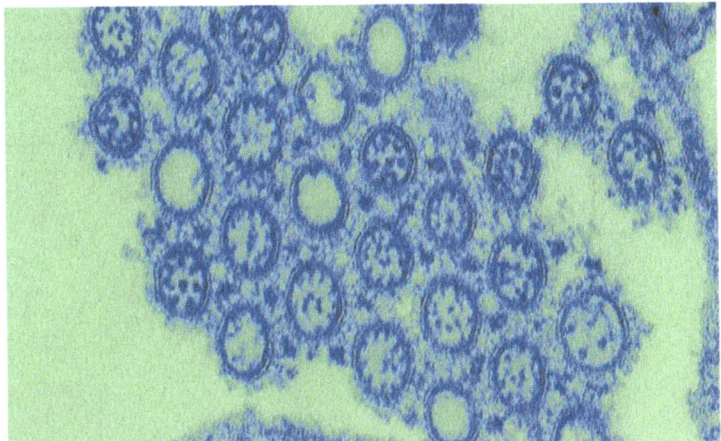

Source: Centers for Disease Control and Prevention (2013). In the public domain.

Fig. 2.5 Image of a number of virions from the novel influenza H1N1. *Source*: Centers for Disease Control and Prevention (2013). In the public domain

As the epidemic evolved, analysts examined its behaviour and effects, and policymakers decided to restore the country's economic, social, and educational sectors. Less than 2 weeks after the declaration of the "sanitary contingency", the government worked to restore life as normal, first with mid-higher and higher education academic institutions resuming their activities and then the primary education activities (Córdova-Villalobos et al., 2009). It is important to note that the return of the education sector depended on the number of new cases.

They registered the first case in California in the US on 15 April 2009. By 19 June, all 50 states, the District of Colombia, Puerto Rico, and the US Virgin Islands had confirmed cases (Centers for Disease Control and Prevention, 2010).

By August 2010, the WHO declared the pandemic over, with the virus causing an estimated 284,400 deaths worldwide (see Fig. 2.6).

2.3   Directing Future Health Responses

Some important lessons from previous pandemics should have been at the forefront for policymakers when COVID-19 hit. Transparency is of significant importance, especially when facing uncertainty (Grant, 2003). Acknowledging people's fears and actively working to maintain their confidence is essential. In today's globalised world, transparency is of even bigger significance, given that a loss of foreign investors' confidence could significantly impact foreign investment flows and economic growth. It also underscores the imperative to strengthen international cooperation regarding disease response.

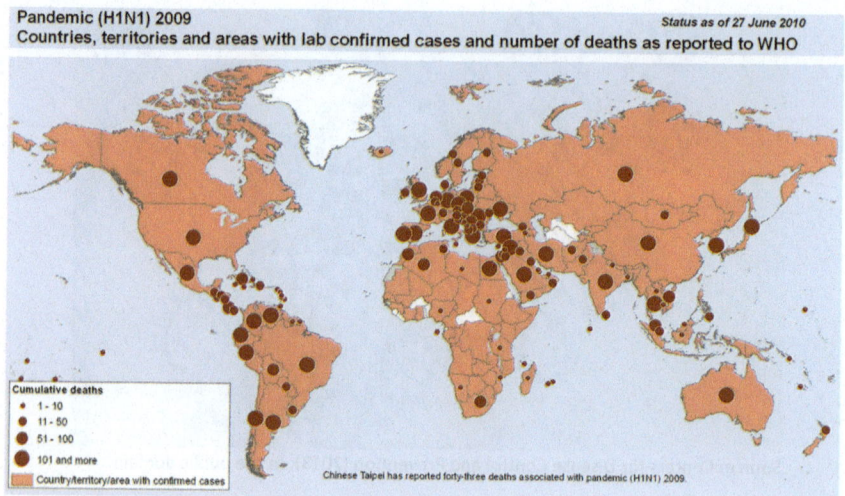

Source: WHO (2010). In the public domain.

Fig. 2.6 Spread of H1N1 at the end of the pandemic in 2010. *Source*: World Health Organization (WHO) (2010). In the public domain

From our pandemic case studies (discussed in-depth in Chaps. 3 and 12), it becomes evident that there was a substantial need to improve the quality of government responses, such as coordination and information sharing between agencies and national and local governments. Better coordination and information sharing among the aforementioned actors is key for an effective and collaborative response to a public health crisis.

Finally, the outbreak of previous pandemics underscores the idea that an important role of governments in an interdependent but uncertain world is to manage risk, establish processes for responding appropriately to unforeseen events, and coordinate policy responses and information sharing globally.

2.4 Macroeconomics of Flu

In macroeconomics, the impact of a health disruption such as a flu outbreak on an economy is typically viewed through the lens of a temporary shock or a short-term economic disturbance (refer to Sect. 11.6 for the effect of non-vaccination on the economy). These disruptions can significantly influence various macroeconomic indicators, including gross domestic product (GDP), inflation, unemployment, and overall economic activity. The consequences of health disruptions are multifaceted and can have broad implications for both the demand and supply sides of the economy.

When a flu outbreak or similar health crisis occurs, it can lead to a decline in economic activity due to a reduction in aggregate demand. People tend to reduce their consumption and avoid public places, impacting sectors like retail, tourism, hospitality, and transportation. Consequently, consumer spending, which is a major component of GDP, decreases, causing a temporary economic downturn. Business investment may also decline as uncertainty rises, affecting the supply side of the economy (Barro, 2013).

The labour market is profoundly affected during a health crisis, with increasing sickness rates leading to a higher number of absences from work. This affects productivity and could potentially cause disruptions in production itself. Furthermore, businesses might implement social distancing measures or operate at reduced capacity, impacting employment levels. Moreover, those workers who become sick or need to care for family members may be unable to work, contributing to higher unemployment rates (Bloom et al., 2018).

Government interventions, such as public health measures and stimulus packages, play a crucial role in mitigating the economic impact of a flu outbreak. Governments often implement measures to contain the spread of the flu, such as lockdowns, travel restrictions, and quarantine protocols. While these measures may dampen economic activity in the short term, they are considered essential for public health and preventing further economic damage in the long run.

Fiscal and monetary policies are key tools used by governments to counter the adverse economic effects of a health disruption. Fiscal policies involve government spending and taxation adjustments, while monetary policies focus on interest rate changes and money supply. During a health crisis, governments may implement fiscal stimulus packages to support affected sectors and individuals, and central banks may lower interest rates to encourage borrowing and investment, aiming to stimulate economic growth (World Bank, 2014).

The majority of earlier studies on the economic effects of epidemics focused on direct medical costs or income losses due to disease-related morbidity and mortality. These costs encompass both private and public expenditures on diagnosing and treating the disease. Costs are also associated with the heightened necessity for maintaining sterile environments, implementing prevention measures, and conducting primary research (Commission on Macroeconomics and Health 2002).

There are three main ways that disease impedes economic well-being and development. The first channel is the most direct: the number of years of healthy life expectancy is reduced by avoidable diseases. The combination of early deaths and chronic disability means society faces shorter lives, and this creates significant economic losses. The second channel is on parental investments in children due to the effect of disease. Societies with high rates of infant[2] and child[3] mortality experience higher fertility rates, partially to counterbalance the frequency with which children die. However, larger numbers of children have a circular effect in that it reduces the ability of low-income families to invest in each child's health and educational needs. The third channel is the adverse effects of disease on returns from business and infrastructure investment; broadly speaking, it does not include worker productivity.

---

[2] Deaths under 1 year of age.

[3] Deaths under 5 years of age.

A high disease prevalence undermines entire agriculture, mining, manufacturing, and tourism industries, as well as essential infrastructure projects. In addition, epidemic and endemic diseases can potentially erode social cooperation and even compromise political and macroeconomic stability (Commission on Macroeconomics and Health, 2002).

Previous researchers have also focused on the long-term demographic consequences of epidemics. Epidemics directly affect the population and labour force, which means this mechanism negatively impacts an economy's long-term growth prospects, given the devastation of human capital (Lee & McKibbin, 2003). Apart from this direct negative effect, epidemics can influence households' fertility decisions, affecting the demographic structures.

2.5   Summary

In this chapter, we explored the timeline of historical pandemics and discussed their impact on health and economic well-being by focusing on three case studies. We discussed how these three pandemics were able to spread and how they ultimately were controlled.

It was interesting to note that the 1918 influenza outbreak that caused the death of approximately 40–50 million worldwide ended through no pharmaceutical interventions, thereby highlighting the human immune system's resilience. In contrast, our study of the SARS and H1N1 pandemics revealed how important government transparency was in managing unnecessary public fears, maintaining people's confidence, securing foreign investment flows and helping economic growth.

Lastly, our discussion on the macroeconomics of flu highlighted the complex relationship between health crises, economic growth and development, and human capital. It emphasised how pandemics can ripple through societies, affecting physical health, slowing productivity and increasing unemployment.

References

Africa Center for Strategic Studies. (2020). Lessons from the 1918-1919 Spanish Flu Pandemic in Africa. Available from https://africacenter.org/spotlight/lessons-1918-1919-spanish-flu-africa/. Accessed on 15.07.24.

Barro, R. J. (2013). Health and economic growth. *Annals of Economics and Finance, 14*(2), 329–366.

Barry, J. M. (2005). *The great influenza. The story of the deadliest pandemic in history.* Penguin Random House LLC.

Bloom, D. E., Cadarette, D., & Sevilla, J. P. (2018). *New and resurgent infectious diseases can have far-reaching economic repercussions. Epidemics & Economics.* International Monetary

Fund publication. https://www.imf.org/en/Publications/fandd/issues/2018/06/economic-risks-and-impacts-of-epidemics-bloom. Accessed on 12.07.23

Britannica, T. (2023). Editors of Encyclopaedia (2023, 28 March). *Influenza pandemic of 1918–19. Encyclopedia Britannica.* https://www.britannica.com/event/influenza-pandemic-of-1918-1919. Accessed on 06.04.23.

Britannica, T. (2024). The Editors of Encyclopaedia (2024, 13 July). *SARS. Encyclopedia Britannica.* https://www.britannica.com/science/SARS. Accessed 15.07.24.

Brodeur, A., Gray, D., Islam, A., & Bhuiyan, S. J. (2020). A Literature Review of the Economics of COVID-19. Institute of Labor Economics (IZA) Discussion Paper No. 13411.

Centers for Disease Control and Prevention. (2010). 2009 H1N1 pandemic timeline. https://www.cdc.gov/flu/pandemic-resources/2009-pandemic-timeline.html. Accessed on 18.01.23.

Centers for Disease Control and Prevention. (2013). CDC SARS Response Timeline. https://www.cdc.gov/about/history/sars/timeline.htm#print. Accessed on 18.01.23.

Commission on Macroeconomics and Health. (2002). Macroeconomics and Health: investing in health for economic development. Report of the Commission on Macroeconomics and Health to the World Health Organization. Geneva.

Coombes, R. (2009). Influenza A/H1N1: questions and answers. *British Medical Journal, 338*(7703), 1104–1105.

Córdova-Villalobos, J. A., Sarti, E., Arzoz-Padrés, J., Manuell-Lee, G., Méndez, J. R., & Kuri-Morales, P. (2009). The influenza A(H1N1) epidemic in Mexico. Lessons learned. *Health Research and Policy Systems, 7*(21), 1–7.

Grant, S. (2003). Risk assessment and SARS, public lecture, National Institute of Economics and Business, The Australian National University, 28 July. http://ecocomm.anu.edu.au/nieb/SGranCNIEB_LectureNotesO30728.pdf. Accessed on 06.06.23.

Jordan, E. O. (1927). *Epidemic influenza: A survey.* American Medical Association.

Lee, J.-W., & McKibbin, W. J. (2003). Globalisation and disease: The case of SARS. *Asian Economic Papers, 3*(1), 113–131.

Lee, J. W., & McKibbin, W. J. (2012). The impact of SARS. In R. Garnaut & L. Song (Eds.), *China: New engine of world growth* (pp. 19–33). ANU Press.

Patterson, K. D., & Pyle, G. F. (1991). The geography and mortality of the 1918 influenza pandemic. *Bulletin of the History of Medicine, 65*(1), 4–21.

Vaughan, W. T. (1921). Influenza: An epidemiologic study. *American Journal of Hygiene*, iii–260.

World Bank. (2014). *The economic impact of the 2014 Ebola epidemic: Short- and medium-term estimates for West Africa.* World Bank.

World Health Organization (WHO). (2010). World: Pandemic (H1N1) 2009 - Countries, territories and areas with lab confirmed cases and number of deaths as reported to WHO (Status as of 27 June 2010). https://reliefweb.int/map/world/world-pandemic-h1n1-2009-countries-territories-and-areas-lab-confirmed-cases-and-number-19. Accessed on 08.07.23.

Chapter 3
Origins, Epidemiology and the COVID-19 Vaccine

Abstract This chapter provides a comprehensive discussion of the origins, epidemiology, and timeline of the COVID-19 pandemic, focusing particularly on developing and deploying COVID-19 vaccines. Beginning with an overview of the virus's emergence and spread, the chapter discusses the authorisation of vaccines amid imperfect information, leading to public mistrust in governments and pharmaceutical companies.

Subsequently, the chapter delves into retrospective revelations concerning the shortcomings of pharmaceutical companies in ensuring the efficacy of the COVID-19 vaccine. This factor significantly contributed to vaccine hesitancy among the public. We emphasise the obligation of pharmaceutical companies to rebuild public trust actively. They must convincingly demonstrate their commitment to rigorous safety protocols during vaccine trials, a transparent approach to potential side effects, and a resolute avoidance of any involvement in controversial gain-of-function research. Additionally, alternative pharmaceutical interventions to alleviate COVID-19 symptoms are discussed, advocating for improved access through policy intervention.

The chapter also outlines the various non-pharmaceutical interventions governments employed to mitigate the spread of COVID-19 and highlights the impact of lockdown regulations. Lastly, it delves into the complexities of pharmaceutical interventions, examining the rapid development and approval of vaccines, transparency issues, and public trust erosion. The chapter concludes with a call for equitable access to antiviral medications to combat future outbreaks effectively.

Keywords COVID-19 · Epidemiology · Non-pharmaceutical interventions · Pharmaceutical interventions

3.1   Introduction

This chapter begins by providing an overview of the origins, epidemiology and timeline of COVID-19. The chapter then briefly introduces government non-pharmaceutical interventions and highlights the impact of lockdown regulations. Next, we discuss the authorisation of COVID-19 vaccines by many countries based on imperfect information, a decision that sowed seeds of mistrust in governments.

Subsequently, the chapter delves into retrospective revelations concerning the shortcomings of pharmaceutical companies in ensuring the efficacy of the COVID-19 vaccine. This factor significantly contributed to vaccine hesitancy among the public. We emphasise the imperative for pharmaceutical companies to rebuild public trust actively. They must convincingly demonstrate their commitment to rigorous safety protocols during vaccine trials, a transparent approach to potential side effects, and a resolute avoidance of any involvement in controversial gain-of-function research.

Furthermore, we acquaint readers with alternative pharmaceutical interventions to alleviate COVID-19 symptoms, which could potentially prevent hospitalisation and advocate for better access through policy intervention.

3.2   Origin and Epidemiology of COVID-19

In what seems now eerily prophetic, Laver and Garman (2001, p. 1776) wrote, "*A worldwide epidemic (pandemic) of type A influenza could occur any time. Such an event will be caused by a 'new' virus against which the human population has no immunity, and past experience indicates that this new virus will probably arise in China. With today's crowded conditions and rapid transportation, the epidemic is expected to reach every corner of the globe. Millions of people will become ill, and many will die*".

Almeida et al. (1968) identified a novel group of viruses isolated from different animals and humans. They suggested they should be named "coronaviruses" (CoVs) since their surface resembled the uppermost layer of the Sun, the "corona" (Fig. 3.1). Since Almeida et al. (1968) discovery, researchers have identified coronaviruses in many animal species and linked them to various illnesses. Although most of them cause respiratory diseases in humans, from the common cold to more rare and serious diseases such as Severe Acute Respiratory Syndrome (SARS) and Middle East Respiratory Syndrome (MERS), both of which have high mortality rates and were detected for the first time in 2003 and 2012, respectively (refer to Chap. 2 for a discussion on SARS) (World Health Organization (WHO) 2020).

We categorise CoVs into four genera: alpha-, beta-, gamma- and delta-CoV. Those CoVs causing human diseases are currently limited to alpha- or beta-CoV; however,

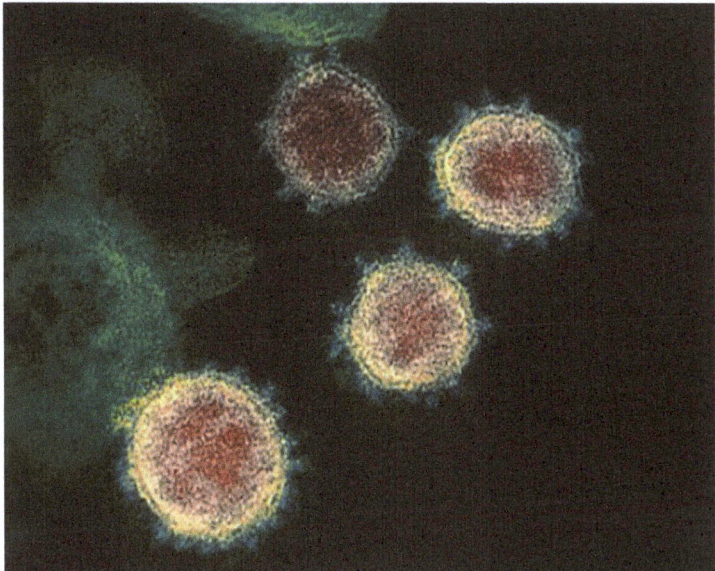

Source: History of Vaccines (2023). In the public domain.

Fig. 3.1 Image of the surface of the coronavirus. *Source*: History of Vaccines (2023). In the public domain

various animal species can also be infected by these CoVs. For example, civet cats and humans were infected by SARS-CoV in 2002, and dromedary camels and humans were infected by MERS-CoV in 2012. A virus regularly transmitted from an animal to a human is called a zoonotic virus, and the initial transmission from animals to humans is referred to as a spillover event (Centers for Disease Control and Prevention, 2021).

To identify the source or origin of a virus, it is helpful to look at the genetic makeup of the virus and see whether it resembles other known viruses since this may offer some clues as to its origin. Genetic similarities with known viruses might imply that they come from a similar source or geographic area.

SARS-CoV-2, the coronavirus responsible for the COVID-19 pandemic, belongs to a group of genetically related viruses, including SARS-CoV and several other CoVs found in bat populations. MERS-CoV also belongs to this group, but its genetic connection is less close. Thorough investigations and interviews with the first known human cases of the disease are crucial to determine where they may have become infected. This may aid in identifying earlier cases and narrow the geographical areas and timeframes, allowing for more specific investigations to identify the source.

At the time of writing this book, we accept largely that the zoonotic source of SARS-CoV-2 came as a result of a leak from a laboratory in Wuhan City, the capital city of Hubei Province of China (The Wall Street Journal, 2023).

3.3   Timeline of COVID-19

Even though a laboratory in Wuhan City leaked the virus, Zhu et al. (2020) note that the first human cases of COVID-19, the coronavirus disease caused by SARS-CoV-2, was reported on 8 December 2019 and came from a wet market in Wuhan. After the initial case, the WHO (2020) reported various clusters of patients throughout late December 2019.

Japan, South Korea and the United States confirmed their first case of COVID-19 approximately 3 weeks after the reported outbreak in China (Fig. 3.2). From then on, disease progression within these countries varied quite a bit. While the US took 42 days to reach 100 confirmed cases, Japan and South Korea reached that number in 31 and 29 days, respectively. Table 3.1 below provides a timeline of key events starting from January 2020.

Once again, we note that China, while praised for its initial handling of the outbreak in Wuhan, refused to assist the WHO in managing the global crisis by not releasing the genetic map, or genome, of the virus for more than a week after three different government labs had fully decoded the information. This lack of transparency from the Chinese government meant that the WHO did not have enough data to assess how effectively the virus spread between people or what risk it posed to the rest of the world, costing valuable time (Associate Press, 2020).

More than three and a half years later (20 July 2023), there have been 768,237,788 confirmed cases of COVID-19, including 6,951,677 deaths. Europe has been the

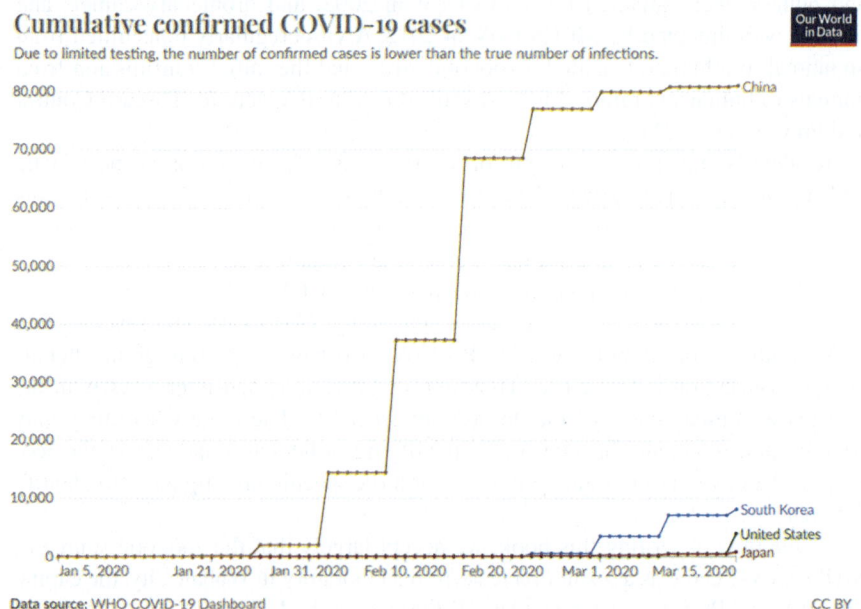

Fig. 3.2 Confirmed cases for Japan, South Korea, the United States and China (January 2020 to March 2020). *Source*: Mathieu et al. (2020)

Table 3.1 Timeline of COVID-19

Date	Events
4 January 2020	WHO reports a cluster of pneumonia cases in Wuhan, Hubei, China
7 January 2020	WHO identifies COVID-19
11 January 2020	China announces first death from COVID-19
13 January 2020	First official case of COVID-19 reported outside China in Thailand
17 January 2020	Authorities in Nepal, France, Australia, Malaysia, Singapore, South Korea, Vietnam and Taiwan confirm cases
21 January 2020	First case of COVID-19 was reported in the United States of America (US)
22 January 2020	WHO finds evidence of human-to-human transmission from China
23 January 2020	China imposes lockdowns in the cities of Wuhan, Xiantao and Chibi in the Hubei province
30 January 2020	WHO declares COVID-19 to be a Public Health Emergency of International Concern
31 January 2020	US declares COVID-19 a domestic public health emergency
2 February 2020	First death due to COVID-19 outside of China in the Philippines
9 February 2020	The death toll in China surpasses that of 2002–03 Severe Acute Respiratory Syndrome (SARS)
14 February 2020	Egypt reports first case of COVID-19, the first case in Africa
15 February 2020	France reports first death from COVID-19 outside of Asia
23 February 2020	COVID-19 cases rise in Italy in what becomes the largest outbreak outside of Asia
26 February 2020	Brazil confirms the first case of COVID-19, the first case in South America
27 February 2020	First case of community transmission reported in the US
29 February 2020	First death due to COVID-19 in the US
8 March 2020	Over 100 countries report COVID-19 cases Italy imposes quarantine in Lombardy region
11 March 2020	WHO declares COVID-19 a pandemic
13 March 2020	Donald Trump declares a national emergency in the US
17 March 2020	All 50 states in the US have at least one confirmed case of COVID-19 California is the first state to implement a 'stay-at-home' order in the US
19 March 2020	Italy's death toll surpasses that of China
21 March 2020	EU suspends public deficit rules to inject fiscal stimulus across countries
25 March 2020	The White House and Senate leaders of both the Democratic and Republican parties in the US agreed on a US$2 trillion stimulus to aid workers, businesses, and the healthcare system in response to the pandemic
26 March 2020	US leads the world in COVID-19 cases
2 April 2020	Global cases of COVID-19 reach one million
8 April 2020	China lifts lockdown in Wuhan, 76 days after sealed off to contain COVID-19
11 April 2020	The US records 2000 deaths in 1 day, the highest single-day death toll recorded by any country
15 April 2020	Global cases of COVID-19 reach two million
24 April 2020	US's death toll surpasses 50,000

(continued)

Table 3.1 (continued)

Date	Events
27 April 2020	Global cases of COVID-19 reach three million
28 April 2020	COVID-19 cases in the US surpass one million
21 May 2020	Global cases of COVID-19 surpass five million
22 May 2020	Brazil surpasses Russia as the country with the second highest number of cases after the US

Source: Brodeur et al. (2020)

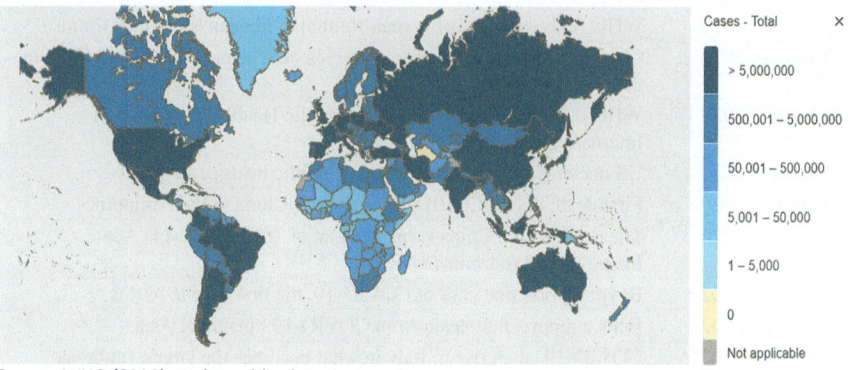

Source: WHO (2023). In the public domain.

Fig. 3.3 Visualisation of total cases globally. *Source*: WHO (2023). In the public domain

hardest hit region, with 275,775,826 confirmed cases, and Africa reported the least number of cases, with 9,681,456 (although there is doubt on the African numbers) (Fig. 3.3). As of 22 July 2023, a total of 13,474,348,801 vaccine doses have been administered (WHO, 2023).

3.4   Previous Pandemic Interventions

The last time the world responded to a global emerging disease epidemic of the scale of the COVID-19 pandemic with no access to pharmaceutical interventions was the 1918–19 H1N1 influenza pandemic. According to Bootsma and Ferguson (2007), some countries, like the United States (US), responded with various non-pharmaceutical interventions[1] during the 1918–1919 H1N1 influenza pandemic. Examples of the policy measures implemented during this time included the closure of schools, churches, bars and other social venues. Subsequently, where cities acted early in the pandemic and implemented these interventions, they successfully reduced case numbers while the interventions remained in place and experienced

---

[1] Measures intended to reduce transmission by reducing contact rates in the general population.

lower mortality overall. However, after lifting these interventions, transmission returned.

Primarily, the US relied on two strategies: suppression and mitigation. During the suppression stage, the aim was to reduce the reproduction number[2] to below one. Therefore, the objective is to reduce case numbers to low levels or (as for SARS) eradicate human-to-human transmission altogether (Bootsma & Ferguson, 2007). During the mitigation stage, the aim was to use non-pharmaceutical interventions (and vaccines) not to interrupt transmission entirely but to reduce the health impact of an epidemic. For example, during the H1N1 pandemic, authorities distributed early vaccine supplies to individuals with pre-existing medical conditions at risk of developing a more severe form of the viral disease. In this scenario, population immunity gradually builds up during the course of the epidemic, resulting in a rapid reduction in case numbers and transmission dropping to low levels (Bootsma & Ferguson, 2007). Refer to Chap. 12 for more detailed policy interventions during previous pandemics.

3.5 COVID-19 Government Non-pharmaceutical Interventions (in General)

Governments worldwide have tried various interventions to slow the spread of COVID-19 and encourage vaccination. Three years after the global pandemic hit and 2 years after administering the first vaccinations, this section briefly summarises interventions and applications and their effectiveness in addressing three key COVID-19 areas: (i) slowing the spread of COVID-19, (ii) encouraging vaccination and (iii) addressing the spread of misinformation and fake news.

3.5.1 Slowing the Spread of COVID-19

To slow the spread of COVID-19, it is best to imagine a spectrum of non-pharmaceutical interventions, with complete lockdown (the extreme) on the one end and simple social distancing and protective measures on the other end. Although every government walked their own path, all fell within this broad spectrum, balancing the need for containment and the level of societal and financial disruption. In Chaps. 4 and 5, we recall combinations of interventions used by the countries we focus on in our empirical studies in Chaps. 7–10. However, most of them implemented a complete lockdown of their citizens. In general, school closures were the most effective non-pharmaceutical intervention, followed by workplace closures, business and venue closures and banning public events. Although less disruptive,

---

[2]The average number of secondary cases each case generates.

public information campaigns and mask-wearing requirements were also effective (Mendez-Britoa et al., 2021).

It should be noted that whereas lockdown is deemed to be the most effective non-pharmaceutical intervention to curb the spread of the virus, it is also one of the policies that caused significant harm to individuals and families and disproportionately affected disabled persons. Many disabled children and their families were affected by a lack of access to face-to-face schooling, sometimes compounded by digital exclusion or inaccessible remote learning methods. The lack of usual support structures had implications for many disabled children's social and emotional development and impacted the physical and mental health of adult disabled persons (Martin, 2022). Many disabled people were more dependent than non-disabled people on medical or rehabilitation interventions, and disruption to services such as routine physiotherapy, speech and language therapy and occupational therapy, therefore, affected them more.

Additionally, we know that lockdowns negatively affected health (Ohrnberger, 2022), the global economy (Naseer et al., 2023), mental health (Adams-Prassl et al., 2022; Brodeur et al., 2021), loneliness (Hamermesh, 2020) and happiness (Rossouw et al., 2021a, b; Greyling et al. 2021a, b).

3.5.2   Encouraging Vaccinations

Countries chose different options to encourage their people to get vaccinated. Once again, imagine a spectrum with mandatory vaccines (the extreme) at one end and using instruments to encourage vaccination at the other. On the less extreme side of the spectrum, countries could use financial incentives to get people vaccinated. However, this requires a balancing act since a study by Cryder et al. (2010) found that if incentives are too small, people won't take it up, and if incentives are too large, people believe receiving the vaccine comes with a higher risk of side effects.

Apart from financial incentives, governments also focused on communicating to people about the vaccine using a combination of effective messaging, trusted communicators and targeting specific vulnerable communities such as the elderly, minority groups and the immunocompromised. Effective messaging such as multiple vaccine appointment reminders (Dai et al., 2021), the safety of the vaccine (Tironi et al., 2021) and protecting your loved ones and community (Freeman et al., 2021) has shown to increase the vaccine uptake. Using trusted communicators such as healthcare professionals (Bartoš et al., 2022) and celebrities (Honora et al., 2022) also positively affected vaccine uptake.

On the extreme side of the spectrum, most governments engaged in behaviour, making it difficult for people to remain unvaccinated. In Chaps. 4, 5 and 14, we discuss individual country policies, but here we note interventions such as default vaccine appointments (people must opt-out), COVID-19 passports and imposing fines or using other disadvantages.

3.5.3   Misinformation and Fake News

In general, to counter misinformation, we use strategies such as pre-bunk, de-bunk and reminders. Pre-bunk teaches common misinformation techniques, such as playing the game *Go Viral!* (Basol et al., 2021) whereas de-bunk uses fact-checkers to address misinformation directly. Reminders on social media platforms such as Twitter and Facebook ask people to check their facts before sharing information.

3.6   COVID-19 Government Pharmaceutical Interventions (in General)

In 2020, with the pandemic in full swing, the race was on to see which government could create the first vaccine to curb the spread of the virus effectively. In August 2020, the government of Russia announced it had fast-tracked the creation of a vaccine named *Sputnik V*. Between April and July 2020, Sinovac Biotech Ltd., a Chinese biotech company, launched clinical trials of an inactivated virus vaccine called *Coronavac*. Around the same time, clinical trials of two novel vaccines (made by biotech companies Moderna and Pfizer-BioNTech) began in the United States. Decades-old technology served as the basis for those vaccines, utilising messenger RNA (mRNA) to deliver a message to immune cells, prompting them to produce a protein resembling the virus's surface proteins. This method enabled the creation of vaccines without the necessity of cultivating the virus in a laboratory. All that was required was the genetic code for the virus's proteins (History of Vaccines, 2023).

In December 2020, the United States Food and Drug Administration (FDA) authorised two mRNA vaccines for emergency use. In February 2021, authorities approved the emergency use of a viral vector vaccine Johnson & Johnson Janssen produced. The Janssen vaccine delivers mRNA to immune cells inside an inactivated adenovirus, triggering the recipient immune cells to create proteins, much like the vaccines made by Moderna and Pfizer-BioNTech do (History of Vaccines, 2023).

Other vaccines have been developed against SARS-CoV-2. The New York Times had a vaccine tracker (Fig. 3.4) on its website; however, since August 2022, it is no longer being updated. Still, the online tool kept track of the development of

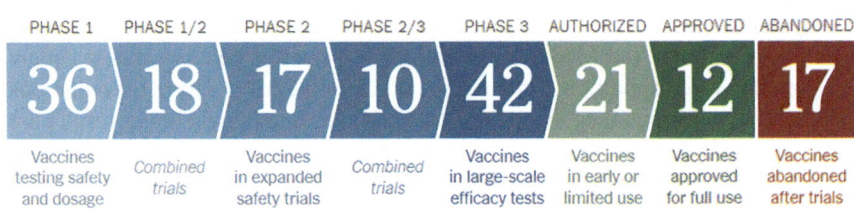

Fig. 3.4 Coronavirus vaccine tracker. *Source*: Zimmer et al. (2022)

COVID-19 vaccines from early 2020 through August 2022. More than 120 clinical trials were underway then and subsequently abandoned.

For example, in January 2021, the Imperial College London abandoned its vaccine and the German CureVac in October 2021. As of August 2022, the tracking tool showed 21 vaccines authorised for emergency use and 12 given full approval for use. Unfortunately, many countries, especially developing countries, cannot develop or produce their own vaccines, and many are too poor to afford to acquire vaccines for their populations.

In addition to the aforementioned concerns, the transparency surrounding the efficacy of COVID-19 vaccines has been a significant issue that has eroded public trust in governments. As countries raced to boost their vaccination rates, the prevailing message was that getting vaccinated would substantially reduce the risk of contracting the virus and ending up in the hospital. For instance, the New Zealand government disseminated an inaccurate advertisement claiming, *"Once you've had both doses of the vaccine, it has been shown to be up to 95 per cent effective at preventing COVID-19"* (Anthony, 2021). Regrettably, this statement proved false, and when vaccinated individuals still fell ill, it sowed doubt in the public's perception of government honesty. Adding to the confusion, data from, for example, the UK indicated that 63.4% of individuals who succumbed to the delta variant within 28 days of a positive COVID-19 test between 1 February and 21 June had received at least one vaccine dose (Yates, 2021). Attempting to elucidate the nuances to the general population, such as using the concept of Simpson's Paradox, appeared futile, as people tended to fixate on these numbers, deepening their scepticism. Furthermore, Godlee (2020) and Gibson (2022a) raised concerns that the potential limited benefits of COVID-19 vaccines compared to the risks posed by breakthrough infections and vaccine-related adverse events could undermine trust in other vaccination initiatives.

Fast-forward to another vaccination initiative, the rollout of booster vaccines, and we witness another contentious chapter in governmental decisions. Despite a 16-2 vote against the widespread use of boosters by an advisory panel of external experts to the FDA, citing a lack of safety data and doubts about the benefits of mass boosting over targeted approaches, the FDA proceeded to authorise boosters for the general population (Perrone & Neergaard, 2021). The advisory panel's critique noted, *"If unnecessary boosting causes significant adverse reactions, it may increase general vaccine hesitancy"*. Even the WHO contended that a vaccination strategy relying on recurrent booster doses of the original vaccine composition was unlikely to be suitable or sustainable (WHO, 2022).

Beyond safety fears and potential hesitancy issues, the efficacy data concerning the Pfizer-BioNTech and Moderna bivalent mRNA booster vaccines is now widely recognised to be disappointing (Wang et al., 2022; Offit, 2023). Given the numerous rounds of vaccinations they've already received, these underwhelming results are unlikely to convince people to take yet another vaccine shot. As stated by Offit (2023), *"Now, boosting everyone with an Omicron shot is trying to prevent, in otherwise healthy people, mild illness for a few months until the next variant comes along to replace it. That doesn't make sense."*

Further exacerbating concerns regarding the Pfizer-BioNTech vaccine is the alleged revelation that emerged on 12 October 2022. Janine Small, an executive, addressed the European Parliament, acknowledging that Pfizer did not test the vaccine's ability to prevent the transmission of COVID-19 before making it accessible to the public. Small stated, *"We had to operate in tandem with the pace of scientific advancements...we had to take calculated risks."* This admission held particular significance because a central premise behind numerous non-pharmaceutical interventions, such as vaccine mandates and passport systems (elaborated in Chap. 13), was that vaccination could safeguard the individual and protect others. When the vaccine's capacity to curtail transmission remained uncertain at the time of its release, governments and private organisations found themselves making crucial decisions without the essential information required for their decision-making process (Housman, 2022).

What dealt the final blow to Pfizer's reputation was the revelation brought to light by Project Veritas through undercover footage. The exposé alleged unsettling facts, including Pfizer's contemplation of (i) deliberately inducing virus mutations for the purpose of developing vaccines in advance, a practice considered illegal gain-of-function research, (ii) characterising COVID-19 as a long-term source of substantial profit, and (iii) insinuating that US federal regulators had shown leniency toward Pfizer with the expectation of future employment opportunities (Daily Wire News, 2023).

Apart from the woes that Pfizer itself has experienced, we have to address the correlation between booster vaccines and excess deaths in various countries. To illustrate this concern, Gibson (2022b) analysed aggregate data for 31 OECD countries from August 2021 to May 2022. This period coincided with the initiation of booster rollouts in many OECD countries, and it ended when excess mortality estimates were set for most of these nations. Gibson (2022b) found a direct link between higher excess mortality rates and increased booster usage. Using monthly average excess mortality p-scores, indicating the percentage by which total deaths exceeded expected deaths, they found that the p-scores are 4.4% points higher for every 10 doses per 100 people ($p < 0.01$) when the mean booster rate is 28 per 100, controlling for the proportion of people who had been fully vaccinated under original protocols.[3] In layman's terms, this means that where and when *booster usage is higher, excess mortality is higher.*

As a result, the campaign to persuade individuals to take booster shots to prevent new outbreaks appears to be an uphill battle, if not already a lost cause.

Nevertheless, the outlook is not entirely bleak with regard to pharmaceutical interventions. Increasingly, people recognise that vaccines are not the sole solution in the fight against the COVID-19 pandemic. Several antiviral medications, such as Paxlovid and Molnupiravir, are available and, when administered early during a COVID-19 infection, can help individuals avoid hospitalisation. Unfortunately, in certain countries, such as New Zealand, these antiviral medicines are accessible

---

[3] Noting that being fully vaccinated is a necessary condition for being boosted.

only to specific demographic groups, including the elderly, immunocompromised individuals, and those with pre-existing conditions (Pharmac, 2023). Government policy should rectify this disparity to ensure broader access to these effective antiviral treatments.

3.7 Summary

This chapter discussed the intricacies of COVID-19, its origin and epidemiology, strategies to curb its spread, and the multifaceted approaches governments adopted. We highlighted that at the time of writing this book, it was largely accepted that the zoonotic source of SARS-CoV-2 came as a result of a leak from a laboratory in Wuhan City. However, the first human case of COVID-19 was reported on 8 December 2019 and came from a wet market in Wuhan.

We briefly introduced interventions and applications and their effectiveness in addressing three key COVID-19 areas. First, slowing the virus's spread through a combination of non-pharmaceutical interventions; second, encouraging vaccination through either financial incentives or government mandates; and third, countering misinformation through strategies such as pre-bunk, de-bunk and reminders.

In our discussion that focused on pharmaceutical interventions, we paid specific attention to the COVID-19 vaccine. We highlighted how its rapid development and approval, transparency surrounding the efficacy, and excess deaths undermined trust in vaccination initiatives. We also touched upon alleged unsettling facts surrounding Pfizer, which significantly impacted people's trust in pharmaceutical companies, whether true or not. Lastly, we presented the need for governments to look at policies regarding antiviral medicines that will see more people gain access and help individuals avoid hospitalisation in future outbreaks.

References

Adams-Prassl, A., Boneva, T., Golin, M., & Rauh, C. (2022). The impact of the coronavirus lockdown on mental health: evidence from the United States. *Economic Policy, eiac002*.

Almeida, J. D., Berry, D. M., Cunningham, C. H., Hamre, D., Hofstad, M. S., Mallucci, L., et al. (1968). Virology: Coronaviruses. *Nature, 220*(650).

Anthony, J. (2021). 'Genuine error' led to incorrect information in Covid-19 vaccine ad, Government says. https://www.stuff.co.nz/business/industries/126242692/genuine-error-led-to-incorrect-information-in-covid19-vaccine-ad-government-says. Accessed on 18.08.23.

Associate Press. (2020). China delayed releasing coronavirus info, frustrating WHO. https://www.cnbc.com/2020/06/02/china-delayed-releasing-coronavirus-info-frustrating-who.html. Accessed on 17.01.23.

Bartoš, V., Bauer, M., Cahlíková, J., & Chytilová, J. (2022). Communicating doctors' consensus persistently increases COVID-19 vaccinations. *Nature, 606*, 542–549.

Basol, M., Roozenbeek, J., Berriche, M., Uenal, F., McClanahan, W. P., & van der Linden, S. (2021). Towards psychological herd immunity: Cross-cultural evidence for two prebunking interventions against COVID-19 misinformation. *Big Data & Society, 8*(1).

Bootsma, M. C. J., & Ferguson, N. M. (2007). The effect of public health measures on the 1918 influenza pandemic in US cities. *Proceedings of the National Academy of Sciences of the United States of America, 104*(18), 7588–7593.

Brodeur, A., Gray, D., Islam, A., & Bhuiyan, S. J. (2020). A Literature Review of the Economics of COVID-19. Institute of Labor Economics (IZA) Discussion Paper No. 13411.

Brodeur, A., Clark, A. E., Fleche, S., & Powdthavee, N. (2021). COVID-19, lockdowns and well-being: Evidence from Google Trends. *Journal of Public Economics, 193*, 104346.

Centers for Disease Control and Prevention. (2021). Zoonotic diseases. https://www.cdc.gov/one-health/basics/zoonotic-diseases.html#:~:text=However%2C%20animals%20can%20some-times%20carry,bacterial%2C%20parasites%2C%20and%20fungi. Accessed on 17.01.23.

Cryder, C. E., London, A. J., Volpp, K. G., & Loewenstein, G. (2010). Informative inducement: Study payment as a signal of risk. *Social Science & Medicine, 70*(3), 455–464.

Dai, H., Saccardo, S., Han, M. A., Roh, L., Raja, N., Vangala, S., et al. (2021). Behavioural nudges increase COVID-19 vaccinations. *Nature, 597*, 404–409.

Daily Wire News. (2023). Project Veritas Video: Pfizer Official Says Firm Considering Ways To 'Mutate' Virus Via 'Directed Evolution'. https://www.dailywire.com/news/project-veritas-video-pfizer-official-says-firm-considering-ways-to-mutate-virus-via-directed-evolution. Accessed on 18.08.23.

Freeman, D., Loe, B. S., Yu, L., Freeman, J., Chadwick, A., Vaccari, C., et al. (2021). Effects of different types of written vaccination information on COVID-19 vaccine hesitancy in the UK (OCEANS-III): a single-blind, parallel-group, randomised controlled trial. *The Lancet Public Health, 6*, e416–e427.

Gibson, J. (2022a). Widespread public misunderstanding of pivotal trials for COVID-19 vaccines may damage public confidence in all vaccines. *Frontiers in Public Health, 10*, 847658.

Gibson, J. (2022b). The Rollout of COVID-19 Booster Vaccines is Associated With Rising Excess Mortality in New Zealand. Working Paper in Economics 11/22, University of Waikato.

Godlee, F. (2020). COVID-19: Less haste, more safety. *British Medical Journal, 370*, m3258.

Greyling, T., Rossouw, S., & Adhikari, T. (2021a). A tale of three countries: How did Covid-19 lockdown impact happiness? *South African Journal of Economics, 89*(1), 25–43.

Greyling, T., Rossouw, S., & Adhikari, T. (2021b). The good, the bad and the ugly of lockdowns during Covid-19. *PLoS One, 16*(1), e0245546.

Hamermesh, D. S. (2020). Life satisfaction, loneliness and togetherness, with an application to Covid-19 lockdowns. *Review of Economics of the Household, 18*, 983–1000.

History of Vaccines. (2023). Diseases. Coronavirus. https://historyofvaccines.org/diseases/corona-virus. Accessed on 18.01.23.

Honora, A., Wang, K. Y., & Chih, W. H. (2022). How does information overload about COVID-19 vaccines influence individuals' vaccination intentions? The roles of cyberchondria, perceived risk, and vaccine scepticism. *Computers in Human Behaviour, 130*(107176).

Housman, D. (2022). Pfizer Exec Admits Vaccines Weren't Tested For Stopping Transmission Before Hitting Market. https://dailycaller.com/2022/10/12/pfizer-coronavirus-covid-vaccine-testing-transmission-european-union-parliament/. Accessed on 18.08.23.

Laver, G., & Garman, E. (2001). The Origin and Control of Pandemic Influenza. *Science, 293*(5536), 1776–1777.

Mathieu, E., Ritchie, H., Rodés-Guirao, L., Appel, C., Giattino, C., Hasell, J., Macdonald, B., Dattani, S., Beltekian, D., Ortiz-Ospina, E., & Roser, M. (2020). Coronavirus pandemic (COVID-19). Published online at OurWorldInData.org. Available from https://ourworldindata.org/coronavirus. Accessed on 15.07.24.

Martin, N. (2022). Impacts of the COVID-19 pandemic on disabled people in New Zealand. Open Access Te Herenga Waka-Victoria University of Wellington. Thesis. https://doi.org/10.26686/wgtn.21202982. Accessed on 18.01.23.

Mendez-Britoa, A., El Bcheraoui, C., & Pozo-Martina, F. (2021). Systematic review of empirical studies comparing the effectiveness of non-pharmaceutical interventions against COVID-19. *Journal of Infection, 83*, 281–293.

Naseer, S., Khalid, S., Parveen, S., Abbass, K., Song, H., & Achim, M. V. (2023). COVID-19 outbreak: Impact on global economy. *Frontiers in Public Health, 10*, 1009393.

Offit, P. A. (2023). Bivalent Covid-19 Vaccines — A Cautionary Tale. *New England Journal of Medicine, 388*(6), 481–483.

Ohrnberger, J. (2022). Economic shocks, health, and social protection: The effect of COVID-19 income shocks on health and mitigation through cash transfers in South Africa. *Health Economics, 31*(11), 2481–2498.

Perrone, M., & Neergaard, L. (2021). FDA advisory panel rejects widespread Pfizer vaccine booster shots. PBS News Hour 17 September 2001. https://www.pbs.org/newshour/health/fdaadvisory-panel-rejects-widespread-pfizer-vaccine-booster-shots. Accessed on 27.07.23.

Pharmac. (2023). COVID-19 antivirals: Access Criteria. https://pharmac.govt.nz/news-and-resources/covid19/access-criteria-for-covid-19-medicines/covid-antivirals/. Accessed on 27.07.23.

Rossouw, S., Greyling, T., & Adhikari. (2021a). The implied volatility of happiness pre and peri-COVID-19: a Markov Switching Dynamic Regression Model. *PLoS One, 16*(12), e0259579.

Rossouw, S., Greyling, T., & Adhikari, T. (2021b). Happiness-lost: Did Governments make the right decisions to combat Covid-19? *South African Journal of Economic and Management Sciences, 24*(1), a3795.

The Wall Street Journal. (2023). Lab Leak Most Likely Origin of Covid-19 Pandemic, Energy Department Now Says. https://www.wsj.com/articles/covid-origin-china-lab-leak-807b7b0a. Accessed on 06.04.23.

Tironi, A. P., Barham, E., Zuckerman, D. S., Gerez, J. E., Marshall, J., & Pocasangre, O. (2021). Messages that increase COVID-19 vaccine acceptance: Evidence from online experiments in six Latin American countries. *PLoS One, 16*(10), e0259059.

Wang, Q., Bowen, A., Valdez, R., Gherasim, C., Gordon, A., Liu, L., et al. (2022). Antibody responses to Omicron BA.4/BA.5 bivalent mRNA vaccine booster shot. bioRxiv, https://doi.org/10.1101/2022.10.22.513349. Accessed on 27.07.23.

World Health Organization (WHO). (2020). Origin of SARS-CoV-2. https://apps.who.int/iris/bitstream/handle/10665/332197/WHO-2019-nCoV-FAQ-Virus_origin-2020.1-eng.pdf. Accessed on 17.01.23.

World Health Organization (WHO). (2022). Interim statement on COVID-19 vaccines in the context of the circulation of the Omicron SARS-CoV-2 variant from the WHO Technical Advisory Group on COVID-19 Vaccine Composition (TAG-CO-VAC). 11 January 2022. https://www.who.int/news/item/11-01-2022-interim-statement-on-covid-19-vaccines-in-thecontext-of-the-circulation-of-the-omicron-sars-cov-2-variant-from-the-who-technicaladvisory-group-on-covid-19-vaccine-composition. Accessed on 18.01.23.

World Health Organization (WHO). (2023). WHO Coronavirus (COVID-19) Dashboard. https://covid19.who.int/. Accessed on 20.07.23.

Yates, C. (2021). Most COVID deaths in England now are in the vaccinated—here's why that shouldn't alarm you. https://theconversation.com/most-covid-deaths-in-england-now-are-in-the-vaccinated-heres-why-that-shouldnt-alarm-you-163671. Accessed 19.01.23.

Zhu, N., Zhang, D., Wang, W., Li, X., Yang, B., Song, J., China Novel Coronavirus Investigating and Research Team, et al. (2020). A Novel Coronavirus from patients with Pneumonia in China, 2019. *The New England Journal of Medicine, 382*(8), 727–733.

Zimmer, C., Corum, J., Wee, S., & Kristoffersen, M. (2022). Coronavirus vaccine tracker. https://www.nytimes.com/interactive/2020/science/coronavirus-vaccine-tracker.html. Accessed on 18.01.23.

Chapter 4
Case Studies: Evolution of the COVID-19 Pandemic in the Northern Hemisphere

Abstract This chapter examines the nuanced dynamics of the COVID-19 pandemic and vaccine hesitancy through case studies of seven Northern Hemisphere countries: Belgium, France, Germany, Great Britain, Italy, the Netherlands, and Spain. It explores the evolution of the pandemic, the adoption of non-pharmaceutical interventions, and the intricate rollout of COVID-19 vaccines in these nations. By scrutinising the government responses and their impacts on public trust and vaccine acceptance, the chapter explains the critical interplay between early regulatory actions and global well-being. It highlights the importance of strategic planning and resource allocation in strengthening healthcare systems and resilience through real-world examples.

The chapter underscores the pivotal role of government interventions in shaping the trajectory of the pandemic, emphasising the effectiveness of measures such as lockdowns and social distancing in curbing virus spread and mitigating casualties. However, it also acknowledges the severe damage inflicted by these policies, including mental health outcomes and economic recessions.

Examining the COVID-19 vaccine rollout, the chapter compares instances of success and failure across different nations. While some countries navigated capacity challenges adeptly, others struggled with initial vaccination hesitancy, resorting to mandates to boost uptake. Notably, successful information campaigns played a transformative role, as evidenced by the Dutch government's turnaround in vaccination rates.

Ultimately, this chapter serves as a reminder of the importance of government responses and institutional trust in safeguarding public health. By extracting lessons from the experiences of Northern Hemisphere countries, it advocates for a collective global effort towards resilience and preparedness in combating health crises, fostering trust, and fostering vaccine acceptance for a healthier future.

Keywords Northern hemisphere · Demand-side factors · Supply-side factors · Trust · Institutions

© The Author(s), under exclusive license to Springer Nature
Switzerland AG 2024
S. Rossouw, T. Greyling, *Resistance to COVID-19 Vaccination*, Human
Well-Being Research and Policy Making,
https://doi.org/10.1007/978-3-031-56529-8_4

4.1   Introduction

This chapter focuses on specific Northern Hemisphere countries included as case studies in analysing the COVID-19 pandemic and vaccine hesitancy. Country introductions for seven Northern Hemisphere countries, Belgium, France, Germany, Great Britain, Italy, the Netherlands, and Spain, will be provided. The chapter will discuss a timeline of the evolution of the COVID-19 pandemic, non-pharmaceutical interventions adopted, and each Northern Hemisphere country's relevant rollout of the COVID-19 vaccine. Particular emphasis will reflect how early government-mandated regulations, such as lockdowns, pre-empt the decrease in well-being experienced globally. In terms of the COVID-19 vaccine rollout, the chapter will provide an in-depth discussion of the strategies of the Northern Hemisphere countries that seemingly got it right. Some Northern Hemisphere countries failed, thereby decreasing trust in institutions and, subsequently, the COVID-19 vaccine.

4.2   Case Study Countries

Before turning to our individual countries concerning the evolution of the COVID-19 pandemic and vaccine rollout, let's first look at some demand and supply-side factors related to our Northern Hemisphere countries.

Addressing the COVID-19 pandemic required interventions on both the supply and demand for healthcare services. In this section, we briefly discuss the effects that the COVID-19 pandemic had on the countries' healthcare system, separately addressing demand-side (Table 4.1) and supply-side factors (Table 4.2). Specifically, we have added real-world examples for some Northern Hemisphere countries in discussing problems such as the ageing population, comorbidities and population density under demand-side factors and healthcare expenditure and hospital beds under supply-side factors.

4.2.1   Demand-Side Factors

1. Ageing Population

Italy's ageing population significantly strained healthcare resources during the COVID-19 pandemic. As Table 4.1 shows, Italy's population over 65 years old was 23 per cent in 2020, making it one of the countries in Europe with the highest proportion of elderly citizens. When COVID-19 struck, Italy faced a significant challenge, seeing as their older individuals were at a higher risk of severe illness and mortality from the virus, placing an increased demand on hospital beds, ventilators, and specialised care, overwhelming the healthcare system. As noted by Onder et al. (2020) and Bonanad et al. (2020), Italy's mortality increased significantly in septuagenarian (70 years and older) and almost tripled in octogenarian (between 80 and

Table 4.1 Demand factors in the Northern Hemisphere countries

Variable	United Kingdom	Germany	Italy	Spain	France	Belgium	Netherlands
Total population	67,080,000 (2020)	83,160,000 (2020)	59,440,000 (2020)	47,370,000 (2020)	67,570,000 (2020)	11,540,000 (2020)	17,440,000 (2020)
Density people/Km²	277 (2020)	238 (2020)	201 (2020)	95 (2020)	123 (2020)	381 (2020)	518 (2020)
Median age	40.4 years (2020)	44.6 years (2020)	47.3 years (2020)	44.9 years (2020)	41.4 years (2020)	40.8 years (2020)	41.7 years (2020)
Life expectancy at birth	80 years (2020)	81 years (2020)	82 years (2020)	82 years (2020)	82 years (2020)	81 years (2020)	81 years (2020)
Population over 65 years old (% of total population)	19 (2020)	22 (2020)	23 (2020)	20 (2020)	21 (2020)	19 (2020)	20 (2020)
Old age dependency ratio	32 (2020)	39.7 (2020)	39.6 (2020)	32.8 (2020)	37.3 (2020)	33.1 (2020)	34.3 (2020)
Population aged 15 and over smoking daily (% of the population aged 15 years and over)	15.8 (2019)	18.8 (2019)	18.6 (2019)	19.8 (2019)	24 (2019)	15.4 (2019)	15.4 (2019)
People reporting a long-standing illness or health problem (%)	37.8 (2019)	43.2 (2019)	15.9 (2019)	29.2 (2019)	38 (2019)	26.1 (2019)	32.2 (2019)
Diabetes I and II prevalence among adults	3.9 (2019)	10.4 (2019)	5 (2019)	6.9 (2019)	4.8 (2019)	6.8 (2019)	5.4 (2019)
GDP per capita (USD)	40,318 (2020)	46,722 (2020)	31,918 (2020)	26,959 (2020)	39,055 (2020)	45,517 (2020)	52,162 (2020)
Unemployment rate (% of the labour force)	3.7 (2020)	3.9 (2020)	9.2 (2020)	15.5 (2020)	8.0 (2020)	6.3 (2021)	3.8 (2020)
Working hours lost due to the COVID-19 crisis expressed as the number of FTE jobs (Based on 40 h per week)	3344.775 (2020)	2141.532 (2020)	2781.353 (2020)	2272.225 (2020)	1907.032 (2020)	335.143 (2020)	240.782 (2020)

Source: Worldometers (2021), World Bank (2021), Office for National Statistics (2022), Eurostat (2021), OECD (2023), European Observatory on Health Systems and Policies (2019), OECD (2021) and ILOSTAT (2023)

Table 4.2 Change in supply factors from pre- to during the COVID-19 pandemic

Variable	United Kingdom	Germany	Italy	Spain	France	Belgium	Netherlands
Name of national healthcare system	The National Health Service	Statutory health insurance	Servizio Sanitario Nazionale	Sistema Nacional de Salud	Statutory health insurance	Social health insurance	Zorginstituut Nederland
Hospital beds per 1000	2.9 (2010) 2.4 (2020)	8.3 (2010) 7.8 (2020)	3.6 (2010) 3.2 (2020)	3.1 (2010) 3.0 (2020)	6.4 (2010) 5.7 (2020)	6.1 (2010) 5.5 (2020)	4.1 (2010) 2.9 (2020)
ICU beds per 100,000	6.6 (2010) 5.6 (2020)	29.2 (2010) 29.7 (2020)	12.5 (2010) 11.5 (2020)	9.7 (2010) 12.5 (2020)	11.6 (2010) 28.2 (2020)	15.9 (2010) 17.3 (2020)	6.4 (2010) 6.9 (2020)
Number of doctors per 1000	2.60 (2010) 3.03 (2020)	3.80 (2010) 4.47 (2020)	3.80 (2010) 4.00 (2020)	3.70 (2010) 4.58 (2020)	3.40 (2010) 3.17 (2020)	2.90 (2010) 3.21 (2020)	3.00 (2010) 3.85 (2020)
Nurses per 1000	8.8 (2010) 8.9 (2020)	11.9 (2010) 12.03 (2020)	5.5 (2010) 6.3 (2020)	5.3 (2010) 6.1 (2020)	9.0 (2010) 11.8 (2019)	10.1 (2010) 11.7 (2020)	11.9 (2010) 11.6 (2020)
Hospitals per 1000,000	27.42 (2012) 28.64 (2020)	40.37 (2010) 36.15 (2020)	20.75 (2010) 17.92 (2020)	16.42 (2010) 16.7 (2020)	41.76 (2010) 44.23 (2020)	17.9 (2010) 14.13 (2020)	25.7 (2010) 35.43 (2020)
Domestic general government health expenditure (GGHE-D) per capita in US$	3207.36 (2010) 4123.35 (2020)	3490.38 (2010) 4651.76 (2020)	2524.39 (2010) 2325.70 (2020)	2076.74 (2010) 2125.07 (2020)	3235.02 (2010) 3658.53 (2020)	3454.79 (2010) 3966.00 (2020)	3552.13 (2010) 4022.26 (2020)

Source: OECD Health Statistics (2023), OECD/European Union (2022), Rhodes et al. (2012), World Health Organization (WHO) (2023) and WHO Global Health Expenditure (2023)

89 years old) patients. These findings are consistent with a higher susceptibility to infection and severe clinical manifestations observed in older adult patients and highlight the necessity for comprehensive planning and resource allocation to address the vulnerabilities of an ageing population during health crises.

2. Comorbidities

Germany, like many other governments, implemented non-pharmaceutical interventions such as lockdowns to counter the increasing numbers of individuals infected by the coronavirus. As a consequence, not only was interpersonal contact reduced to handle infection, but there was a decline in standard medical care for chronic diseases like diabetes mellitus (DM). As indicated in Table 4.1, Germany had a prevalence rate of 10.4% for DM types I and II in adults in 2019 prior to the emergence of COVID-19. Schmitt et al. (2023) investigated the impact of DM on morbidity and mortality in patients with COVID-19 based on all COVID-19 hospitalisations in Germany throughout the year 2020. Their findings revealed that 25.7% of people hospitalised for COVID-19 also had DM. Furthermore, the hospitalisation rate for COVID-19 patients with DM increased with advancing age, a concern given that Germany's population over 65 years old reached 22% in 2020. The study concluded that the risk of in-hospital death for COVID-19-infected patients was 2.9 times higher in patients with additional type I DM and 1.8 times higher in type II DM patients.

3. Population Density

We know that population density plays a pivotal role in the onset and dissemination of infectious diseases (Ali & Keil, 2007). Larger urban centres exhibit high concentrations of people and crowding, heightening the likelihood of disease outbreaks and rapid transmission. The Netherlands, with the highest population density among our Northern Hemisphere countries (518 per km^2), did not escape this phenomenon. Boterman (2023) examined the role of population density in the spread of the coronavirus in the Netherlands. The study showed that during the summer months and the initial phase of the second wave, densely populated regions of the Netherlands, preeminent cities like Amsterdam, Rotterdam, and The Hague, exhibited the highest concentrations of cases.

Boterman (2023) also found that during the first stage of the second wave, population density had a strong and significant effect on infections and hospitalisations. However, the author concluded that when lockdown measures were implemented, the correlation between population density and infections and hospitalisations disappeared.

4.2.2 Supply-Side Factors

1. Health expenditure

According to Ricci et al. (2020), Italy's public health sector was utterly unprepared when the COVID-19 pandemic broke out. The pandemic exposed the vulnerabilities of the Italian health system, driven by budgetary constraints over the past decade prioritising economic efficiency and savings, often at the expense of investment in healthcare and highlighted the Italian government's lack of foresight in the political and socio-health domains. As reflected in Table 4.2, Italy's domestic general government health expenditure per capita decreased by 7.87 per cent from 2010 to 2020, resulting in a shortage of intensive care beds (a reduction of 8 per cent from 2010 to 2020) and overburdened health personnel (4 doctors and 6.3 nurses per 1000 people). Epifanio et al. (2023) found that the healthcare workforce struggled to face all the challenges related to the pandemic, especially in the northern regions of Italy. Demanding work shifts due to the shortage of colleagues led to feelings of hopelessness and burnout among nurses and physicians. Furthermore, healthcare workers frequently contracted the virus (446,875 by November 2020), and physicians experienced high mortality rates. Modenese et al. (2022) found that the mortality rate for Italian physicians was 12 times higher in March–May 2020 compared to the same time period after the start of the Italian vaccination campaign.

2. Hospital Beds

Several of our Northern Hemisphere countries faced limitations in terms of hospital bed capacity. For example, in the UK, which had the lowest number of hospital beds per 1000 people among our Northern Hemisphere countries at 2.4 (Table 4.2), there was a significant effect on the ability to provide time-critical access to healthcare services. By March 2020, hospitals suspended cancer screening activities, delayed routine diagnostic procedures, and only urgent symptomatic cases received priority for diagnostic interventions. Maringe et al. (2020) conducted a study to assess the effects of these circumstances on patients with breast, colorectal, oesophageal, and lung cancer. They found that, compared to pre-pandemic figures, there was an estimated increase of 7.9 to 9.6, 15.3 to 16.6, 5.8 to 6.0, and 4.8 to 5.3%, respectively, in mortality rates up to 5 years after diagnosis for these four cancer types. This translated to an additional 3291 to 3621 deaths across the scenarios within a 5-year period. Maringe et al. (2020) determined that the total additional years of life lost across these cancers is estimated to be an astonishing 59,204—63,229 years.

Considering the above, we can see how the COVID-19 pandemic has highlighted the complicated relationship between demand-side and supply-side factors in healthcare systems in our Northern Hemisphere countries. Our real-world examples emphasise how, for example, an ageing population, comorbidities, and population density can exert pressure on vital supply-side resources like healthcare professionals and hospital beds.

Now, let's turn to our individual Northern Hemisphere country case studies.

4.2.3   UK's COVID-19 Journey: Challenges and Triumphs

The United Kingdom (UK), a nation of 66.65 million with an average happiness level of 7.165 in 2019 (Helliwell et al., 2020), commenced its battle with the COVID-19 pandemic on a positive economic note, boasting a 1.4% annual GDP

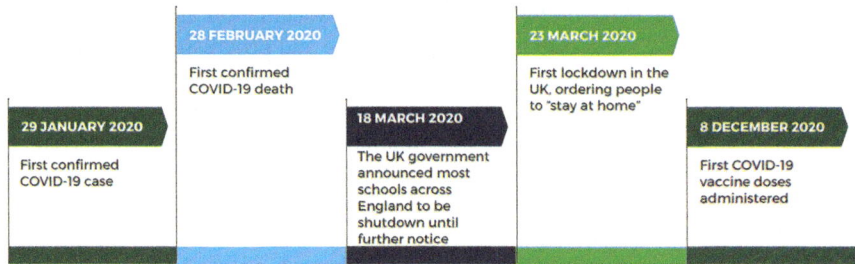

Fig. 4.1 Evolution of the COVID-19 pandemic in the United Kingdom. *Source*: Authors' own Figure

growth rate in the year leading up to December 2019. However, challenges loomed with a substantial debt-to-GDP ratio of 85.9% and an unemployment rate of 3.8% (Eurostat, 2020).

On 29 January 2020, officials confirmed the pandemic's first case, and on 28 February, the first COVID-19-related death was reported (see Fig. 4.1), prompting the closure of all schools on 20 March. By 23 March, the government imposed a stay-at-home order, restricted gatherings to two individuals and permitted outdoor exercise once daily. The UK didn't declare a formal state of emergency but introduced 'emergency powers' to tackle the crisis. By 31 March, the Oxford Stringency Index[1] registered a score of 79.63 (the stringency index ranges from 0 to 100, with 100 being the most stringent), underlining the rigour of the lockdown measures (Hale et al., 2020).

A conditional plan to lift lockdown was announced on 10 May 2020. The plan allowed those unable to work from home to return to their workplace. However, those travelling had to avoid using public transport. Schools re-opened on 1 June 2020, and non-essential shops opened by 15 June 2020 (Institute for Government Analysis, 2022). Unfortunately, their freedom was short-lived as the UK entered its second lockdown on 31 October. The second lockdown was justified by stating it would prevent a "medical and moral disaster" for the National Health Services. After enduring another 4 weeks of lockdown, the UK returned to a stricter three-tier system of restrictions on 2 December 2020 (Institute for Government Analysis, 2022).

On the same day that the UK returned to a stricter three-tier system of restrictions, the Pfizer-BioNTech COVID-19 vaccine was approved for use in the UK, becoming the first to be authorised anywhere in the world. By 8 December 2020, the UK administered the first COVID-19 vaccine. The cheaper and easier-to-distribute Oxford-AstraZeneca vaccine was approved on 30 December, followed by the Moderna in January 2021 (Institute for Government, 2021).

In terms of the UK's vaccine rollout strategy, the government published a list of nine priority groups on 30 December 2020. This vaccine policy came about due to

---

[1] Consisting of the following indicators: school closing, workplace closing, cancelling of public events, restrictions on gatherings, stay at home requirements, restrictions on internal movement, restrictions on international travel and restrictions on public information campaigns.

advice from the independent Joint Committee on Vaccination and Immunisation (JCVI). The rollout started with the most vulnerable and progressed down through age groups and risk levels. The government started to offer vaccines to 12–15-year-olds in September 2021. Additionally, since evidence from the international committee confirmed the potential of waning immunity from vaccinations received at the end of December 2020/early January 2021, they began the rollout of their 'booster' vaccines programme for the priority groups identified in the original rollout (Institute for Government, 2021).

Despite notable successes, the UK government faced criticism because of their vaccination policy since 12–15-year-olds only received approval to get the COVID-19 vaccine in September 2021 (Mason & Elgot, 2021). This meant resuming in-person schooling for children without adequate COVID-19 mitigation, risking widespread infections and more disruptions to the learning environment. Additionally, people's trust in the government's ability to manage the pandemic effectively diminished after announcing their so-called 'Freedom Day' (Donovan, 2021). Freedom Day removed all COVID-19 restrictions amid a backdrop of 47,000 new cases reported in the previous 24 h (Donovan, 2021). The decision of Freedom Day drew global criticism from approximately 1200 scientists, saying it constituted a global threat if daily cases increased exponentially and vaccine-resistant virus mutations were allowed to develop (Ball, 2021).

4.2.4 Spain's COVID-19 Response and Vaccination Triumphs

Spain has a total population of 47 million spread among 17 Autonomous Communities (AC)[2], further divided into provinces. The average happiness level for 2019 was 6.401 (Helliwell et al., 2020), and the annual GDP growth rate in the year to December 2019 was 2.4%. Unfortunately, their debt as a percentage of GDP was high at 97.6 per cent, and the unemployment rate was 13.6 per cent, the highest out of the Northern Hemisphere countries under investigation (Eurostat, 2020).

Spain confirmed their first case of COVID-19 on 31 January (Fig. 4.2). However, Spanish health authorities did not undertake any measures to stop the spread of the virus until 1 month later, when confirmed cases reached 100. By 12 March, parliament was suspended, and four districts in Cataluñã were placed under lockdown for 2 weeks. On 13 March (10 days after recording its first COVID-19 death on 3 March), Madrid closed the hospitality sector and schools. By 14 March, a" state of alarm" was declared, and Spain's citizens were requested to stay at home, with a complete ban on gatherings and people only allowed to walk their dogs until 11 April (Henríquez et al., 2020). According to the Oxford Stringency Index, Spain scored 85.19 (ranges between 0 and 100, with 100 being the most stringent in terms of lockdown) by 31 March 2020 (Hale et al., 2020).

---

[2] AC are the main managers of the health system coordinating the provider networks and purchasing resources.

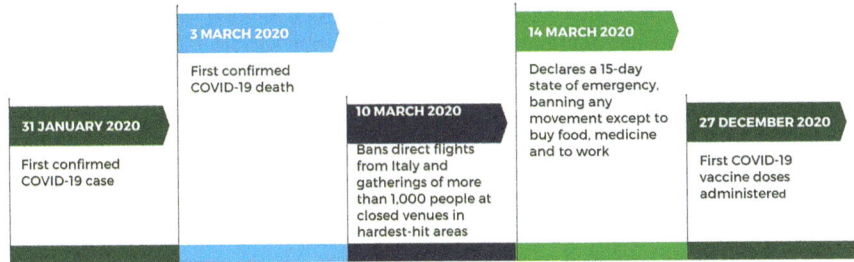

Fig. 4.2 Evolution of the COVID-19 pandemic in Spain. *Source*: Authors' own Figure

Table 4.3 Vaccine acquired by the European Commission

Vaccine company/type	Dose for Spain (approx.)	Dose per person
Pfizer/BioNTech/mRNA	177.6 million	2 doses
Moderna/mRNA	52 million	2 doses
AstraZeneca/Vector adenovirus	31 million	2 doses
Janssen/Vector adenovirus	20 million	1 dose
Novavax/S protein	2.2 million	2 doses
Sanofi Pasteur/S protein	496,000	2 doses
CureVac/S protein	Didn't realise	2 doses

Source: Gobierno de España (2022)

Spain started their plan to roll back the restrictions in April 2020, with non-essential workers being allowed to return on 13 April. However, those who were able to were still obliged to stay home until 26 April. As noted by Henríquez et al. (2020), Spain implemented two additional policies: i) on 23 April, minors (younger than 14) were allowed to go outside, and ii) on 2 May, those 14 years and older were allowed to exercise outside during different timeslots. On 3 May, the government revealed their "Plan of return to the New Normality[3]", and on 11 May, some territories transitioned to phase 1, which meant that family and friends reunions of up to 10 people could take place. On 20 May, mandatory mask-wearing was mandated if a distance of 2 m could not be kept, and by 21 June 2020, the lockdown was officially over.

Spain engaged in joint procurement of COVID-19 vaccines through the European Union (EU) with other member states as part of the EU vaccine strategy coordinated by the European Commission. Advance purchase agreements negotiated with various pharmaceutical companies ensured vaccine availability (Table 4.3).

Spain's vaccination strategy aimed to reduce morbidity and mortality, prioritise vulnerable groups and ensure vaccine safety. The rollout, commencing on 27 December 2021, initially prioritised residents and healthcare personnel in care

---

[3] The plan established 4 phases: Phase 0 (State of Alarm) and 3 additional phases (Phase 1: family and friends' reunions of up to 10 people; Phase 2: 15 people: Phase 3: mobility between provinces of the same AC).

homes, front-line health staff, other healthcare workers, and dependent individuals with disabilities who required intensive support (Gobierno de España, 2020). As vaccine supplies increased, health authorities progressively included younger cohorts, and during the summer, they extended vaccination eligibility to all age groups. By 1 September 2021, 78% of Spain's population had received at least one vaccine dose, ranking third in Europe (after Portugal and Malta) despite the absence of a national vaccine mandate (Wang et al., 2023).

According to Antonini et al. (2022), Spain's population traditionally exhibited a high level of trust in vaccines, resulting in vaccination rates that exceeded those of many high-income countries. Trust in the public health system, efficient vaccine distribution, and a vivid recollection of the high death toll and infection rates during the initial COVID-19 waves were attributed to the success of the vaccination strategy. Spain's national health system and healthcare professionals enjoyed more trust than other institutions or professional groups in the country (Jovell et al., 2007).

However, Spain's delayed response at the outset of the pandemic and a lack of workable contingency plans nearly overwhelmed the healthcare system. It contributed to one of the highest COVID-19 death rates (Casasnovas et al., 2021).

4.2.5   Navigating the Uncharted Waters: Italy's Response to the COVID-19 Pandemic

In contrast to Spain, Italy was not faring well in terms of its economic well-being when COVID-19 hit. Their annual GDP growth rate in the year to December 2019 was less than 1% (0.8), and their debt as a percentage of GDP was an astounding 134.8%. The unemployment rate nearly reached double digits at 9.7%, the second highest among the countries under investigation in Chapters 7–10 (Eurostat, 2020). Unfortunately, Italy's total population of 60.36 million also had the lowest average happiness level among our European countries in 2019 at 6.387 (Helliwell et al., 2020).

Italy, the first EU country confronted with the COVID-19 pandemic, confirmed its first case on the very day a six-month state of emergency was declared (Fig. 4.3). On 31 January, Italy also became the first European nation to suspend flights from China after confirming two cases in Rome. The first Italian COVID-19-positive patient death was reported on 21 February by local health authorities in Lombardy's Codogno (Lodi). The government took the decisive step of closing all schools and universities on 4 March. Additional social distancing measures were implemented on 9 March, just 5 days later. On 11 March, a national "partial lockdown" was announced, culminating in a complete lockdown on 22 March. During this period, authorities prohibited gatherings but allowed solitary outdoor exercise. Within 2 months of the initial outbreak, Lombardy, the hardest-hit region in Italy, witnessed a peak of over 23,000 excess deaths, an excess mortality rate of +118% compared to the average mortality rate from 1 January—30 April for the years 2015–2019

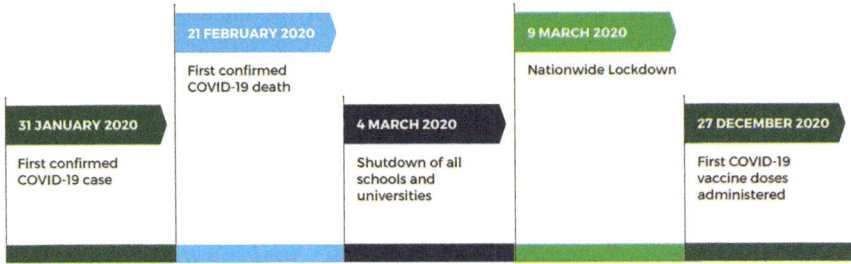

Fig. 4.3 Evolution of the COVID-19 pandemic in Italy. *Source*: Authors' own Figure

(Bosa et al., 2021). By the end of March 2020, Italy's stringency measures on the Oxford Stringency Index reached 85.19 (Hale et al., 2020).

On 10 April, Prime Minister Giuseppe Conte established a "committee of experts in economic and social subjects" to formulate plans for transitioning from a complete lockdown to a broader re-opening of the country. Italy's response, as documented in the DPCM (2020), moved from Phase 1 (ending on 3 May) to Phase 2 (4 May—2 June), during which most primary and secondary sectors, professionals, private healthcare clinics, retail shops, businesses, and customer services resumed activities under specific COVID-19 safety protocols. Authorities lifted restrictions on free movement but limited it to one's residential region.

Italy's vaccination rollout, which began on 27 December 2020, adopted distinct priority groups for vaccination:

- Phase 1: Health and social health workers, residential elderly facility residents and staff, individuals over 80 years, and people aged 60 to 79 with chronic illnesses.
- Phase 2: Law enforcement, teachers, school staff, pharmacists, and veterinarians.
- Phase 3: Individuals under 60 with comorbidities not categorised as extremely vulnerable and the remaining cohorts under 60 years (European Centre for Disease Prevention and Control, 2020).

By 31 July 2021, Italy, ranked as the second-worst Northern Hemisphere country in terms of people not fully vaccinated (52%), faced a challenging road to increase COVID-19 vaccine uptake (Roberts, 2021). The Italian government took a robust stance by enacting emergency legislation mandating COVID-19 vaccines for all healthcare workers, including pharmacy staff—those who declined vaccination faced reassignment or suspension without pay for up to a year. Additionally, Italy introduced vaccine passports.

Bosa et al. (2020) argue that the absence of a well-prepared emergency plan, mismanagement of "patient 1" and other initial cases, lack of transparency in communication, and an initially ill-suited surveillance system all contributed to Italy's primarily hospital-centred response during the early stages of the COVID-19 crisis, particularly in Lombardy. The emergency legislation faced fierce resistance from

Italy's deeply ingrained anti-vaccine movement, partly nurtured by populist political forces such as the 5 Star Movement that entered government in 2018 while promoting vaccine hesitancy. Moreover, public trust in vaccines waned when Italy temporarily suspended the use of the Oxford/AstraZeneca vaccine following reports of several deaths (Roberts, 2021).

4.2.6 Germany's Response to COVID-19: Striking a Balance Between Freedom and Health

Germany, Europe's largest economy, has a total population of 83.02 million people and an average happiness level for 2019 of 7.076 (Helliwell et al., 2020). The economic outlook was primarily positive before COVID-19 struck. The annual GDP growth rate in the year to December 2019 was 1.5%, debt as a percentage of GDP was 61.9%, and the unemployment rate was low at 3.2%, the lowest among our group of Northern Hemisphere countries (Eurostat, 2020).

The first case of COVID-19 was confirmed on 27 January 2020 when an employee for a company based in the southern Bavarian town of Starnberg tested positive for SARS-CoV-2 (Fig. 4.4). On 9 March, Germany registered their first death linked to COVID-19, and 2 days later, the virus was reported in all of Germany's 16 federal states. The government also closed all schools on the same day as Spain, 13 March and nearly 1 month after their first confirmed case, on 22 March, Germans were requested to stay at home through the implementation of a partial lockdown. Restaurants and cinemas were closed, although gatherings were allowed of up to two individuals, and people were allowed solo outdoor exercise. Visits to hospitals, care homes and homes for the elderly were no longer allowed.

Whereas the German state, Bavaria, declared a state of emergency on 17 March, the rest of Germany did not follow suit. However, the government secured emergency powers on 25 March to unlock a historic rescue package. The new spending

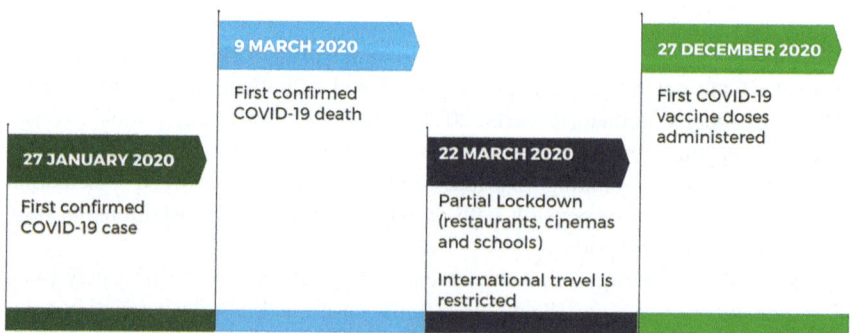

Fig. 4.4 Evolution of the COVID-19 pandemic in Germany. *Source*: Authors' own Figure

plans foresaw an extra €156 billion ($169 billion) in new government debt in 2020, around 100 billion more than would have been permitted under Germany's notorious debt ceiling that limits annual borrowing (Deutsche Welle, 2020). According to the Oxford Stringency Index, Germany scored 76.85 (ranges between 0 and 100, with 100 being the most stringent in terms of lockdown) by the end of March 2020, the lowest among the Northern Hemisphere countries under investigation (Hale et al., 2020).

On 4 May, Germany lifted its first coronavirus lockdown after seven difficult weeks. However, by August 2020, Germany faced a second wave of COVID-19 infections, and by October, Berlin implemented a new curfew, followed by a "Lockdown Light" on 2 November 2020. Under this "Lockdown Light", meetings in public were limited to two households and a maximum of 10 people. The catering, hospitality and tourism sectors were closed down, but schools remained open. Unfortunately, with new infections spiralling out of control, there was no alternative than to impose strict lockdown again on 6 January (Deutsche Welle, 2021a).

In April 2020, before initiating its own vaccine rollout, Germany committed to ensuring the fair global distribution of vaccines and played a pivotal role as one of the founding members of the Country Coordinating Mechanism Access to COVID-19 Tools Accelerator (ACT-Accelerator). By August 2022, Germany was the second-largest donor, contributing a total of €3 billion. Germany primarily channelled its support through the international COVAX Facility, a part of the ACT-Accelerator, which, by August 2022, had distributed more than 1.6 billion doses to over 146 countries and territories (Federal Foreign Office, 2022).

Germany rolled out their own vaccination programme on 27 December 2020, along with the rest of the EU. However, the first month of the rollout was plagued by a raft of logistical challenges. On 19 January 2021, almost 1 month into the vaccine rollout, the Robert Koch Institute (2023) reported that in the previous 24 hours, just over 62,000 vaccinations (the majority of which were first doses) were carried out. This was in stark contrast to the target of 300,000 vaccinations daily.

Despite an extensive German vaccination media campaign spanning 2021 and 2022, a considerable portion of the population had refused the COVID-19 vaccination or remained hesitant (as of 7 July 2021, 9.2 million people aged 18 years and older) (Robert Koch Institute, 2022). Sterl et al. (2023), who retrospectively investigated why Germans did not get vaccinated, found clear evidence that West Germany was more likely to be vaccinated than East Germany. A possible reason for this geographical divide is cited by Deutsche Welle (2021b), where the right-wing populist party Alternative for Germany (AfD) had significant influence. The AfD, which is sceptical of or refuses COVID-19 measures, such as wearing masks, had a direct effect on lowering trust in public and state institutions.

The introduction of vaccine passports in Germany failed to alleviate the situation, with many Germans expressing discontent that unvaccinated people would not be allowed to enter venues like sports stadiums, movie theatres or restaurants because they deemed the residual risk high in such places (Sprengholz et al., 2021). Germans felt they should be allowed to make their own decisions about their bodies, which were taken away by government mandates (Sterl et al., 2023).

4.2.7   France: The Dual Impact of Government Responses

France has a total population of 66.99 million people and an average happiness level for 2019 of 6.664 (Helliwell et al., 2020). The economic outlook was positive when COVID-19 entered the country with an annual GDP growth rate in the year to December 2019 of 1.7%, debt as a percentage of GDP was 98.4%, and the unemployment rate was relatively low at 8.1% (Eurostat, 2020).

The picture looks significantly different for France than for the rest of our European countries. A patient initially treated for suspected pneumonia on 27 December 2019 was tested in May 2020, and the results returned positive. This means that the virus may have arrived a month earlier than expected. The 'official' first three cases were confirmed on 24 January and were directly connected to the Wuhan region of China; the first COVID-19 death was reported on 14 February (Fig. 4.5). The government also closed all schools on the same day as Spain and Germany, 13 March. From 17 March, the French government requested everyone to stay at home with no gatherings allowed, but people were allowed a maximum of 1 h outdoors per day. A "sanitary state of emergency" was declared on 18 March with a total number of 1404 confirmed cases. According to the Oxford Stringency Index, by the end of March 2020, France scored 87.96 (ranges between 0 and 100, with 100 being the most stringent in terms of lockdown) (Hale et al., 2020).

Like the other EU countries, France started their COVID-19 vaccination rollout on 27 December 2020 after the Pfizer–BioNTech COVID-19 vaccine was approved by the European Union Commission.

In France, introducing a stringent vaccination policy known as 'COVID-19 vaccine passports' created a negative attitude towards the COVID-19 vaccine, potentially eroding public trust and impacting vaccine acceptance (The Economist, 2021). By August 2021, the French government introduced the so-called "health pass" and made it mandatory for all events or venues with more than 50 people, including restaurants, cafes, and large shopping centres. Although the government intended to incentivise vaccination to facilitate a return to normalcy, this approach polarised public opinion. The announcement that movie theatres, museums and sports venues now required visitors to provide proof of a COVID-19 vaccination or a negative test

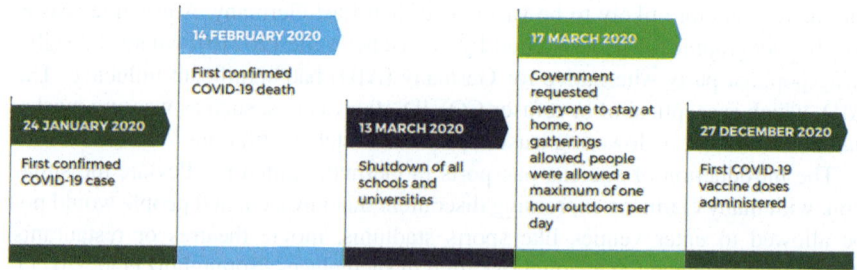

Fig. 4.5 Evolution of the COVID-19 pandemic in France. *Source*: Authors' own Figure

had many French nationals angry but willing to take the vaccine if this meant that life would go back to normal (The Economist, 2021). Unfortunately, in January 2022, when the French government enacted a law making vaccination a legal requirement for access to cultural events, theme parks, ski lifts, eateries, bars, and most forms of long-distance transport, it triggered widespread protests and civil unrest (BBC News, 2022).

Similar to Germany, the French government committed to the fair global distribution of vaccines to ensure equity in global health. In April 2021, France became the first nation to donate vaccines through the COVAX Facility. France surpassed its original vaccination donation target by August 2022, providing 124 million doses and establishing itself as the third-largest donor, following the United States and Germany (Ministry for Europe and Foreign Affairs, 2023).

4.2.8   The Belgian Balancing Act

Belgium has a total population of 11.6 million and an average happiness level for 2019 of 6.864 (Helliwell et al., 2020). The annual GDP growth rate in the year to December 2019 was 2.2%, which boded positively for them. Unfortunately, their debt as a percentage of GDP was high at 98.6%, and the unemployment rate was 5.3% (Eurostat, 2020).

Belgium confirmed its first case of COVID-19 on 4 February 2020, and the government closed all schools, discos, cafes and restaurants and cancelled all public gatherings on 13 March (Fig. 4.6). According to the Oxford Stringency Index, Belgium scored 81.48 (ranges between 0 and 100, with 100 being the most stringent in terms of lockdown) 2 weeks after they went into lockdown (Hale et al., 2020).

On the same day as Germany, 14 February, Belgium recorded its first COVID-19-related death, and by 21 June, the end date of the country's first wave, 9591 deaths had been recorded, bringing their mortality rate up among the highest worldwide (Sierra et al., 2020). Sadly, about 60 per cent of the COVID-19 deaths in 2020 were among residents in long-term care facilities (OECD/European Observatory on Health Systems and Policies, 2021). By the end of August 2021, the mortality rate

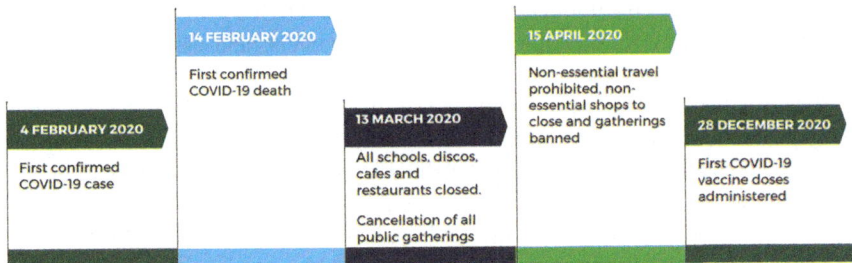

Fig. 4.6 Evolution of the COVID-19 pandemic in Belgium. *Source*: Authors' own Figure

from COVID-19 was almost 40 per cent higher than the EU average (2200 per million population compared with 1590), mainly due to higher death rates seen during the first wave (OECD/European Observatory on Health Systems and Policies, 2021). Belgium's high mortality rate is partly due to the government only cancelling all non-essential travel, closing non-essential shops and banning gatherings by 15 April 2020.

Belgium started their lockdown exit strategy in May 2020, even though positive cases exceeded 40,000. The lockdown exit strategy posited that by June 2020, pools, wellness centres, amusement parks, and casinos would be re-opened. Additionally, people could gather and interact with up to 15 individuals per week (Boogaerts et al., 2022). Unfortunately, by August 2020, daily cases surged again, with the 14-day incidence rising from 11 per 100,000 on 5 July to 71 on 9 August. This time, they saw that the 20–29 age group was mainly affected. The typical Belgian commuting customs exacerbated the spread of the virus, and by 1 October 2020, a significant increase in incidence occurred (Natalia et al., 2022). On 2 November 2020, Belgium entered its second lockdown, meaning all non-essential shops closed, family visits were prohibited, and people were permitted only one close contact outside the household. Belgium's school holidays coincided with this period and were extended until 15 November. This lockdown was enforced until January 2021, and given that people were allowed only one close contact outside the household, the Christmas period was one of the strictest in Europe.

Belgium started their COVID-19 vaccination rollout on 28 December 2020; however, according to Vanham (2021), Belgium faced capacity issues (only 320,000 instead of 600,000 vaccines promised by Pfizer by late December) and struggled to get vaccination centres up and running because of vaccine delivery delays. This meant that COVID-19 vaccinations had to be rolled out on a phased basis, focusing first on residents and staff in residential care facilities and hospital staff, followed by ambulatory healthcare professionals and the general population. Unfortunately, by 2 January 2021, only about 700 residents and care home staff had received their first doses. To put this in perspective, during the same time period, Germany and Italy had administered approximately 317,000 and 182,000 doses, respectively. There was a notable erosion of trust among the Belgian people in the information disseminated by their government, especially following reports of political favouritism in allocating the limited vaccine stock (Vanham, 2021). The above events led to widespread anger towards the politicians for making COVID-19 a political game, undermined trust in the government's pandemic management, and cast doubts on the COVID-19 vaccine rollout.

However, the government implemented several measures to correct the situation, likely positively changing the attitude towards the COVID-19 vaccine. The Belgian government established a dedicated COVID-19 task force responsible for addressing logistical and capacity challenges. According to Vanham (2021), the increased acceptance of the COVID-19 vaccine could also be attributable to lockdown policy measures being relaxed during spring, which would be contingent on vaccination rates rather than case numbers or hospitalisation rates. This policy resonated with people wanting to return to 'normal'.

4.2.9   *Navigating the Dutch Dilemma*

The Netherlands, with a population of 17.44 million and the highest average happiness level among our Northern Hemisphere countries, with 7.449 in 2019 (Helliwell et al., 2020), started the COVID-19 pandemic from a position of economic stability. In the year leading up to December 2019, the country achieved an annual GDP growth rate of 2%, showcasing robust economic prospects. Additionally, the nation boasted a comparatively low debt-to-GDP ratio of 48.6% and an unemployment rate of 3.38% (Eurostat, 2020). The Dutch experience during the pandemic reveals a nuanced story of government responses, including instances of effective regulations and government failures, which influenced public trust in institutions and, by extension, COVID-19 vaccine acceptance.

The Netherlands' early responses to the COVID-19 pandemic underscored their proactive approach. The country confirmed its first case on 27 February 2020 and its first COVID-19-related death on 6 March (Fig. 4.7). The Dutch government moved fast and, a mere 9 days later, closed all schools, restaurants and pubs on 15 March and initiated an 'intelligent lockdown' on 23 March. According to the Oxford Stringency Index, the Netherlands scored 78.70 after roughly 2 weeks of lockdown, ranking as the second-lowest European score after Germany (Hale et al., 2020).

On 11 May, there was a relaxation of some of the 'intelligent lockdown' measures: primary schools opened (splitting groups, children spend half the normal time at school), children's daycare centres opened completely, outdoor exercise at a 1.5-meter distance was permitted, libraries opened, and contact professions were allowed back to work (wearing a mask was not obligated, just a health check questionnaire when booking/entering). By 1 June, restaurants, pubs, theatres and museums re-opened for a maximum of 30 visitors. Restaurants and pubs could accommodate more customers if they could adhere to the 1.5-meter rule. And by 2 June, all high schools re-opened.

However, the Dutch experience with the COVID-19 vaccine rollout revealed significant challenges that impacted trust in the government and vaccine acceptance. The Netherlands was notably the last European country to commence its vaccine rollout on 6 January 2021, lagging behind its neighbours. Prime Minister Mark Rutte admitted that this was due to the government's approach not being agile

Fig. 4.7 Evolution of the COVID-19 pandemic in the Netherlands. *Source*: Authors' own Figure

enough when they realised that instead of the Oxford/AstraZeneca vaccine, which does not require storage at extremely low temperatures, they would have to administer the BioNTech/Pfizer vaccine, which is more challenging to use in small-scale vaccination centres because it must be stored in dry ice. The upgrading of an IT system compounded this delay to allow the Dutch health authority (GGD) to track appointments as well as which vaccine was used on different patients. The GGD also needed to establish at least one mass vaccination point in each of its 25 regions (Schaart, 2021). These challenges cast doubt on the government's ability to manage the vaccine distribution process effectively.

Additionally, in the initial stage of the vaccine rollout, young Dutch adults (18–34 years, comprising about 25% of the total population) who were willing to receive the COVID-19 vaccine constantly trailed about ten percentage points after the average percentage of the whole population (Vollmann & Salewski, 2021). To encourage vaccine uptake, the Dutch government spent around €6 million (by July 2021) on information campaigns informing the public about the safety of the various COVID-19 vaccines (Bahceli, 2021). Vollmann and Salewski (2021) showed that higher vaccine uptake resulted from information campaigns positively influencing attitudes towards vaccines. The Netherlands' fully vaccinated population increased significantly from 2430 people on 31 January 2021 to 9,288,187 by 1 August 2021 (Mathieu et al., 2021). This result underscores the effectiveness of information campaigns and the Dutch government's commitment to addressing vaccine hesitancy.

4.3   Summary

This chapter first discussed how addressing the COVID-19 emergency required interventions on both the supply and demand side of healthcare services. We highlighted real-world examples from our Northern Hemisphere countries. Specifically, we looked at challenges such as the ageing population, comorbidities, and population density under demand-side factors and constraints related to healthcare expenditure, as well as the impact on healthcare workers and hospital beds under supply-side factors. These challenges and constraints necessitated adaptive government responses ensuring the resilience of healthcare systems, highlighting the importance of strategic planning in political and socio-health domains and effective resource allocation.

Next, we comprehensively discussed the COVID-19 pandemic timeline, including non-pharmaceutical interventions and the vaccine rollout across our seven Northern Hemisphere countries: the UK, Spain, Italy, Germany, France, Belgium and the Netherlands. By doing the aforementioned, we highlighted government responses that affected public trust and vaccine acceptance.

The pandemic's timeline revealed variations in the evolution of the crisis, underscoring the importance of early government interventions. The effectiveness of non-pharmaceutical measures, including lockdowns and social distancing, was pivotal in shaping each country's pandemic trajectory—these regulations aimed to curb the virus's spread and save lives. However, as we discuss in Chap. 13, many of these policies directly led to the immense mental harm done to individuals and families, severely impacted businesses and caused a global economic recession.

When it came to countries' COVID-19 vaccine rollout and vaccination policy, we discussed instances of both success and failure. For example, the UK seemingly did not face significant capacity issues, and their rollout could be seen as a success. However, the government faced severe criticism for not vaccinating the 12-15-year-old age group sooner. On the other hand, Italy struggled to get its population vaccinated initially, and the government had to rely on vaccine mandates (something France did as well)—impacting trust in the government and the vaccine.

What did become apparent from this chapter was the effectiveness of well-organised information campaigns to address vaccine hesitancy. The Dutch government stands as a testimony to this by using information campaigns to turn their initial sluggish vaccination programme into a success story by increasing vaccination numbers from 31 January 2021 to 1 August 2021 by 157%.

In essence, this chapter acted as a reminder of the significance of government responses and trust in institutions when wanting to safeguard public health. The case studies from our Northern Hemisphere countries provide us with valuable lessons for navigating similar crises in the future. By learning from both the successes and failures of these countries, government and non-government agencies can work towards a more resilient and prepared global response to health challenges, reinforcing trust and promoting vaccine acceptance.

References

Ali, S. H., & Keil, R. (2007). Contagious cities. *Geography Compass, 1*(5), 1207–1226.

Antonini, M., Eid, M. A., Falkenbach, M., et al. (2022). An analysis of the COVID-19 vaccination campaigns in France, Israel, Italy and Spain and their impact on health and economic outcomes. *Health Policy and Technology, 11*(2), 100594.

Bahceli, Y. (2021). Wealthy, efficient Dutch play catch-up in vaccine rollout. Health News. https://www.reuters.com/article/us-health-coronavirus-netherlands-vaccin-idUKKBN2AH1CC. Accessed 15.08.21.

Ball, P. (2021). Why England's COVID 'Freedom Day' alarms researchers. *Nature*. https://www.nature.com/articles/d41586-021-01938-4. Accessed 15.08.21.

BBC News. (2022). Covid: Thousands protest in France against proposed new vaccine pass. https://www.bbc.com/news/world-europe-59925408. Accessed on 18.08.21.

Bonanad, C., García-Blas, S., Tarazona-Santabalbina, F., Sanchis, J., Bertomeu-González, V., Fácila, L., Ariza, A., Núñez, J., & Cordero, A. (2020). The effect of age on mortality in patients with COVID-19: A meta-analysis with 611,583 subjects. *Journal of Post-Acute and Long-term Care Medicine, 21*(7), P915–P918.

Boogaerts, T., Quireyns, M., De Prins, M., Pussig, B., De Loof, H., et al. (2022). Temporal monitoring of stimulants during the COVID-19 pandemic in Belgium through the analysis of influent wastewater. *International Journal of Drug Policy, 104*, 103679.

Bosa, I., Castelli, A., Castelli, M., Ciani, O., Compagni, A., & Garofano, M. (2020). Italy's response to the coronavirus pandemic. Cambridge Core Blog [Online]. https://www.cambridge.org/core/blog/2020/04/16/italys-response-to-the-coronavirus-pandemic/. Accessed on 18.08.23.

Bosa, I., Castelli, A., Castelli, M., Ciani, O., Compagni, A., Galizzi, M. M., Garofano, M., Ghislandi, S., Giannoni, M., Marini, G., & Vainieri, M. (2021). Response to COVID-19: Was Italy (un)prepared? *Health Economics, Policy and Law, 17*(1), 1–13.

Boterman, W. (2023). Population density and SARS-CoV-2 pandemic: Comparing the geography of different waves in The Netherlands. *Urban Studies, 60*(8), 1377–1402.

Casasnovas, J. L., Seguí, F. L., & Goset, A. A. (2021). Sustainability and Resilience in the Spanish Health System. London School of Economics and Political Science (LSE) in partnership with Health System Sustainability and Resilience (PHSSR). LSE Consulting.

de España, G. (2020). COVID-19 vaccination strategy in Spain: Key points. https://www.sanidad. gob.es/gabinetePrensa/notaPrensa/pdf/24.11241120144436287.pdf. Accessed on 18.08.23.

de España, G. (2022). Strategy of COVID-19 vaccination. https://www.vacunacovid.gob.es/ preguntas-y-respuestas/que-vacunas-tendremos-disponibles-en-espana. Accessed on 18.08.23.

Deutsche Welle. (2020). What's in Germany's emergency coronavirus budget? https://www.dw.com/ en/whats-in-germanys-emergency-coronavirus-budget/a-52917360. Accessed on 18.08.23.

Deutsche Welle. (2021a). Chronology: How COVID has spread in Germany. https://www. dw.com/en/covid-how-germany-battles-the-pandemic-a-chronology/a-58026877. Accessed on 18.08.23.

Deutsche Welle. (2021b). COVID Highlights a Geographic Split in Germany. https://www.dw.com/ en/covid-highlights-a-geographic-split-in-germany/a-59884113. Accessed on 18.08.23.

Donovan, E. T. (2021). The Detail: UK's 'Freedom Day' comes amid soaring Covid-19 cases. https://www.stuff.co.nz/national/the-detail/300362357/the-detail-uks-freedom-day-comes-amid-soaring-covid19-cases. Accessed 15.08.21.

DPCM. (2020). Decreto del Presidente del Consiglio dei Ministri (DPCM) 26/04/2020—Ulteriori disposizioni attuative del decreto-legge 23 febbraio 2020, n. 6, recante misure urgenti in materia di contenimento e gestione dell'emergenza epidemiologica da COVID-19, applicabili sull'intero territorio nazionale. In: GOVERNMENT, I. (ed.).

Epifanio, M. S., Grutta, S. L., Piombo, M. A., Riolo, M., Spicuzza, V., Franco, M., et al. (2023). Hopelessness and burnout in Italian healthcare workers during COVID-19 pandemic: The mediating role of trait emotional intelligence. *Frontiers in Psychology, 14*.

European Centre for Disease Prevention and Control. (2020). *Overview of COVID-19 vaccination strategies and vaccine deployment plans in the EU/EEA and the UK—2 December 2020.* Stockholm.

European Observatory on Health Systems and Policies. (2019). State of Health in the EU United Kingdom Country Health Profile 2019. https://eurohealthobservatory.who.int/docs/ librariesprovider3/country-health-profiles/country-health-profile-2019-united-kingdom.pdf ?sfvrsn=a7699a06_1&download=true#:~:text=Among%20those%20who%20do%2C%20 more,they%20had%20at%20least%20two. Accessed on 18.08.23.

Eurostat. (2020). Digital Economy and Society. https://ec.europa.eu/eurostat/tgm/table.do?tab=tab le&init=1&plugin=1&language=en&pcode=tin00073. Accessed on 18.08.23.

Eurostat. (2021). EU's median age increased to 44.1 years in 2021. https://ec.europa.eu/eurostat/ web/products-eurostat-news/-/ddn-20220228-1. Accessed on 18.08.23.

Federal Foreign Office. (2022). COVID-19: Germany's commitment to fair distribution of vaccines. https://www.auswaertiges-amt.de/en/aussenpolitik/themen/covax/2396914#:~:text=To%20 date%2C%20Germany%20has%20donated,particularly%20in%20Africa%20and%20Asia. Accessed on 18.08.23.

Hale, T., Angrist, N., Cameron-Blake, E., Hallas, L., Kira, B., Majumdar, S., et al. (2020). Oxford COVID-19 government response tracker. https://www.bsg.ox.ac.uk/research/research-projects/ covid-19-government-response-tracker. Accessed 28.07.21.

Helliwell, J. F., Layard, R., Sachs, J. D., De Neve, J.-E., Aknin, L. B., Huang, H., et al. (Eds.). (2020). *World happiness report 2020.* Sustainable Development Solutions Network.

Henríquez, J., Gonzalo-Almorox, E., García-Goñi, M., & Paolucci, F. (2020). The first months of the COVID-19 pandemic in Spain. *Health Policy and Technology, 9*(4), 560–574.

ILOSTAT. (2023). COVID-19 and labour statistics. https://ilostat.ilo.org/topics/covid-19/#. Accessed on 18.08.23.

Institute for Government. (2021). Coronavirus vaccine rollout. https://www.instituteforgovernment.org.uk/article/explainer/coronavirus-vaccine-rollout. Accessed on 09.05.23.

Institute for Government Analysis. (2022). Timeline of UK government coronavirus lockdowns and restrictions. https://www.instituteforgovernment.org.uk/data-visualisation/timeline-coronavirus-lockdowns. Accessed 9.05.23.

Jovell, A., Blendon, R. J., Navarro, M. D., Fleischfresser, C., Benson, J. M., DesRoches, C. M., et al. (2007). Public trust in the Spanish healthcare system. *Health Expectations, 10*, 350–357.

Maringe, C., Spicer, J., Morris, M., Purushotham, A., Nolte, E., Sullivan, R., et al. (2020). The impact of the COVID-19 pandemic on cancer deaths due to delays in diagnosis in England, UK: A national, population-based, modelling study. *The Lancet Oncology, 21*(8), 1023–1034.

Mason, R., & Elgot, J. (2021). JCVI 'largely opposed' to Covid vaccination for children under 16. The Guardian. https://www.theguardian.com/society/2021/aug/07/jcvi-largely-opposed-to-covid-vaccination-for-children-under-16. Accessed 04.02.22.

Mathieu, E., Ritchie, H., Ortiz-Ospina, E., Roser, M., Hasell, J., Appel, C., et al. (2021). A global database of COVID-19 vaccinations. *Nature Human Behaviour*. https://www.nature.com/articles/s41562-021-01122-8. Accessed 01.02.22.

Ministry for Europe and Foreign Affairs. (2023). With COVAX: France is a major player in vaccine solidarity. https://www.diplomatie.gouv.fr/en/french-foreign-policy/development-assistance/priority-sectors/health/news/article/with-covax-france-is-a-major-player-in-vaccine-solidarity. Accessed on 18.08.23.

Modenese, A., Loney, T., & Gobba, F. (2022). COVID-19-related mortality amongst physicians in Italy: Trend pre- and post-SARS-CoV-2 vaccination campaign. *Healthcare, 10*(7).

Natalia, Y. A., Faes, C., Neyens, T., & Molenberghs, G. (2022). The COVID-19 wave in Belgium during the fall of 2020 and its association with higher education. *PLoS One, 17*(2), e0264516.

OECD. (2021). Health at a glance 2021: OECD indicators, OECD Publishing., https://doi.org/10.1787/ae3016b9-en. Accessed on 18.08.23.

OECD. (2023). Old-age dependency ratio (indicator). https://data.oecd.org/pop/old-age-dependency-ratio.htm. Accessed on 15.10.23.

OECD. Stat. (2023). Health Statistics. https://stats.oecd.org/Index.aspx?ThemeTreeId=9. Accessed on 18.08.23.

OECD/European Observatory on Health Systems and Policies. (2021). *Belgium: Country health profile 2021, state of health in the EU*. OECD Publishing. Paris/European Observatory on Health Systems and Policies, Brussels.

OECD/European Union. (2022). Hospital beds per 1,000 population, 2010 and 2020 or nearest year. In health at a glance: Europe 2022: State of health in the EU cycle, OECD Publishing., https://doi.org/10.1787/0628c7c7-en. Accessed on 18.08.23.

Office for National Statistics (ONS). (2022). Population estimates for the UK, England, Wales, Scotland and Northern Ireland: mid-2021. https://www.ons.gov.uk/peoplepopulationandcommunity/populationandmigration/populationestimates/bulletins/annualmidyearpopulationestimates/mid2021. Accessed 18.08.23.

Onder, G., Rezza, G., & Brusaferro, S. (2020). Case-fatality rate and characteristics of patients dying in relation to COVID-19 in Italy. *JAMA, 323*(18), 1775–1776.

Rhodes, A., Ferdinande, P., Flaatten, H., et al. (2012). The variability of critical care bed numbers in Europe. *Intensive Care Medicine, 38*, 1647–1653.

Ricci, G., Pallotta, G., Sirignano, A., Amenta, F., & Nittari, G. (2020). Consequences of COVID-19 outbreak in Italy: Medical responsibilities and governmental measures. *Frontiers in Public Health, 8*.

Robert Koch Institute. (2022). Monitoring Des COVID-19-Impfgeschehens in Deutschland: Monatsbericht des RKI Vom. https://www.rki.de/DE/Content/Infekt/Impfen/ImpfungenAZ/COVID-19/Monatsberichte/2022-07-07.pdf?__blob=publicationFile. Accessed on 23.06.23.

Robert Koch Institute. (2023). Digital vaccination rate monitoring for COVID-19 vaccination. https://www.rki.de/DE/Content/InfAZ/N/Neuartiges_Coronavirus/Daten/Impfquoten-Tab.html. Accessed on 23.06.23.

Roberts, H. (2021). Italy's uphill battle to force health workers to get vaccinated. Politico. 2021. https://www.politico.eu/article/italy-health-workers-coronavirus-vaccinations/.   Accessed 15.08.21.

Schaart, E. (2021). Back-of-the-pack Dutch under fire for slow coronavirus vaccine rollout. Politico. https://www.politico.eu/article/netherlands-coronavirus-vaccination-slow-start-mark-rutte-hugo-de-jonge/#:~:text=However%2C%20the%20Dutch%20lagged%20behind,each%20 of%20its%2025%20regions. Accessed on 15.06.21.

Schmitt, V. H., Hobohm, L., Sagoschen, I., Sivanathan, V., Hahad, O., Münzel, T., et al. (2023). Diabetes mellitus and its association with adverse in-hospital outcomes in patients with COVID-19—A Nationwide study. *Viruses, 15*(8), 1627.

Sierra, B. N., Bossuyt, N., Braeye, T., et al. (2020). All-cause mortality supports the COVID-19 mortality in Belgium and comparison with major fatal events of the last century. *Archives of Public Health, 78*, 117.

Sprengholz, P., Betsch, C., & Böhm, R. (2021). Reactance revisited: Consequences of mandatory and scarce vaccination in the case of COVID-19. *Applied Psychology, Health and Well-Being, 13*, 986– 995.

Sterl, S., Stelzmann, D., Luettschwager, N., & Gerhold, L. (2023). COVID-19 vaccination status in Germany: Factors and reasons for not being vaccinated (yet). *Frontiers in Public Health, 11*, 1070272.

The Economist. (2021). Why vaccine-shy French are suddenly rushing to get jabbed. 2021. https://www.economist.com/graphic-detail/2021/07/14/why-vaccine-shy-french-are-suddenly-rushing-to-get-jabbed. Accessed 15.06.21.

Vanham, P. (2021). Belgium's COVID-19 Comeback Is a Model for the World. https://foreignpolicy.com/2021/08/15/belgium-covid-19-pandemic-vaccination-campaign-model-europe-eu/. Accessed 15.08.21.

Vollmann, M., & Salewski, C. (2021). To get vaccinated, or not to get vaccinated, that is the question: Illness representations about COVID-19 and perceptions about COVID-19 vaccination as predictors of COVID-19 vaccination willingness among young adults in The Netherlands. *Vaccine, 9*(9), 941.

Wang, Y., Kentikelenis, A., McKee, M., & Stuckler, D. (2023). The far-right and anti-vaccine attitudes: Lessons from Spain's mass COVID-19 vaccine rollout. *European Journal of Public Health, 33*(2), 215–221.

WHO Global Health Expenditure. (2023). Global Health Expenditure Database. https://apps.who.int/nha/database. Accessed on 12.08.23.

World Bank. (2021). World Bank Open Data 2021. https://data.worldbank.org/. Accessed on 12.08.23.

World Health Organization (WHO). (2023). Global Health Workforce Statistics 2010, OECD, supplemented by country data. https://data.worldbank.org/indicator/SH.MED.PHYS. ZS?end=2010&start=1960. Accessed on 16.08.23.

Worldometers. (2021). Population. https://www.worldometers.info/. Accessed on 12.08.23.

Chapter 5
Case Studies: Evolution of the COVID-19 Pandemic in the Southern Hemisphere

Abstract This chapter discusses the complex dynamics of the COVID-19 pandemic and vaccine hesitancy through case studies of three Southern Hemisphere countries: Australia, New Zealand, and South Africa. Examining the evolution of the pandemic, non-pharmaceutical interventions, and vaccine rollout in these nations reveals the diverse impacts of government responses on public trust and well-being.

The chapter begins by examining the multifaceted challenges faced by Southern Hemisphere countries on both the supply and demand sides of healthcare services, including an ageing population, comorbidities, and unemployment. Through real-world examples, it underscores the profound mental health issues and burnout experienced by healthcare workers, highlighting the importance for policymakers to address these concerns proactively.

A comprehensive analysis of the pandemic timeline reveals the varying trajectories shaped by early government interventions, particularly focusing on the effectiveness of measures such as Managed Isolation and Quarantine, lockdowns, and social distancing. While aimed at curbing the spread of the virus, these policies inflicted significant mental harm on individuals and families, exacerbating economic challenges and social unrest.

Examining the specific experiences of Australia, New Zealand, and South Africa, the chapter explains the nuances of government strategies and their impacts. Australia's decentralised approach to lockdown regulations resulted in prolonged restrictions in certain regions, leading to civil unrest and loss of trust in the government's crisis management. New Zealand's initial elimination strategy gained international praise but faced criticism for prolonged isolation measures and vaccine rollout setbacks. Meanwhile, South Africa's stringent lockdowns exacerbated economic woes and spurred widespread civil unrest, compounded by allegations of government corruption undermining vaccine trust.

Drawing lessons from these experiences, the chapter emphasises the importance of adaptive policymaking and community engagement in creating effective responses to future health crises. By learning from the successes and failures of Southern Hemisphere countries, policymakers can foster resilience and trust, paving the way for more robust public health interventions and vaccine acceptance in the face of emerging challenges.

Keywords Southern hemisphere · Demand-side factors · Supply-side factors · Trust · Institutions

5.1   Introduction

This chapter focuses on specific Southern Hemisphere countries included as case studies in analysing the COVID-19 pandemic and vaccine hesitancy. Country introductions for three Southern Hemisphere countries, Australia, New Zealand and South Africa, will be provided. By including a country from Africa, we can see the effect on individuals who remain outside the current reach of effective prevention and treatment approaches to COVID-19. The chapter will discuss a timeline of the evolution of the COVID-19 pandemic, non-pharmaceutical interventions adopted, and each Southern Hemisphere country's relevant rollout of the COVID-19 vaccine. Particular emphasis will reflect how early government-mandated regulations, such as lockdowns, negatively impacted well-being while intended to preserve lives. In terms of the COVID-19 vaccine rollout, the chapter will provide an in-depth discussion of the strategies of Southern Hemisphere countries that mostly failed, thereby decreasing trust in institutions and, subsequently, the COVID-19 vaccine.

5.2   Case Study Countries

Before turning to our individual countries concerning the evolution of the COVID-19 pandemic and vaccine rollout, let's first look at the demand and supply factors related to our Southern Hemisphere countries.

Similar to the Northern Hemisphere, addressing the COVID-19 pandemic required interventions on both the supply and demand for healthcare services in our Southern Hemisphere countries. In this section, we briefly discuss the effects that the COVID-19 crisis had on the countries' healthcare systems by referring to demand and supply-side factors (Table 5.1). Specifically, we have added real-world examples for our Southern Hemisphere countries in discussing problems such as the ageing population, comorbidities and unemployment under demand-side factors and healthcare expenditure, the availability of healthcare professionals (nurses and doctors) and hospital beds under supply-side factors.

By November 2020, South Africa had 757,000 reported infections and 20,500 COVID-19-related deaths, with children making up 8% of COVID-19 confirmed cases (UNICEF, 2020). The deaths were attributed to limited access to medical care, especially for women who require antenatal and postnatal care services, as more women opted for home births. Limited access to health care was partly due to the

Table 5.1 Demand and supply factors in the Southern Hemisphere countries

Demand factors			
Variable	Australia	New Zealand	South Africa
Total population	25,660,000 (2020)	5,090,000 (2020)	58,800,000 (2020)
Density people/Km^2	3 (2020)	19 (2020)	48 (2020)
Median age	36.7 years (2020)	36.4 years (2020)	27.6 years (2020)
Life expectancy at birth	83 years (2020)	82 years (2020)	65 years (2020)
Population over 65 years old (% of total population)	16 (2020)	16 (2020)	6 (2020)
Old age dependency ratio	27.7 (2020)	28.9 (2020)	9.6 (2020)
Population aged 15 and over smoking daily (% of the population aged 15 years and over)	11.2 (2019)	12.5 (2019)	17.3 (2019)
People reporting a long-standing illness or health problem (%)	45.6 (2019)	25 (2019)	16.3 (2021)
Diabetes I and II prevalence among adults	5.6 (2019)	6.2 (2019)	12.7 (2019)
Tuberculosis notification rates per 100,000	6 (2019)	6.6 (2019)	615 (2019)
HIV prevalence rate (% of population ages 15–49)	0.1 (2019)	0.1 (2019)	18.6 (2019)
GDP per capita (USD)	51,722 (2020)	41,760 (2020)	5741 (2020)
Unemployment rate (% of the labour force)	6.5 (2020)	4.6 (2020)	24.3 (2020)
Working hours lost due to the COVID-19 crisis expressed as the number of FTE jobs (based on 40 h per week)	501.411 (2020)	−6.416 (2020)	1798.406 (2020)
Change in supply factors from pre- to during the COVID-19 pandemic			
Name of national healthcare system	Medicare	Te Whatu Ora	National Health Insurance
Hospital beds per 1000	3.8 (2016) 2.5 (2021/2022)	2.4 (2009) 2.5 (2020)	2.3 (2010) 2.0 (2020)
ICU beds per 100,000	8.9 (2006) 8.1 (2020)	5.5 (2006) 3.4 (2020)	8.9 (2015) 5.6 (2020)
Number of doctors per 1000	3.3 (2010) 3.9 (2020)	2.6 (2010) 3.4 (2020)	0.7 (2004) 0.8 (2021)
Nurses per 1000	10.4 (2010) 13.1 (2020)	10.6 (2010) 11.8 (2020)	3.9 (2004) 5.00 (2018)
Hospitals per 1,000,000	61.05 (2010) 52.19 (2020)	37.92 (2010) 31.24 (2020)	1.00 (2014) -
Domestic general government health expenditure (GGHE-D) per capita in US$	3600.12 (2010) 4431.03 (2020)	2531.12 (2010) 3241.86 (2020)	322.40 (2010) 304.09 (2020)

Source: Australian Bureau of Statistics (2021), Statistics New Zealand (2021), Statistics South Africa (2021), Worldometers (2021), World Bank (2021), OECD (2023), Australian Institute of Health and Welfare (2022, 2023), Akindele and Useh (2021), OECD (2021), ILOSTAT (2023), OECD. Stat (2023), Mokhele et al. (2021), Wallace et al. (2015), Martin et al. (2010), WHO (2023), WHO Global Health Expenditure (2023), WHO (2020), Ministry of Health (2020a) and NSW Government (2019)

decrease in domestic general government health expenditure per capita from 2010 to 2020 of nearly 6% (Table 5.1). The need for medical professionals, equipment, and hospital beds escalated, creating challenges in resource allocation. These deaths were also due to more attention being given to COVID-19, which prompted the resurgence of other deadly non-communicable diseases, such as cardiovascular diseases, cancer, diabetes and chronic lower respiratory diseases, during the lockdown and the neglect of comorbidities like HIV (18.6%), Tuberculosis (615 per 100,000 population) and diabetes mellitus (12.7%) (Table 5.1). A multi-site observational study conducted in the Western Cape Province, South Africa, found a two-fold risk of COVID-19 death adjusted for age and sex in people living with HIV regardless of viremia or immunosuppression (Western Cape Department of Health in collaboration with the National Institute for Communicable Diseases, 2021). The death of the breadwinner of a family caused hardships, hunger and pain, especially in vulnerable families that are living below the poverty line.

South Africa already had an unemployment rate of 24.3% in 2020 (Table 5.1), when an estimated 2.2 million jobs were lost between April and June 2020, causing a further loss in livelihoods and exacerbating the direct impact on families. This substantial loss of jobs and income meant that 47% of households ran out of money for food in April during lockdown (UNICEF, 2020). High unemployment rates additionally hinder the healthcare system in South Africa by limiting funding (approximately 9% of the population paid taxes in 2020) and resources for healthcare infrastructure, recruitment of healthcare workers, and investment in critical medical equipment.

The picture for New Zealand and Australia looks significantly different compared to South Africa. By November 2020, New Zealand and Australia had reported 1594 and 27,569 infections and 25 and 914 COVID-19-related deaths, respectively (Mathieu et al., 2021).

However, both New Zealand and Australia face the problem of an ageing population (10% higher than South Africa in 2020) (Table 5.1). By 1 September 2020, 462 of the 657 deaths in Australia had occurred in aged care services, with the median age being 86 years (Australian Government Department of Health, 2020). As noted by Smallwood et al. (2021), Australian healthcare workers (3.9 doctors and 13.1 nurses per 1000 people) (Table 5.1) faced many challenges, including heavy workloads due to the high number of elderly patients being hospitalised, redeployment or job insecurity, social change and increased risks to their own lives and their family members. The authors who conducted a national, cross-sectional study found that between 7 August and 23 October 2020, healthcare workers had experienced mental illness during the pandemic, with 59.8% experiencing mild to severe anxiety, 70.9% moderate to severe burnout and 57.3% mild to severe depression. This undoubtedly poses a risk to workforce retention, which is concerning, seeing as the number of Australians aged 85 years and over is projected to double by 2042, constituting 3% of Australia's population (Australian Bureau of Statistics, 2018).

Considering the above, we can see how the COVID-19 pandemic has highlighted the complicated relationship between demand-side and supply-side factors in healthcare systems in our Southern Hemisphere countries. Our real-world examples emphasise how, for example, an ageing population, comorbidities, and unemployment can exert pressure on vital supply-side resources like healthcare expenditure and professionals and hospital beds. We also note that the COVID-19 pandemic has highlighted significant mental health issues and burnout in our healthcare workers, which have significant repercussions in the years to come if better crisis preparedness and psychological support services are not seen as urgent for policymakers.

Now, let's turn to our individual Southern Hemisphere country case studies.

5.2.1   Government-Mandated Regulations and the Impact on Public Trust During COVID-19: A Focus on Australia

Australia has a population of 25.5 million and an average happiness score of 7.223 for 2019 (Helliwell et al., 2020). When COVID-19 hit, Australia had an annual GDP growth rate of 1.9% in the year to December 2019, debt as a percentage of GDP was 41.73%, and the unemployment rate was 6.2% (Australia Bureau of Statistics, 2020).

Australia, which follows a federal government system, never went into complete lockdown, such as that implemented by New Zealand and South Africa. The first confirmed case on Australian soil was reported on 25 January 2020, and it recorded the first COVID-19-related death on 1 March (Fig. 5.1). However, it wasn't until 15 March (50 days after the first confirmed case) that the Australian government banned gatherings of more than 500 people. This number changed to a maximum of 100 people on 18 March, and on 19 March, the border was closed to non-residents, a strategy to limit the importation of the virus. From 23 March onwards, different states implemented various lockdown regulations related to clubs, bars, places of worship, cinemas, gyms and casinos, and in some states, schools were closed down.

On 29 March, the government urged (not mandated) that Australians should stay at home other than for food shopping, medical care needs, exercise or work/education that could not be done from home. Additionally, a ban was placed on congregating with more than two people in public. But this was the most stringent lockdown regulation mandated by the Australian government. The mean Stringency index

Fig. 5.1 Evolution of the COVID-19 pandemic in Australia. *Source*: Authors' own Figure

(Hale et al., 2020) for Australia's time period was 40, lower than that of either New Zealand or South Africa.

The multi-faceted Australian response continued to develop as different states within the federation implemented varying degrees of lockdown measures. However, the decentralisation of power within Australia's federal structure allowed the Premier of Victoria, Daniel Andrews, to keep the city of Melbourne, with a population exceeding five million, under strict lockdown for a total of 262 days since March 2020. This meant that Melbourne spent more time under COVID-19 lockdowns than any other city worldwide. Melbourne's sixth lockdown finally ended when the city reached its 70% double dose target for the COVID-19 vaccine on 21 October 2021 (BBC News, 2021a). This decision by Premier Andrews divided the state of Victoria and earned him the name of "Dictator Dan" since he was the face of pain and misery to many Victorians. The unimaginable length of the lockdowns led to several violent protests and civil unrest. For example, when protesters showed up in the thousands at the Shrine of Remembrance in September 2021, they were met by police in tanks packing gas grenade launchers and rubber bullets. There were ugly scenes that saw men, women, children and dogs blasted for practising their democratic right to protest. Property was destroyed, cars were damaged, and ordinary people were injured (Flower, 2023).

Australia launched its COVID-19 vaccine rollout on 22 February 2021, a week after taking delivery of the first COVID-19 (Pfizer-BioNTech) vaccines and approving the usage of AstraZeneca (Australian Government Department of Health, 2021). The early phase of the rollout was marked by the prioritisation of quarantine and border workers, frontline healthcare workers and aged and disability care residents and staff. When the vaccination rollout started in late February, the government aimed to administer four million doses by the end of March 2021 (Australian Government Department of Health, 2021). However, the government failed miserably and missed their target by a staggering 3.4 million doses and could only administer 600,000 doses by the end of March, which equated to only 2.57% of the population who received at least one dose (Mathieu et al., 2021). The initial challenges faced with getting momentum behind the rollout were primarily due to international supply issues, natural disasters, including the New South Wales floods, errors and booking issues (BBC News, 2021b).

5.2.2   New Zealand's COVID-19 Response: From Accolades to Contempt

New Zealand, Australia's cousin, has a significantly smaller population of 5.5 million and a higher average happiness score of 7.3 in the year 2019 (Helliwell et al., 2020). The economic outlook was positive, featuring an annual GDP growth rate of 2.3% (somewhat higher than Australia's) in the year leading up to December 2019. The country's debt as a percentage of GDP and unemployment rate were relatively lower than Australia's at 25 and 4.2%, respectively (Statistics New Zealand, 2020).

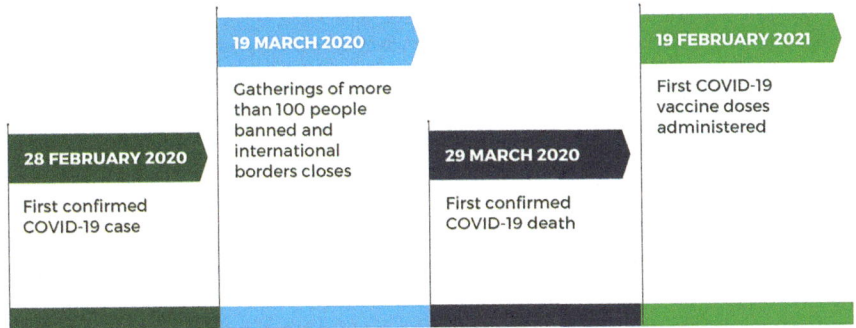

Fig. 5.2 Evolution of the COVID-19 pandemic in New Zealand. *Source*: Authors' own Figure

After the first confirmed case of COVID-19 emerged on 28 February 2020 (Fig. 5.2), New Zealand committed to an 'elimination strategy' in response to the COVID-19 pandemic, which provided a sustained approach to *keep it out, find it and stamp it out*. Under the elimination strategy, all activities focused on getting to and maintaining 'zero COVID-19', and an Alert Level Framework was implemented to support this elimination strategy (Ministry of Health, 2023).

New Zealand acted swiftly after announcing its elimination strategy and closed its international borders on 19 March to anyone but New Zealand citizens and residents (see discussion below about Managed Isolation and Quarantine). A mere week later, New Zealand declared a nationwide lockdown (alert level 4—the most stringent) on 26 March. Under level 4 lockdown, people could leave their homes only for essential reasons, but mask-wearing in supermarkets and health facilities was mandatory. Additionally, people were told to work from home except if they were deemed essential personnel. No international or national travel between cities was allowed, and all levels of educational institutions were closed. However, New Zealanders were allowed to exercise outside their homes at any given time as long as people stayed 2 m apart. New Zealand's Stringency Index for the period, ranging from 1 January to 30 May, averaged 41.35, indicating a higher level of stringency than Australia but lower than South Africa (Hale et al., 2020).

On 27 April 2020, New Zealand moved to alert level 3, which loosened some restrictions. By 8 June, New Zealand's elimination strategy seemed to have worked when the Ministry of Health (2020b) reported that there were no more active cases of COVID-19 in New Zealand. This brought accolades worldwide, applauding the New Zealand government's ability to eradicate COVID-19 amidst the struggles of most countries to contain the spread of the virus. After 102 days of being COVID-19-free, a mere five new cases sent New Zealand back into lockdown on 12 August 2020, but this time, different levels of stringency were imposed across the country. For Auckland, the largest city in New Zealand with 33 per cent of the population, alert level 3 lockdown was reinstated while the rest of New Zealand transitioned to alert level 2. After a span of 19 days, Auckland transitioned to alert level 2, but free movement, which comes with alert level 1, was only allowed on 7 October 2020.

Fast-forward to 2021, and New Zealand's zero-COVID-19 policy became the laughingstock of the world. On 14 February, Auckland was again placed back into level 3 lockdown for three confirmed cases. Seeing that 28% of the Auckland workforce was not permitted to work under alert level 3, the estimated cost to the economy for the period spent in level 3 lockdown was a considerable $60–$69 million (ASB, 2021a). Incredibly, on 28 February, the government sent Auckland back into level 3 lockdown for 1 week because of a single case of COVID-19. Despite no other positive cases being reported, Auckland only moved to level 1 on 12 March 2021. This time, the cost to the economy was an insurmountable $240 million (ASB, 2021b).

On 19 April 2021, a Trans-Tasman quarantine-free travel bubble started allowing people to move between New Zealand and Australia without quarantining. However, this bubble travel was paused and started several times during the year. And again, on 17 August 2021, when the first case of COVID-19 since June was reported, Auckland was placed under level 4 lockdown. The government was severely criticised for this move by health experts worldwide who called the decision archaic and misinformed, earning the country the less than flattering nickname, 'hermit nation' (Cohen, 2022). Quarantine-free travel with Australia was also suspended until February 2022 (New Zealand Doctor, 2023).

New Zealand set up a Managed Isolation and Quarantine (MIQ) system as part of the *keep it out, find it and stamp it out* policy (Ministry of Business, Innovation, & Employment, 2023). This meant that citizens or residents entering the border of New Zealand were legally required to stay in an MIQ facility for 14 days at their own expense[1] (changed to 7 days in October 2021) and had to have a negative COVID-19 test and confirmation from a Medical Officer of Health stating they were a low risk of having or transmitting COVID-19 before they could leave the facility (Ministry of Business, Innovation, & Employment, 2023). This policy was accredited for its success in keeping New Zealand's infected and fatality numbers low.

However, this policy was also accredited for the immense mental harm done to individuals and families. The MIQ lottery system meant travellers needed a voucher to enter the country. Still, soon, there were reports of automated scripts and bots being used on the MIQ website, allowing those willing to pay or with the technical skills to jump the queue. It led to exasperated travellers refreshing the MIQ site up to 10,000 times and still not getting a room. An inadequate number of rooms was available, which meant that, for example, 26,000 New Zealanders abroad fought for 3000 spots, which sold out in 67 min (Stewart, 2021). The flow-on effect of this was that many Kiwis were being kept separated from the people closest to them, missing weddings and milestone birthdays, not being allowed into New Zealand to see dying parents or siblings, and subsequently missing their funerals. In 2022, New Zealand's Ombudsman slammed the MIQ system as unreasonable and demanded that the New

---

[1] $1610 for the first or only person in the family travel group, $460 for each additional adult in the family travel group, $230 for each additional child (3 to 17 years old, inclusive) in the family travel group.

Zealand government apologise to thousands of Kiwis who couldn't get back into New Zealand. The Prime Minister, Jacinda Ardern, refused to apologise (Wade, 2022). Only in February 2022 could fully vaccinated New Zealanders and other eligible travellers returning to New Zealand from Australia enter New Zealand and self-isolate for 14 days rather than enter MIQ (Ministry of Business, Innovation, & Employment, 2023).

For the *stamp it out* part of the policy, people who tested positive for COVID-19 had to self-isolate for 10 days, which decreased to 7 days, and this last COVID-19 mandate was only dropped in Augustus 2023 more than 3 years after its implementation. Long after, the rest of the world got on with life.

In terms of New Zealand's COVID-19 vaccine rollout, the government commenced the vaccination campaign on 19 February 2021, with border workers and those working in MIQ facilities being the first group to receive the Pfizer/BioNTech vaccine. Subsequently, other priority groups, such as healthcare workers and essential personnel, came next in the rollout plan. However, the rollout faced several setbacks and mistakes that eroded public trust. For example, the Aged Care Association described the rollout as a 'shambles' since by April 2021 (2 months after initiating the rollout), rest homes around New Zealand were still waiting for the government to announce the start date for vaccinating elderly people (Wallis, 2021). The waiting period before even announcing the vaccination date of this particular high-priority group was baffling since rest homes such as Rosewood in Christchurch in the South Island were linked to one of the deadliest COVID-19 clusters (Lourens, 2020).

A significant issue was the government's decision to rely heavily on a single vaccine, Pfizer/BioNTech, rather than diversifying to use other vaccines such as AstraZeneca. This led to supply constraints as global demand for the vaccine surged. This decision, influenced by the prioritisation of vaccine effectiveness over cost, hindered New Zealand's ability to secure a steady vaccine supply, and the plan to vaccinate the general population by the end of 2021 faltered and fell behind schedule (Satherley, 2021). For example, by June 2021, New Zealand had only managed to vaccinate 9.2% (fully and partly vaccinated) of the population compared to Australia, which managed to vaccinate 17% and started its vaccine rollout 2 days later than New Zealand. Apart from the aforementioned, New Zealand's government's messaging also lacked transparency, leaving the public uninformed about the vaccination process. These missteps, combined with complacency following New Zealand's success in controlling the virus, fostered scepticism and frustration among the population (Vance, 2021).

In addition to vaccine-related challenges, the proliferation of misinformation and conspiracy theories about the COVID-19 vaccine has eroded trust in vaccination efforts (Thaker & Floyd, 2021). This problem is particularly prominent within New Zealand's ethnic minority and vulnerable communities (Tukuitonga, 2021). The failure to prioritise and reach these marginalised groups as part of the vaccination campaign and the perceived shortcomings in the government's vaccine rollout created fertile ground for spreading misinformation and, subsequently, a significant challenge in the battle against COVID-19 in New Zealand.

5.2.3   Navigating the Storm: South Africa's Resilience and Challenges During the COVID-19 Pandemic

South Africa has the largest population of the three Southern Hemisphere countries, with 57.7 million people. It also had the lowest average happiness score, with 4.814 for the year 2019 (Helliwell et al., 2020). The economy grew at a meagre 0.15% in 2019, debt as a percentage of GDP was 62.2%, and the unemployment rate was significantly higher than that of the other countries at 29% (Statistics South Africa, 2020). In light of the bleak economic outlook, the country's sovereign credit rating was downgraded to junk status by Moody's in March 2020, which impacted political stability and increased national debt and debt interest payments.

To combat the spread of COVID-19, South Africa adopted a similar strategy to New Zealand and decided on "*going fast and going hard*". South Africa reported its first confirmed case on 5 March 2020 (Fig. 5.3). Just 21 days later, on 27 March, the country implemented strict lockdown regulations comparable only to those of the Philippines and Jordan. During South Africa's level 5 lockdown, people were subjected to the same regulations as the New Zealanders; however, there were additional stringency measures, such as a ban on the sale of alcohol and tobacco and no exercise being permitted outside their homes. In addition, the South African government called for the help of the defence force to ensure compliance with the restrictions. The mean Stringency Index (Hale et al., 2020) for South Africa for this time period was 44.90, thus somewhat higher than that of New Zealand.

South Africa progressively moved down from level 5 lockdown to level 1 by September 2020. Alert level 1 meant people could move around freely while wearing masks, and shops, facilities, and schools were open (South African Government, 2022). South Africa continued to move between alert levels throughout 2021 and the beginning of 2022 until their National State of Disaster was lifted on 5 April 2022.

For South Africa, the impact of the coronavirus was devastating on the economy, with the first hard lockdown in 2020 causing three million job losses within a few months. In a survey conducted in 2020, nearly half (46%) of South Africans said their households frequently experienced hunger due to insufficient funds to buy

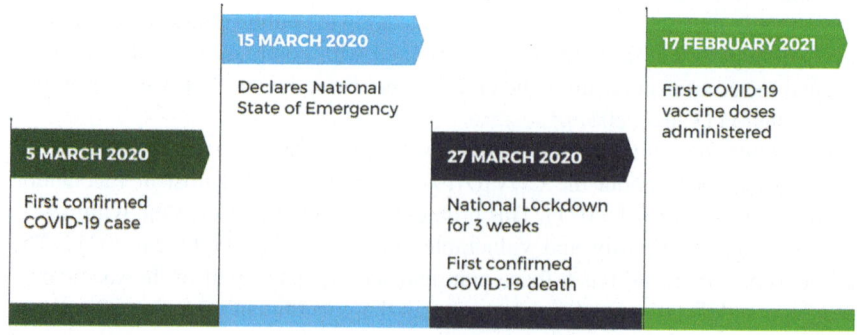

Fig. 5.3 Evolution of the COVID-19 pandemic in South Africa. *Source*: Authors' own Figure

food (IPSOS, 2021). Additionally, approximately six in every ten South Africans (58 per cent) said that *"The Covid-19 pandemic has a negative impact on the income of my household"*, and a half (50%) said, *"People in my household suffer more from stress and other illnesses during the Covid-19 pandemic"* (IPSOS, 2021).

Furthermore, unemployment (according to the strict definition) hit a new record high of 32.6% in the first quarter of 2021, with more than seven million people unemployed (Reuters, 2020). The rate was the highest since the quarterly labour force survey began in 2008.

In an attempt to mitigate the effects of the pandemic and lockdowns, the South African government topped up child support grants, first introduced in 1998, and introduced new relief schemes (Social Relief of Distress Grant and Temporary Employer-Employee Relief Scheme) but was forced to stop these benefits in April 2021, as the government could not afford them any longer. In June 2021, South Africa went into a third lockdown, causing massive hardship for poor families who rely on daily wage labour like construction and domestic workers, creating a 'tinder box ready to ignite' (van der Berg & Patel, 2021). The COVID-19 period was also marked by the worst violence in decades when rioters sent factories and malls up in flames, looters stripped supermarkets bare, and the army was used to stem the incredible civil unrest (Harrisberg, 2021). This unrest originated from the arrest and imprisonment of former president Jacob Zuma on 7 July 2021 due to his refusal to appear at an inquiry into high-level corruption during his 9 years in office until 2018. Following his arrest, his supporters took to the streets initially to demand his release. However, the protests quickly escalated into widespread looting, with rioters blocking major highways and setting fire to chemical plants, farms and food storage facilities. The violence resulted in the death of more than 300 lives and caused billions worth of damage (Harrisberg, 2021). This all added to South Africa's woes and pushed the economy closer to the brink of destruction.

As South Africa navigated the COVID-19 pandemic, it encountered various challenges that impacted both its response to the virus and vaccine rollout. These issues ranged from capacity constraints to the prevalence of anti-vaccination campaigns and mistrust in the government due to corruption allegations (Cocks, 2021). In January 2022, President Cyril Ramaphosa sanctioned an inquiry into his government's coronavirus spending in 2020, prompted by a series of scandals that caused public outrage. This was done since South African investigators flagged COVID-19 contracts worth around 2.1 billion rand (US$137.12 million) for possible corruption and fraud (Reuters, 2022). The Special Investigating Unit (SIU), which led the investigation, had said previously that it had uncovered instances of inflated pricing for personal protective equipment, violations of procurement rules, and non-delivery of services despite payments being made. Subsequently, the SIU referred 224 government departments or entities officials for disciplinary action after finding that 2803 contracts were irregular. It identified some of those facing accusations and estimated that the value of cash and assets to be recovered was around 552 million rand.[2]

---

[2] $1 = 15.3149 rand.

South Africa started their vaccine rollout in February 2021. However, it is safe to say that when they found themselves in the grip of a resurgence with the Delta virus in June 2021, the government failed South Africa's people by not ensuring they were timeously vaccinated. While the vaccine programme was underway, it struggled to meet even the National Department of Health's revised targets. By June 2021, a mere 3.3 per cent of South Africans had been vaccinated, including less than one-third of those older than 60 who were targeted to be vaccinated by the end of June 2021 (Department of Health, 2023).

Challenges in the vaccine supply chain meant significant constraints for South Africa, like many other African countries, who could not secure sufficient COVID-19 vaccine doses. This has been due to the global inequity in vaccine distribution (refer to Chap. 10.2). These failures, however, also underscore a lack of planning. South Africa's delayed engagement with pharmaceutical companies in bilateral discussions meant they couldn't ensure getting vaccines early. South Africa only started earnestly engaging with companies in January 2021. This simply put it at the back of the queue for vaccine acquisition. Equally important have been the impediments to widespread access and effective community mobilisation, especially for those within the high-risk groups targeted for vaccination. This hampered the rapid scaling-up of vaccinations (Madhi, 2021).

5.3   Summary

This chapter first looked at the effect of the COVID-19 pandemic concerning the supply and demand side of healthcare services. We highlighted real-world examples from our Southern Hemisphere countries. Specifically, we looked at challenges such as the ageing population, comorbidities (Diabetes and Tuberculosis) and unemployment under demand-side factors and constraints related to healthcare expenditure, the availability of healthcare professionals (nurses and doctors) and hospital beds under supply-side factors. Through exploring these challenges and constraints, we saw that significant mental health issues and burnout in healthcare workers could have significant repercussions in the future if not addressed by policymakers.

Next, we comprehensively discussed the COVID-19 pandemic timeline, including non-pharmaceutical interventions and the vaccine rollout across our three Southern Hemisphere countries: Australia, New Zealand and South Africa. By doing the aforementioned, we highlighted government responses that affected public trust and vaccine acceptance and caused mental harm.

The pandemic's timeline revealed variations in the evolution of the crisis but underscored governments' early interventions. The effectiveness of non-pharmaceutical measures, including Managed Isolation and Quarantine, lockdowns and social distancing, shaped each country's pandemic trajectory—these regulations aimed to curb the virus's spread and save lives. However, as we discuss in

Chap. 13, many of these policies directly led to the immense mental harm done to individuals and families, severely impacted businesses and caused a global economic recession.

We explored how Australia, which follows a federal government system, never went into lockdown as a country but instead allowed different states to implement different lockdown regulations. While Australia's lockdown stringency was the lowest of our three Southern Hemisphere countries, we did see how an abuse of power in Victoria meant the city of Melbourne spent 262 days in lockdown—longer than any other city in the world. The consequence of this was several violent protests and civil unrest, destroying property and cars and causing injuries to people. Australia's vaccine rollout did not start well, and as a result, people lost trust in the government's ability to manage the crisis effectively.

New Zealand's elimination strategy in response to the COVID-19 pandemic at first received accolades worldwide, but this turned into mocking the longer the government kept New Zealand cut off from the rest of the world. Additionally, when the government overreacted in 2021 and kept Auckland (where 28 per cent of the country's workforce resides) in lockdown for 12 days, it devastated the economy. New Zealand's Managed Isolation and Quarantine system, as part of the *keep it out, find it and stamp it out* policy, has been responsible for causing immense mental harm to individuals and families. Many Kiwis were kept separated from the people closest to them, missing weddings and milestone birthdays, not being allowed into New Zealand to see dying parents or siblings, and subsequently missing their funerals. New Zealand's vaccine rollout faced several setbacks and mistakes that eroded public trust.

South Africa imposed strict lockdown regulations comparable only to those of the Philippines and Jordan. The government went as far as banning the sale of alcohol and tobacco, and no exercise outside of homes was permitted. South Africans did not agree with these strict lockdowns, and subsequently, the government had to rely on the defence force to ensure compliance with the restrictions. For South Africa, COVID-19 decimated the economy, with the first hard lockdown in 2020 causing three million job losses within months, and almost 46% of South African households often went hungry because they did not have enough money to buy food. The COVID-19 period was also marked by the worst violence in decades when rioters sent factories and malls up in flames, looters stripped supermarkets bare, and the army was used to stem the incredible civil unrest which added to South Africa's woes and pushed the economy closer to the brink of destruction. South Africa's vaccine rollout faced issues such as capacity constraints and mistrust in the government due to corruption allegations. Subsequently, 224 government or government officials are being investigated for around 2.1 billion rand (US$137.12 million) worth of corruption and fraud.

The lessons learned from the experiences of our three Southern Hemisphere countries related to non-pharmaceutical and pharmaceutical interventions will undoubtedly contribute to more effective responses to future crises and public health challenges.

References

Akindele, M. O., & Useh, U. (2021). Multimorbidity of chronic diseases of lifestyle among south African adults. *The Pan African Medical Journal, 38.* Accessed on 23.10.23.

ASB. (2021a). Here we go again, again. Economic Weekly. https://www.asb.co.nz/content/dam/asb/documents/reports/economic-weekly/economicweekly_150221.pdf. Accessed on 18.03.21.

ASB. (2021b). Bringing out the f-word. Economic Weekly. https://www.asb.co.nz/content/dam/asb/documents/reports/economic-weekly/economicweekly_010321.pdf. Accessed on 18.03.21.

Australian Bureau of Statistics. (2018). Population Projections, Australia. https://www.abs.gov.au/statistics/people/population/population-projections-australia/2017-base-2066. Accessed on 18.08.23.

Australian Bureau of Statistics. (2020). Labour Force, Australia. https://www.abs.gov.au/statistics/labour/employment-and-unemployment/labour-force-australia/latest-release. Accessed on 18.08.23.

Australian Bureau of Statistics. (2021). Snapshot of Australia. https://www.abs.gov.au/statistics/people/people-and-communities/snapshot-australia/latest-release#:~:text=The%20median%20age%20of%20all%20Australians%20remains%20at%2038%20years%20in%202021. Accessed on 18.08.23.

Australian Government Department of Health. (2020). Coronavirus (COVID-19) at a glance. https://www.health.gov.au/resources/publications/coronavirus-covid-19-at-a-glance. Accessed on 18.08.23.

Australian Government Department of Health. (2021). COVID-19 vaccine rollout. https://www.health.gov.au/initiatives-and-programs/covid-19-vaccines. Accessed on 18.08.23.

Australian Institute of Health and Welfare. (2022). Chronic conditions and multimorbidity. https://www.aihw.gov.au/reports/australias-health/chronic-conditions-and-multimorbidity. Accessed on 18.08.23.

Australian Institute of Health and Welfare. (2023). Australia's hospitals at a glance. https://www.aihw.gov.au/reports/hospitals/australias-hospitals-at-a-glance/contents/access-to-hospitals. Accessed on 18.08.23.

BBC News. (2021a). Melbourne: Celebrations as city exits sixth lockdown. https://www.bbc.com/news/world-australia-58998418. Accessed on 23.10.23.

BBC News. (2021b). What's gone wrong with Australia's vaccine rollout? https://www.bbc.com/news/world-australia-56825920. Accessed on 23.10.23.

Cocks, T. (2021). As vaccines arrive, South Africa faces widespread scepticism over safety. https://www.reuters.com/article/uk-health-coronavirus-safrica-anti-vacci-idUSKBN2A90YT. Accessed 04.02.22.

Cohen, D. (2022). How Jacinda Ardern turned New Zealand into a 'hermit kingdom'. The Telegraph. https://www.telegraph.co.uk/news/2022/02/12/jacinda-ardern-turned-new-zealand-hermit-kingdom/. Accessed on 23.10.23.

Department of Health. (2023). COVID-19 online resources and news portal. https://sacoronavirus.co.za/latest-vaccine-statistics/. Accessed on 23.10.23.

Flower, W. (2023). How Daniel Andrews divided Victoria with world's longest Covid lockdown that earned him the name 'Dictator Dan'. Daily Mail. https://www.dailymail.co.uk/news/article-12560657/How-Daniel-Andrews-divided-Victoria.html. Accessed on 23.10.23.

Hale, T., Angrist, N., Cameron-Blake, E., Hallas, L., Kira, B., Majumdar, S., et al. (2020). Oxford COVID-19 government response tracker. https://www.bsg.ox.ac.uk/research/research-projects/covid-19-government-response-tracker. Accessed 28.07.21.

Harrisberg, K. (2021). What's behind the rioting that rocked South Africa? Reuters News. https://news.trust.org/item/20210722170436-n1a8z. Accessed on 23.10.23.

Helliwell, J. F., Layard, R., Sachs, J. D., De Neve, J.-E., Aknin, L. B., Huang, H., & Wang, S. (Eds.). (2020). *World happiness report 2020.* Sustainable Development Solutions Network.

ILOSTAT. (2023). COVID-19 and labour statistics. https://ilostat.ilo.org/topics/covid-19/#. Accessed on 23.10.23.

IPSOS. (2021). Almost half of South African households go hungry due to Covid-19. https://www.ipsos.com/en-za/almost-half-south-african-households-go-hungry-due-covid-19. Accessed on 23.10.23.

Lourens, M. (2020). Rosewood rest home, NZ's deadliest Covid-19 cluster, breached obligations. https://www.stuff.co.nz/national/health/coronavirus/121791737/rosewood-rest-home-nzs-deadliest-covid19-cluster-breached-obligations. Accessed on 23.10.23.

Madhi, S. A. (2021). South Africa's latest COVID-19 lockdown puts spotlight back on vaccination failures. The Conversation. https://theconversation.com/south-africas-latest-covid-19-lockdown-puts-spotlight-back-on-vaccination-failures-163521#:~:text=This%20has%20been%20due%20to,it%20could%20get%20vaccines%20early. Accessed on 23.10.23.

Martin, J. M., Hart, G. K., & Hicks, P. (2010). A unique snapshot of intensive care resources in Australia and New Zealand. *Anaesthesia and Intensive Care, 38*, 149–158.

Mathieu, E., Ritchie, H., Roser, M., Hasell, J., Appel, C., & Giattino, C. (2021). A global database of COVID-19 vaccinations. *Nature Human Behaviour, 5*(7), 947–953.

Ministry of Business, Innovation & Employment. (2023). Isolation and quarantine. https://www.mbie.govt.nz/immigration-and-tourism/isolation-and-quarantine/. Accessed on 23.10.23.

Ministry of Health. (2020a). Immunisation Handbook 2020/2021. Tuberculosis. https://www.health.govt.nz/system/files/documents/pages/immunisation-handbook-21-tuberculosis-v8.pdf. Accessed on 23.10.23.

Ministry of Health. (2020b). No active cases of COVID-19. https://www.health.govt.nz/news-media/media-releases/no-active-cases-covid-19. Accessed on 23.10.23.

Ministry of Health. (2023). COVID-19: Protecting Aotearoa New Zealand. https://www.health.govt.nz/our-work/diseases-and-conditions/covid-19-novel-coronavirus/covid-19-response-planning/covid-19-protecting-aotearoa-new-zealand#:~:text=Elimination%20Strategy,-In%20March%202020&text=This%20was%20an%20important%20approach,was%20implemented%20to%20support%20this. Accessed on 23.10.23.

Mokhele, T., Sewpaul, R., Sifunda, S., Weir-Smith, G., Dlamini, S., Manyaapelo, T., et al. (2021). Spatial analysis of perceived health system capability and actual health system capacity for COVID-19 in South Africa. *The Open Public Health Journal, 14*, 388–398.

New South Wales (NSW) Government. (2019). Tuberculosis in New South Wales. Surveillance Report 2019. https://www.health.nsw.gov.au/Infectious/tuberculosis/Publications/2019-tb-report.pdf. Accessed on 23.10.23.

New Zealand Doctor. (2023). Timeline - coronavirus - COVID-19. https://www.nzdoctor.co.nz/timeline-coronavirus. Accessed on 23.10.23.

OECD. (2021). *Health at a glance 2021: OECD indicators*. OECD Publishing. https://doi.org/10.1787/ae3016b9-en. Accessed on 18.08.23.

OECD. (2023). Old-age dependency ratio (indicator). https://data.oecd.org/pop/old-age-dependency-ratio.htm Accessed on 18.08.23.

OECD. Stat. (2023). Health Statistics. https://stats.oecd.org/Index.aspx?ThemeTreeId=9. Accessed on 12.08.23.

Reuters. (2020). UPDATE 1-South Africa's unemployment rate reaches new record high in first quarter. https://www.reuters.com/article/safrica-economy-unemployment-idUSL2N2NJ0NV. Accessed on 15.10.2023.

Reuters. (2022). South African corruption probe flags COVID contracts worth $137 million. https://www.reuters.com/world/africa/safrican-corruption-probe-flags-covid-contracts-worth-137-million-2022-01-25/. Accessed on 15.10.23.

Satherley, D. (2021). Coronavirus: Almost everyone in NZ will need a vaccine to stop Delta variant spreading—study. https://www.newshub.co.nz/home/new-zealand/2021/06/coronavirus-almost-everyone-in-nz-will-need-a-vaccine-to-stop-delta-variant-spreading-study.html. Accessed 04.02.22.

Smallwood, N., Karimi, L., Bismark, M., Putland, M., Johnson, D., Dharmage, S. C., et al. (2021). High levels of psychosocial distress among Australian frontline healthcare workers during the COVID-19 pandemic: A cross-sectional survey. *General Psychiatry, 34*(5).

South African Government. (2022). Coronavirus COVID-19 Alert level 1. https://www.gov.za/covid-19/about/coronavirus-covid-19-alert-level-1. Accessed on 15.10.23.

Statistics New Zealand. (2020). Unemployment rate hits 5.3 percent due to COVID-19. Available from https://www.stats.govt.nz/news/unemployment-rate-hits-5-3-percent-due-to-covid-19. Accessed on 21.08.23.

Statistics New Zealand. (2021). National population estimates: At 30 June 2021. https://www.stats.govt.nz/information-releases/national-population-estimates-at-30-june-2021/. Accessed on 12.08.23.

Statistics South Africa. (2020). Quarterly employment statistics. http://www.statssa.gov.za/publications/P0277/P0277December2019.pdf. Accessed on 12.08.23.

Statistics South Africa. (2021). Mid-year population estimates 2021. https://www.statssa.gov.za/publications/P0302/Mid%20year%20estimates%202021_presentation.pdf. Accessed on 12.08.23.

Stewart, A. (2021). Our tribal nature explained: The team of 5 million v the kiwis who just want to come home. Stuff article. https://www.stuff.co.nz/travel/300412931/our-tribal-nature-explained-the-team-of-5-million-v-the-kiwis-who-just-want-to-come-home. Accessed on 13.09.23.

Thaker, J., & Floyd, B. (2021). Shifting COVID-19 vaccine intentions in New Zealand: Next steps in the vaccination campaign. *The Lancet Regional Health, 15*(100278).

Tukuitonga, C. (2021). COVID-19 in Pacific Islands people of Aotearoa/New Zealand: Communities taking control. In Y. Campbell & J. Connell (Eds.), *COVID in the islands: A comparative perspective on the Caribbean and the Pacific*. Palgrave Macmillan.

UNICEF. (2020). COVID-19 is a child rights crisis. Responding and reimagining for every child. https://www.unicef.org/southafrica/media/4721/file/ZAF-How-COVID-19-is-changing-childhood-in-SA-November-2020.pdf. Accessed on 13.09.23.

van der Berg, S., & Patel, L. (2021). COVID-19 pandemic has triggered a rise in hunger in South Africa. The Conversation. https://theconversation.com/covid-19-pandemic-has-triggered-a-rise-in-hunger-in-south-africa-164581. Accessed on 13.09.23.

Vance, A. (2021). We've been patient, but the vaccination rollout is not going to plan. https://www.stuff.co.nz/national/politics/opinion/300358215/weve-been-patient-but-the-vaccination-rollout-is-not-going-to-plan Accessed 15.08.21.

Wade, A. (2022). Jacinda Ardern doesn't apologise over MIQ lottery system as documents reveal Govt considered imprisoning Kiwis who used loophole. Newshub article. https://www.newshub.co.nz/home/politics/2022/12/jacinda-ardern-doesn-t-apologise-over-miq-lottery-system-as-documents-reveal-govt-considered-imprisoning-kiwis-who-used-loophole.html. Accessed on 22.08.23.

Wallace, D. J., Angus, D. C., Seymour, C. W., Barnato, A. E., & Kahn, J. M. (2015). Critical care bed growth in the United States. A comparison of regional and national trends. *American Journal of Respiratory and Critical Care Medicine, 191*(4), 410–416.

Wallis, S. (2021). Rest homes still waiting for Covid-19 vaccination start date. Checkpoint. 2021. https://www.rnz.co.nz/national/programmes/checkpoint/audio/2018790783/rest-homes-still-waiting-for-covid-19-vaccination-start-date. Accessed 08.02.22.

Western Cape Department of Health in collaboration with the National Institute for Communicable Diseases, South Africa. (2021). Risk factors for coronavirus disease 2019 (COVID-19) death in a population cohort study from the Western Cape Province, South Africa. *Clinical Infectious Diseases, 73*(7), e2005–e2015.

WHO Global Health Expenditure. (2023). Global Health Expenditure Database. https://apps.who.int/nha/database. Accessed on 12.08.23.

World Bank. (2021). World Bank Open Data 2021. https://data.worldbank.org/. Accessed on 12.08.23.

World Health Organization (WHO). 2020. Global tuberculosis report, 2020. https://www.who.int/ publications/i/item/9789240013131. Accessed on 12.08.23.

World Health Organization (WHO). (2023). Global Health Workforce Statistics 2010, OECD, supplemented by country data. https://data.worldbank.org/indicator/SH.MED.PHYS. ZS?end=2010&start=1960. Accessed on 12.08.23.

Worldometers. (2021). Population. https://www.worldometers.info/ Accessed on 12 August 2023.

Part II
Big Data and Behavioural Insights in the COVID-19 era

Part II starts with discussing the importance of high-frequency real-time information policymakers need regarding well-being. Something that became more apparent during the COVID-19 pandemic when policymakers were confronted with short-term horizons and imperfect information during the decision-making process.

Part II further conducts a comprehensive examination to understand the factors contributing to COVID-19 vaccine hesitancy, which the World Health Organization named one of the top ten threats to global health. Additionally, Part II investigates trends in attitudes toward the COVID-19 vaccine in a cross-country analysis. Using topic modelling and word clouds, we explain how a 'cocktail of emotions' driven by, for example, fear can contribute to why some countries face growing vaccine hesitancy. Subsequently, using supervised machine learning models, Part II illustrates how increasing people's happiness can bolster COVID-19 vaccine acceptance, helping societies attain the desirable "golden standard" of vaccination rates. Part II concludes by investigating the possible adverse consequences of non-vaccination on well-being, health, social relationships and the economy.

Part II
Big Data and Behavioural Insights in the COVID-19 era

Chapter 6
Big Data, Big Data Analytics, and Policymaking During a Global Pandemic

Abstract This chapter discusses the transformative role of Big Data and Big Data analytics in informing policymaking during global pandemics, focusing on the COVID-19 crisis. Exploring various applications of Big Data analytics, including sentiment analysis, predictive modelling, and behavioural analysis, the chapter explains how high-frequency data provides unprecedented insights into human behaviour, attitudes toward government responses, and disease dynamics.

The chapter begins by introducing the concept of Big Data and its advantages over traditional survey data, emphasising the need for real-time information to guide policymakers effectively. It illustrates how Big Data analytics enables the early detection and tracking of outbreaks, facilitates predictive modelling for disease spread, advances vaccine development and distribution, and optimises healthcare resource allocation.

Drawing on examples from the COVID-19 pandemic, the chapter highlights the invaluable contributions of Big Data analytics in understanding the virus's transmission patterns, assessing intervention effectiveness, and identifying vulnerable populations. It underscores the role of machine learning algorithms in analysing vast datasets to inform targeted public health messaging and mitigate misinformation.

Furthermore, the chapter outlines how Big Data empowers policymakers to monitor public sentiment, identify regions with low compliance rates, and assess the economic impact of the pandemic. By leveraging real-time insights from diverse data sources, policymakers can make data-driven decisions, respond swiftly to evolving challenges, and save lives.

Keywords Big Data · Analytics · Sentiment analysis · Emotions · Real-time information · Policymaking

6.1   Introduction

This chapter will introduce the reader to Big Data and Big Data analytics and discuss sentiment analysis as an example of applying Big Data analytics to Big Data. We consider the benefits of Big Data over survey data to demonstrate the need for high-frequency data rather than data released with significant time lags. Furthermore, we argue that high-frequency data is needed to allow policymakers access to virtually *real-time* information, giving them unprecedented insight into human behaviour and people's attitudes towards governments' responses to COVID-19. These findings will provide governments with significant future predictive powers regarding global pandemics.

6.2   What Is Big Data?

Big Data describes a complex and voluminous set of information. It includes *structured, unstructured, and semi-structured datasets* generated through information and communication technologies (ITC) like the Internet (Ularu et al., 2012). It is a challenge to manage Big Data, and *traditional* software *is not adequate. Therefore, it requires specific infrastructure to govern, analyse, and convert data to retrieve information.*

6.2.1   The Characteristics of Big Data

Big Data has five essential characteristics: volume, velocity, variety, veracity and value (Géczy, 2014). See Fig. 6.1, portraying the 5 V's of Big Data that we subsequently discuss.

6.2.1.1   Volume

The volume describes how much data is measured in bytes (Géczy, 2014). A byte is a group of binary digits or bits, usually eight digits (bits), or the amount of storage needed to store a single text character, for example, an "A". A byte is, therefore, a unit of memory size. To give you an idea of the volume of data, your home network might be able to download data at one million bytes every second, generally referred to as eight megabits per second or 8 Mb/s.

Big Data is measured in much bigger units than a byte and is instead measured in gigabytes (GB) (one billion bytes), a terabyte (TB) (1 trillion bytes), a zettabyte (ZB) (1 sextillion bytes), and yottabytes (YB) (a quadrillion GB). To put this into

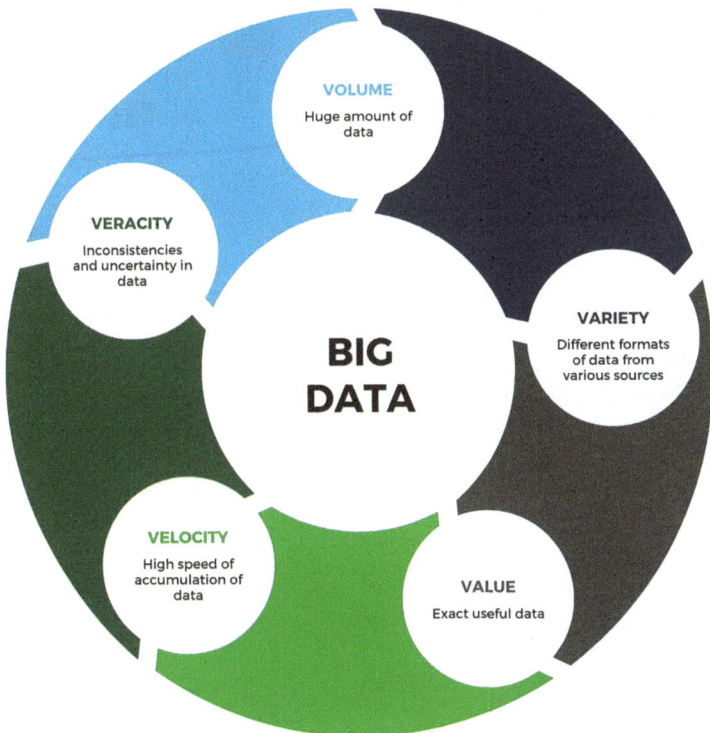

Source: Authors' own Figure.

Fig. 6.1 The 5 V's of Big Data. Source: Authors' own Figure

perspective, assume that a terabyte was a kilometre; it would be equivalent to 1300 round trips to the moon and back (768,800 km).

The rate at which Big Data is created increases exponentially over time. Former Google CEO Eric Schmidt explained that from the very beginning of humanity to 2003, an estimated 5 exabytes of information was created, corresponding to 0.5% of a zettabyte. In 2013, that amount of information (5 exabytes) took only 2 days to create, and that pace is continuously growing (Schmidt, 2010). Previously, it was a challenge to store and analyse Big Data, but nowadays (in 2023), we can gather data from different sources and organise and store it using distributed systems.

6.2.1.2 Velocity

Velocity describes how quickly data is processed (Géczy, 2014). Any Big Data operation or analysis must run at a high rate. Data originating from sensors, social media platforms, and application logs continuously generate vast volumes of data. The incoming data must be stored in the appropriate format for analysis. These processes must be done at a high frequency with the least effort.

Source: SAP business technology platform, n.d. What is big data? In the public domain (https://www.sap.com).

Fig. 6.2 Sources of Big Data. *Source*: SAP business technology platform (n.d.)) What is big data? In the public domain (https://www.sap.com)

6.2.1.3   Variety

There are many sources of Big Data, which we call variety (Géczy, 2014). See Fig. 6.2 for examples of sources of Big Data.

The wide variety of significant data sources is a challenge as it is vital to organise the diverse types of incoming data effectively in a user-friendly format (data analysts and coders are faced with these problems). Examples of data sources include Facebook, Twitter, Instagram, emails, WhatsApp, SMS, Health sector databases, financial institutions databases, and YouTube and Google searches (see Fig. 6.2).

6.2.1.4   Veracity

Data accuracy is referred to as veracity (Géczy, 2014). Inconsistencies and uncertainty in data, thus weak veracity, can influence the robustness of results, as is often said in data analytics: '*garbage in, garbage out*'. Veracity is one of the most crucial data qualities as it specifies the level of data reliability.

6.2.1.5   Value

The value of Big Data is how effectively you can use it (Géczy, 2014). For example, during the COVID-19 pandemic, real-time measures were derived from Big Data, informing policymakers about citizens' emotional reactions towards COVID-19 regulations and vaccines. This information was valuable for steering decision-making.

Structured data   Unstructured data   Semi-structured data

Source: SAP business technology platform. n.d. What is big data? In the public domain (https://www.sap.com)

Fig. 6.3 Different types of Big Data. *Source*: SAP business technology platform (n.d.)) What is big data? In the public domain (https://www.sap.com)

6.3   Types of Big Data

This section discusses the three types of data that most often constitute Big Data: structured, semi-structured, and unstructured. See Fig. 6.3 (Sagiroglu & Sinanc, 2013).

6.3.1   Structured Data

This data type is well-defined and organised. It is often structured in a spreadsheet format, familiar to people, for example, an Excel spreadsheet. Structured data can easily be stored in a database and accessed using traditional methods. This type of data is the easiest to manage and is the type of data we use to predict the most important factors to reach specified vaccination rates (refer to Chap. 10).

6.3.2   Semi-structured Data

Semi-structured data, as the term implies, is somewhat structured data. It is information that is tagged in a manner that has the potential to identify specific groups of data. Semi-structured data may be found in relational database management system (DBMS) table definitions. Often, at first, it seems to be unstructured data, for example, a file saved in a CSV format. However, a CSV file can easily be transformed into a data table (spreadsheet).

6.3.3   Unstructured Data

Unstructured data is data that has no recognised structure. Its size and heterogeneity are significantly more extensive than structured data. Unstructured data refers to any collection of data that is not organised or clearly defined. This data type is messy and challenging to handle, comprehend, and evaluate. The majority of Big Data falls into this category. Unstructured data includes social media comments, tweets, and 'shares', for example, Facebook posts and WhatsApp text messages.

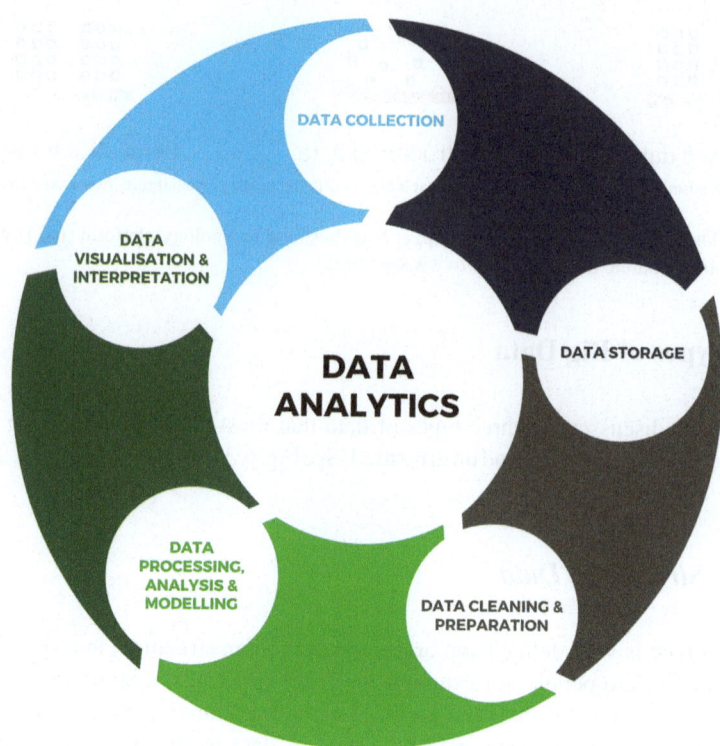

Source: Authors' own Figure.

Fig. 6.4 Data analytics steps. *Source*: Authors' own Figure

6.4   What Is Big Data Analytics?

Big Data analytics is the complex process of examining Big Data to uncover information, such as hidden patterns, correlations, market trends and the sentiments of people that can inform researchers and guide policymakers to make informed decisions. At a high level, data analytics technologies and techniques give means to analyse data sets and gather new information (Chandarana & Vijayalakshmi, 2014).

Data analytics used in Big Data analytics includes different steps, namely data collection, storage, cleaning and preparation, processing, analyses and modelling, visualisation, and interpretation. These steps are represented in Fig. 6.4, and we discuss each briefly below.

6.4.1   Data Collection

This step involves gathering data from various sources, such as social media, sensors, logs, transaction records and economic data.

6.4.2 Data Storage

After collection, the data must be stored for efficient retrieval and processing. Ample data storage often uses distributed storage systems like Hadoop. Distributed file systems, NoSQL databases, and cloud-based storage solutions (e.g., Amazon, Google Cloud Storage) are commonly used.

6.4.3 Data Cleaning and Preparation

Cleaning and preparing Big Data are crucial to ensure data quality and consistency. This may involve handling missing values, outlier detection, and data transformation. Due to the scale of Big Data, specialised tools and frameworks (e.g., Apache Spark) are often used for parallel processing.

6.4.4 Data Processing, Analysis and Modelling

This step involves using various techniques and algorithms to process and analyse the data. It may include tasks like data transformation, aggregation, statistical analysis, Natural Language Processing (sentiment analysis, see Sect. 6.5) and machine learning.

6.4.5 Data Visualisation and Interpretation

The results must be interpreted and presented meaningfully once the data has been processed and analysed. Data visualisation tools are used to create graphs, charts, dashboards, and reports, making it easier to understand and interpret the data to gain insights into a topic. However, traditional visualisation tools may not be able to handle the scale of Big Data. Specialised tools and techniques like Power BI or Tableau are compatible with Big Data.

6.5 Sentiment and Emotion Analyses (Natural Language Processing) Applied to Big Data

In this section, we extend our explanation of data analytics and refer to sentiment analysis as an extensive data analysis method. We describe the sentiment analysis process often used to evaluate the mood or emotions of people or citizens of a country towards a specific topic. The process of emotion analysis is very similar to sentiment analysis; thus, we complement the discussion on sentiment analysis with references to emotion analysis. Chapter 10 explains additional Big Data analytics methods using machine-learning algorithms in predictions.

6.5.1   Sentiment and Emotion Analysis

Sentiment analysis and emotion analysis determine whether text expresses a positive, negative, or neutral opinion about a topic (Zhang et al., 2014) or a specific emotion towards a topic. Using Big Data, we employ Natural Language Processing (NLP) to execute sentiment and emotion analysis. NLP combines computational linguistic, rule-based modelling of human language with statistical, machine learning, and deep learning models. Together, these technologies enable computers to process human language in text or voice data and 'understand' its whole meaning, including the sentiment and emotion captured in the text (Wolff, n.d.).

The different methods of sentiment analysis include:

I. Rules-based Systems: using, for example, lexicons.
II. Automatic systems: relying on machine learning techniques to learn from data.
III. Hybrid systems: combining both rule-based and automatic approaches.

6.5.2   Rules-Based Sentiment Analysis

Rules-based sentiment analysis systems adopt a lexicon to perform sentiment or emotion analysis. This is done by counting and weighting sentiment-related words that have been evaluated and tagged or words carrying a particular emotion. We distinguish between eight emotions: anger, fear, anticipation, trust, surprise, sadness, joy, and disgust. Three main approaches are used to collect the word list mentioned before: manual –, dictionary-based, and corpus-based.

(i) Manual approach: This approach is very time-consuming, and thus, it is not usually used alone but combined with automated approaches. The manual approach is then employed as a final validation method because automated methods make mistakes.
(ii) Dictionary-based approach: This approach uses a predefined dictionary of words where each word is associated with a specific sentiment polarity strength. Feelings of people, such as being happy, sad or depressed, can be determined by comparing words against lexicons from dictionaries.
(iii) Corpus-based approach: This approach tries to find co-occurrence patterns of words to determine their sentiment. This approach is based on the seeding list of opinion words and then finding another opinion word that has a similar context. This method assigns a happiness factor to words depending on the frequency of their occurrences in "happy" or "sad" blog posts.

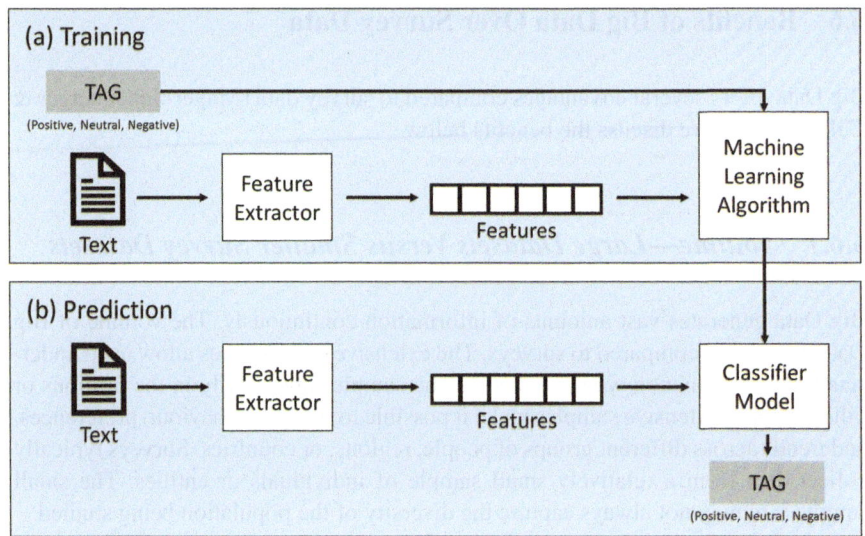

Source: (Wolff n.d)

Fig. 6.5 Automatic sentiment analysis system. *Source*: (Wolff, n.d.)

6.5.3 Automatic Sentiment Analysis Systems

Unlike lexicon or crafted manual rules, automatic system analysis relies on machine learning techniques, such as classification, to determine the polarization of words.

The system must first be fed sample text to automatically classify words before returning a category, such as positive, negative, or neutral. Following this, two stages are involved in implementing automatic systems: training and prediction. In the training stage, the sentiment analysis model is trained to correctly tag text as *negative, neutral* or *positive* using sample data (see Fig. 6.5). The feature extractor then transforms the text into a feature vector, which creates pairs of feature vectors and tags, for example, positive, negative, or neutral, fed into the machine learning algorithm to generate a model. In the prediction stage, the feature extractor transforms the unseen text into feature vectors fed to the model, enabling it to make sentiment predictions.

6.5.4 Hybrid Sentiment Analysis Systems

Using hybrid systems, they combine rule-based and automatic techniques to analyse texts' sentiment or emotions. This method often delivers more accurate results than using the systems individually.

6.6   Benefits of Big Data Over Survey Data

Big Data offers several advantages compared to survey data (Mayer-Schönberger & Cukier, 2013). We discuss the benefits below.

6.6.1   Volume—Large Datasets Versus Smaller Survey Datasets

Big Data generates vast amounts of information continuously. The volume of Big Data is a benefit compared to surveys. The extensive sample sizes allow us to understand the phenomenon we study better. The samples are usually in the millions or billions; these extensive samples make it possible to analyse behaviour, preferences, and trends across different groups of people, regions, or countries. Surveys typically collect data from a relatively small sample of individuals or entities. The small sample size may not always capture the diversity of the population being studied.

6.6.2   Velocity and Continuity

Using Big Data, we can receive data swiftly and continuously (every second of the day) in almost real-time; thus, data classified as Big Data is directly and almost instantaneously observable. Moreover, it can inform policymakers on the current moods of nations. Survey data are observable only with a time lag, which sometimes makes the policymaker's intervention less effective as decisions are made on historical information.

6.6.3   Continuous Updating Versus a Snapshot in Time

Big Data provides a continuous updating and a comprehensive view of a phenomenon over time rather than a snapshot. This allows for a deeper understanding of trends evolution and the ability to detect changes as they occur.

6.6.4   Unbiased and Passive Data Collection Versus Direct Responses Collected in Surveys

Big Data is collected passively as a natural byproduct of various activities, such as online interactions, social media posts, or sensor data. This minimises response bias and recall bias. This is an essential benefit over survey data and eliminates the need for survey administration.

6.6.5   Granularity and Detail Are Not Always Available in Survey Data

Big Data can offer extremely granular and detailed insights, capturing individual behaviours, interactions, and transactions at an acceptable level of detail that surveys typically cannot achieve. For example, the details of a Twitter account or influencer can be followed over time.

6.6.6   Attain Behavioural Insights Without the Biases Found in Survey Data

Big Data provides information on people's actual behaviour as we observe people's opinions in an "objective" manner. Thus, people's opinions are not captured directly by answering predefined explicit questions. When responding to a survey, the order of the questions or the respondent's mood can influence the answers. Therefore, Big Data captures evaluative questions more "objectively" and is more reliable than self-reported survey answers.

6.6.7   Real-Time Analysis and Decision-Making Versus Lagged Information Sharing (Surveys)

Big Data's real-time or near-real-time nature makes it ideal for making timely decisions and responding to emerging trends or issues in dynamic environments. We live in a world characterised by fast living and where circumstances change almost instantaneously, such as the onslaught of the COVID-19 pandemic. Using Big Data, the changes can be observed in near real-time, which can inform policymakers to take affirmative action as needed. With survey data, there is usually a significant time lag associated with releasing information gathered.

6.6.8   Reduced Costs and Efficient Analysis Compared to Costly Survey Collection with Prolonged Analysis

Collecting and processing Big Data can be more cost-effective and time-efficient, especially when dealing with large populations, which can, in minutes, be analysed using machine learning algorithms with servers with high processing power. The design, administration, and analysis of surveys are lengthy processes.

6.6.9   Machine Learning and Predictive Analysis

Big Data is well-suited for machine learning algorithms and predictive analytics, enabling the discovery of hidden patterns, correlations, and trends that might also be revealed in survey data. However, using machine learning speeds up the process, and answers to questions are quickly available, which is not valid for survey data.

6.6.10   Variety of Data Types Versus Limited Data Types Found in Surveys

As discussed in Sect. 6.3, Big Data contains various data types, including structured, semi-structured, and unstructured data, making it suitable for analysing diverse information sources such as text, images, videos, and sensor data. Surveys mostly rely on the responses, either captured in text or reflecting nominal, categorical, ordinal or continuous data.

6.6.11   Flexibility and Adaptability Versus a Set Structure (Survey Data)

In collecting Big Data, we can use different coding and scripts to automate the extraction of data, which can adapt to changing data sources and incorporate new variables and other types of data sources, allowing for flexibility. Using survey data, the structure is set beforehand according to the type of questions included in the survey and does not allow for the flexibility and adaptability of Big Data analyses.

6.7   Limitations of Big Data

Big Data not only has benefits but also suffers from limitations (Masinissa, 2023).

Firstly, Big Data are not a representative sample of the whole population; therefore, any data or analyses of Big Data cannot be immediately extended to the entire population. However, some methods can be applied to adjust the data to make the results more representative (see Iacus & Porro, 2021). Secondly, Big Data has privacy and security concerns, as machine learning algorithms are often trained on personal data, including emails or social media posts. Thirdly, all data sources are vulnerable to cyberattacks, which could result in the theft or manipulation of sensitive data. Therefore, we must protect sensitive information and comply with legal and ethical standards. Fourthly, to analyse Big Data, we need sophisticated methodologies only known to experts in Big Data analysis. Fifthly, Big Data is not always a substitute for surveys, as surveys can provide context, nuance, and specific information that may not be captured in large-scale datasets. Finally, the quality of the data is crucial. If the data is inaccurate, incomplete, or biased, it can lead to incorrect conclusions and decisions. Therefore, the veracity of the data is essential.

6.8   Is Big Data Relevant to COVID-19 and Vaccination Research?

Big Data is highly relevant to COVID-19 and vaccination research. The COVID-19 pandemic brought unprecedented challenges to healthcare systems, economies, and societies worldwide. The pandemic generated enormous data from various sources, including clinical trials, healthcare records, epidemiological studies, and genomic sequencing efforts. Integrating Big Data analytics and machine learning into pandemic responses contributed to understanding the intricacies of the data. The data informed us about the virus, its transmission patterns, the effectiveness of different interventions, and the development of vaccines, which assisted in mitigating and managing the impact of the pandemic.

The COVID-19 pandemic led to many advances in using Big Data and Big Data analytics in managing pandemics and revealed the immense potential of integrating these methods into pandemic response efforts (Haleem et al., 2020). The information we gained from using Big Data and Big Data analytics in grasping various matters related to the COVID-19 pandemic will be instrumental in shaping our approach to future pandemics and public health challenges.

For example, Big Data and Big Data analytics were used for early detection, predictive models for disease spread, vaccine development, resource allocation, behavioural analysis and identifying regions with low compliance rates. We discuss these topics below:

6.8.1   Early Detection and Tracking

One of the most critical aspects of pandemic management is the early detection and tracking of outbreaks. Big Data has become a powerful tool, encompassing vast amounts of information from various sources. Data points such as travel patterns, social interactions, and healthcare records were used to identify potential hotspots and monitor the spread of the virus (Bello-Orgaz et al., 2016).

6.8.2   Predictive Models for Disease Spread

Machine learning algorithms, trained on historical epidemiological data and real-time information feeds, were crucial in creating predictive models for disease spread. These models enabled public health officials to make informed decisions about resource allocation, lockdown measures, and targeted interventions. By identifying potential outbreak zones in advance, authorities were better equipped to allocate healthcare resources effectively, thereby saving lives (Vaishya et al., 2020).

6.8.3   Vaccine Development

The race to develop and distribute effective vaccines against COVID-19 was a monumental undertaking. Big Data and machine learning played a crucial role in expediting this process. Researchers utilised genetic sequencing data from the virus and patient health records to identify potential vaccine candidates. Machine learning algorithms helped simulate the behaviour of potential vaccines, expediting the selection process (Arora et al., 2021).

6.8.4   Vaccine Distribution

Big Data analytics contributes to the optimisation of vaccine distribution strategies. Demographic data, population density, and healthcare infrastructure were considered to ensure equitable and efficient vaccine dissemination. Machine learning models were used to predict vaccine demand, allowing governments to allocate doses where they were most needed (Al-Sai et al., 2022).

6.8.5   Healthcare Resource Allocation

Managing healthcare resources was a formidable challenge, especially during the pandemic's peak. Big Data analytics provided real-time insights into hospital capacities, ventilator availability, and ICU bed occupancy rates. Using machine learning algorithms, predictive models forecasted patient influx, enabling hospitals to adjust staffing levels and prepare for surges in demand (Dash et al., 2019).

6.8.6   Identification of Vulnerable Populations

Big Data and Big Data analytics facilitated the identification of vulnerable populations. By analysing demographic data, comorbidity rates, and socioeconomic factors, healthcare providers could prioritise resources for those at the highest risk. This targeted approach saved lives and ensured a more efficient utilisation of limited resources (Raghupathi & Raghupathi, 2014).

6.8.7   Behavioural Analysis and Public Health Messaging

Understanding human behaviour and compliance with preventive measures is crucial in controlling the spread of a pandemic. Big Data analytics provided insights into public sentiment (such as vaccine-related moods), social media activity, and mobility patterns. We used machine learning models to predict trends in behaviour, which enabled authorities to tailor public health messaging and interventions to meet specific needs (Andreu-Perez et al., 2015).

6.8.8   Identifying Regions with Low Compliance Rates

Public health officials and policymakers could create messaging campaigns to increase adherence to preventive measures or increase vaccination rates by identifying regions or demographics with low compliance rates. Additionally, sentiment analysis allowed public health officials to gauge public perception and adjust messaging strategies accordingly (Javaid et al., 2020).

6.9   How Can Big Data Inform Policymakers During a Pandemic?

In Sects. 6.6 and 6.8, we discussed the benefits of Big Data and its relevance for COVID-19 research. In this section, we expand on our discussion and explain the relevance of Big Data to inform policymakers. We know that Big Data plays a crucial role in informing policymakers during a pandemic on diverse topics, as it can process vast amounts of information from various sources like social media, healthcare systems, and public health agencies to provide real-time updates (Shakeel et al., 2021).

Big Data can inform policymakers on the spread of the disease. This allows policymakers to track and respond to outbreaks quickly. Furthermore, Big Data analytics can aid contact tracing efforts by identifying individuals who may have been exposed to the virus based on location data from mobile devices or other sources. This information can help authorities notify and isolate potentially infected individuals.

Big Data allows us to analyse posts on social media platforms, from which we can predict public behaviour and compliance. These predictions can help policymakers understand the effectiveness of their messages. This assists them to make timely adjustments to their communication strategies.

Big Data and Big Data analytics can help identify misinformation and monitor public sentiment, allowing policymakers to target their communication efforts towards addressing concerns and disseminating accurate information. Additionally,

Big Data can also be used to analyse the economic impact of the pandemic, helping policymakers make decisions regarding financial support, stimulus packages, and economic recovery strategies.

6.10 Summary

In this chapter, we discussed the different kinds of Big Data (structured, unstructured, and semi-structured) as well as the characteristics of Big Data, volume, velocity, variety, veracity and value. We introduced the audience to Big Data analytics and discussed the steps that must be taken. Additionally, we discussed sentiment and emotion analysis in-depth to expand our audiences' knowledge of the power of Big Data analytics.

From there, we discussed the advantages Big Data holds over traditional survey data, also reporting on the limitations of working with Big Data. Next, we informed the audience of the relevance of Big Data in COVID-19 and vaccination research. We highlighted how Big Data analytics contributed to our understanding of the intricacies within the vast amount of data generated from various sources during the COVID-19 pandemic, which assisted in mitigating and managing the impact of the pandemic.

Lastly, we discussed how Big Data can inform policymakers. We conclude that overall, Big Data provides a powerful toolset for policymakers to make data-driven decisions during a pandemic, enabling them to respond faster and more effectively to the evolving situation and ultimately save lives.

References

Al-Sai, Z. A., Husin, M. H., Syed-Mohamad, S. M., Abdin, R. M. D. S., Damer, N., Abualigah, L., & Gandomi, A. H. (2022). Explore big data analytics applications and opportunities: A review. *Big Data and Cognitive Computing, 6*(4), 157.

Andreu-Perez, J., Poon, C. C., Merrifield, R. D., Wong, S. T., & Yang, G. Z. (2015). Big data for health. *IEEE Journal of Biomedical and Health Informatics, 19*(4), 1193–1208.

Arora, G., Joshi, J., Mandal, R. S., Shrivastava, N., Virmani, R., & Sethi, T. (2021). Artificial intelligence in surveillance, diagnosis, drug discovery and vaccine development against COVID-19. *Pathogens, 10*(8), 1048.

Bello-Orgaz, G., Jung, J. J., & Camacho, D. (2016). Social big data: Recent achievements and new challenges. *Information Fusion, 28,* 45–59.

Chandarana, P., & Vijayalakshmi, M. (2014). Big data analytics frameworks. In *2014 international conference on circuits, systems, communication and information technology applications (CSCITA)* (pp. 430–434). IEEE.

Dash, S., Shakyawar, S. K., Sharma, M., & Kaushik, S. (2019). Big data in healthcare: Management, analysis and future prospects. *Journal of Big Data, 6*(1), 1–25.

Géczy, P. (2014). Big Data Characteristics. https://api.semanticscholar.org/CorpusID:114086496. Accessed on 3.11.23.

Haleem, A., Javaid, M., Khan, I. H., & Vaishya, R. (2020). Significant applications of big data in COVID-19 pandemic. *Indian Journal of Orthopaedics, 54,* 526–528.

Iacus, S. M., & Porro, G. (2021). *Subjective Well-being and social media*. CRC Press.

Javaid, M., Haleem, A., Vaishya, R., Bahl, S., Suman, R., & Vaish, A. (2020). Industry 4.0 technologies and their applications in fighting COVID-19 pandemic. *Diabetes & Metabolic Syndrome: Clinical Research & Reviews, 14*(4), 419–422.

Masinissa, S. (2023). 5 Reasons Why Artificial Intelligence Will Fail. https://www.ontechnology.com.ly/5-reasons-why-artificial-intelligence-will-fail/. Accessed on 03.11.23.

Mayer-Schönberger, V., & Cukier, K. (2013). *Big data: A revolution that will transform how we live, work, and think*. Houghton Mifflin Harcourt.

Raghupathi, W., & Raghupathi, V. (2014). Big data analytics in healthcare: Promise and potential. *Health Information Science and Systems, 2*, 1–10.

Sagiroglu, S., & Sinanc, D. (2013). Big Data: A review. In *In 2013 international conference on collaboration technologies and systems (CTS)* (pp. 42–47). IEEE.

SAP business technology platform. (n.d.). What is big data? https://www.sap.com/hk/products/technology-. Accessed 10.11.23.

Schmidt, E. (2010). Every 2 Days We Create As Much Information As We Did Up To 2003. TechCrunch. https://techcrunch.com/2010/08/04/schmidt-data/. Accessed on 02.11.23.

Shakeel, S. M., Kumar, N. S., Madalli, P. P., Srinivasaiah, R., & Swamy, D. R. (2021). COVID-19 prediction models: A systematic literature review. *Osong Public Health and Research Perspectives, 12*(4), 215.

Ularu, E. G., Puican, F. C., Apostu, A., & Velicanu, M. (2012). Perspectives on big data and big data analytics. *Database Systems Journal, 3*(4), 3–14.

Vaishya, R., Javaid, M., Khan, I. H., & Haleem, A. (2020). Artificial intelligence (AI) applications for COVID-19 pandemic. *Diabetes & Metabolic Syndrome: Clinical Research & Reviews, 14*(4), 337–339.

Wolff, R. (n.d.). Quick introduction to sentiment analysis. https://towardsdatascience.com/quick-introduction-to-sentiment-analysis-74bd3dfb536c. Accessed on 12.02.20.

Zhang, H., Gan, W., & Jiang, B. (2014). Machine learning and lexicon-based methods for sentiment classification: A survey. In *In 2014, the 11th web information system and application conference* (pp. 262–265). IEEE.

References

Chapter 7
The Measurement of COVID-19 Vaccine Hesitancy

Abstract The content presented in this chapter to Chap. 9 comes from our published research in PLOS ONE. This chapter serves as the initial examination into measuring COVID-19 vaccine hesitancy, laying the groundwork for a comprehensive cross-country panel analysis utilising Big Data in Chaps. 8 and 9. By providing an in-depth literature review on vaccine hesitancy and detailing the methodology employed in data acquisition and analysis, this chapter explains the complexities of gauging attitudes towards COVID-19 vaccines using real-time Twitter data.

The chapter focuses on studies utilising Big Data analytics to understand vaccine hesitancy. It explains the process of constructing time-series data by extracting tweets and employing Natural Language Processing techniques to determine sentiment and emotions surrounding COVID-19 vaccines. The chapter introduces key lexicons utilised in sentiment analysis and outlines the methodology for topic modelling and word cloud visualisation.

Central to the chapter is the detailed explanation of data acquisition and processing methodologies, wherein over a million tweets are extracted, translated, and analysed to derive sentiment and emotion time series. Robustness tests, including frequency and volume analyses, validate the reliability of the derived time-series data, ensuring the accuracy of subsequent analyses.

Moreover, the chapter discusses the importance of topic modelling and word clouds in identifying trends and narratives within the tweet corpus, enhancing our understanding of attitudes towards COVID-19 vaccines. By employing advanced analytical techniques, such as the Latent Dirichlet Allocation model, the chapter aims to organise unstructured text data into meaningful themes, providing valuable insights for policymakers and researchers alike.

Keywords COVID-19 · Vaccine hesitancy · Twitter · Lexicons · Topic modelling · Word clouds

S. Rossouw, T. Greyling, *Resistance to COVID-19 Vaccination*, Human Well-Being Research and Policy Making,
https://doi.org/10.1007/978-3-031-56529-8_7

7.1   Aim of This Chapter to Chap. 9

The primary aim of this chapter to Chap. 9 is to conduct a comprehensive cross-country panel analysis using Big Data to uncover the evolving trends in positive attitudes towards COVID-19 vaccines over time. A secondary aim lies in identifying those variables related to having a positive attitude, as these factors could potentially increase the uptake of vaccines and provide valuable insights for policymakers.

The content presented in this chapter to Chap. 9 comes from our published research in PLOS ONE. In this Chapter, we provide an in-depth review of the literature pertaining to COVID-19 vaccine hesitancy, explicitly focusing on studies that used Big Data in their analysis. Additionally, we explain how we constructed our time series data through the real-time extraction of tweets from Twitter's vast repository of information. Furthermore, we explain the role of Natural Language Processing in gauging sentiment and emotions pertaining to the COVID-19 vaccine. Furthermore, we briefly explain sentiment and emotion analysis (for a more extensive discussion, please refer to this Chap. 6) and highlight the various lexicons employed in our analysis. Moreover, this chapter introduces the concepts of topic modelling and word clouds, providing insights into their application, which we elaborate on in Chap. 8.

Apart from the above, Chap. 8 continues where this Chapter leaves off and details the methodology employed to create our COVID-19 vaccine positive attitude index (VPAI). Additionally, this Chap. 7 uses descriptive statistics, graphs and topic modelling to analyse the trend in the VPAI over time and compare the results for the Northern and Southern Hemispheres and across the ten countries in our sample (refer to Chaps. 4 and 5). Chapter 9 focuses on identifying those variables significantly related to the VPAI, which, when addressed, can potentially foster a more positive attitude towards COVID-19 vaccines, ultimately bolstering vaccine acceptance rates.

7.2   Introduction

Previous studies (Lyu et al., 2021; Xue et al., 2021; Chopra et al., 2021) analysed the emotions in vaccine-related tweets. However, their primary aim was to understand better the public perceptions, concerns, and emotions related to *COVID-19 vaccine topics and discussions* on social media. They determined the sentiments related to topics and discussions and investigated the strength of discussions and sentiments over time. The main limitations of these studies include that they: (i) only analysed English tweets, with no attention being paid to specific geographical areas or comparing the sentiment across different countries; (ii) did not use sentiment analysis in further analyses; and (iii) did not investigate the variables related to positive vaccine attitudes.

We overcome these limitations by constructing a daily time series called the Vaccine Positive Attitude Index (VPAI), a real-time measure of people's positive attitudes toward the COVID-19 vaccine across ten countries for the period 1 February 2021–31 July 2021. The countries span both the Northern and Southern Hemispheres and include the countries discussed in Chaps. 4 and 5: Australia, Belgium, Germany, Great Britain, France, Italy, the Netherlands, New Zealand, South Africa and Spain.

7.3 Country Background and Literature Review

7.3.1 Country Background

Primarily, the choice of countries is determined by data availability. However, future studies can extend the dataset to include more countries. The current selection of countries from both Hemispheres provides unique insights into people's attitudes to the COVID-19 vaccine. Table 7.1 summarises key facts (see Chaps. 4 and 5 for in-depth discussions) for each country used in this chapter to Chap. 9.

From Fig. 7.1, we can see that the country performing the worst during our investigation period, in terms of the total number of people fully vaccinated, was New Zealand (approximately 750,000 people). However, if we consider the vaccinated as a percentage of the total population, South Africa performed the worst with 5% by 31 July 2021. Of interest is the Northern-Southern Hemisphere split. The Northern Hemisphere outperforms all three Southern Hemisphere countries (Australia, New Zealand and South Africa). France was the worst performer of the Northern Hemisphere countries, with 48% fully vaccinated, whereas Belgium was the best performer (60%) (Mathieu et al., 2021).

7.3.2 Literature on COVID-19 Vaccine Hesitancy

There has been an exponential growth of studies on COVID-19 vaccine hesitancy in the literature as researchers from all disciplines attempted to address one of the biggest global health threats.

Research regarding COVID-19 vaccine hesitancy spanned across both *online surveys* (see, for example, Akarsu et al., 2020; Fisher et al., 2020; Freeman et al., 2020; Ward et al., 2020; Seale et al., 2021) and *in-person surveys* (see, for example, Paul et al., 2021; Sallam, 2021). Primarily, these studies found people's hesitancy and refusal of the COVID-19 vaccine were mostly attributed to (i) fear driven by possible side effects of the vaccine and (ii) the unreliability of what is seen as a new

Table 7.1 Key summary facts of countries in this study

Country	Total population	Average happiness levels[a] (2020)	Oxford Stringency Index (Average for the period)	First confirmed COVID-19 case (2020)	Date of first lockdown (2020)	Total confirmed COVID-19 cases (28 August 2021)	Total confirmed COVID-19 deaths (28 August 2021)	Date of vaccine rollout	Percentage of the population fully vaccinated (31 July 2021)
Australia	25.5 million	7.09	58.64	25 January	17 March[b]	51,256	999	22 February 2021	15%
Belgium	11.6 million	6.98	58.30	4 February	13 March	1.18 million	25,360	28 December 2020	60%
France	66.99 million	6.66	63.15	24 January	17 March	6.81 million	114,506	27 December 2020	48%
Germany	83.02 million	7.08	72.71	27 January	22 March	3.93 million	92,136	27 December 2020	52%
Great Britain	66.65 million	7.17	66.70	31 January	23 March	6.73 million	132,699	8 December 2020	56%
Italy	60.36 million	6.39	74.90	30 January	9 March	4.52 million	129,002	27 December 2020	52%
Netherlands	17.28 million	7.73	64.88	27 February	15 March[c]	1.97 million	18,339	6 January 2021	54%
New Zealand	5.5 million	7.14	26.80	28 February	26 March	3465	26	19 February 2021	15%
South Africa	57.7 million	6.32	51.90	6 March	27 March	2.76 million	81,461	17 February 2021	5%
Spain	46.94 million	6.40	64.33	31 January	14 March	4.83 million	84,000	27 December 2020	58%

[a] The happiness scores cited here reflect the average for the period in 2020 before the first COVID-19 case was announced
[b] Australia never officially went into a complete lockdown such as that seen in the other countries. We used the day when the closure of international borders was announced as a proxy for "lockdown"
[c] The Netherlands started a so-called 'intelligent lockdown' on this date

Sources: Hale et al. (2020), Greyling et al. (2019), Google (2020, 2021), Roser et al. (2020) and Mathieu et al. (2021).

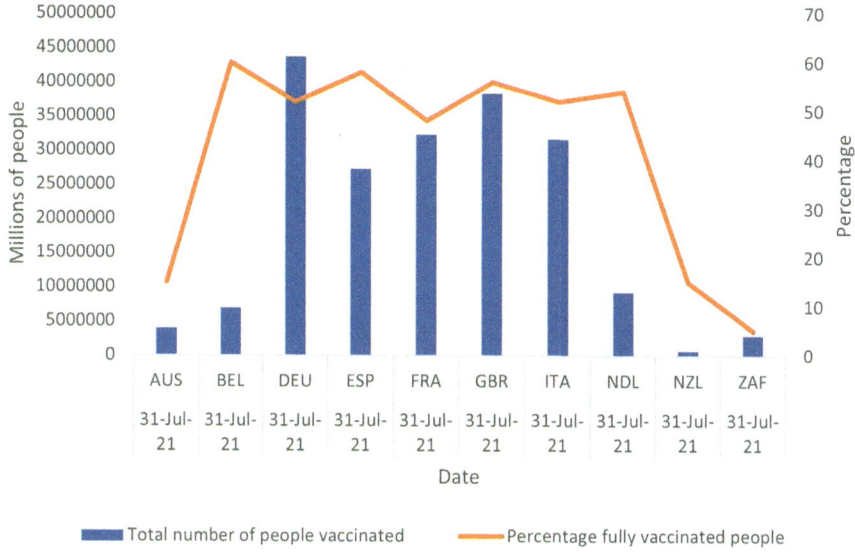

Fig. 7.1 COVID-19 number of people vaccinated and the percentage of fully vaccinated people per country (31 July 2021). *Source*: Mathieu et al. (2021)

vaccine. Paul et al. (2021) surveyed 32,361 participants from 7 September to 5 October 2020. The authors found that distrustful attitudes towards vaccination were higher amongst individuals from ethnic minority backgrounds, with lower levels of education, lower annual income, poor knowledge of COVID-19, and poor compliance with government COVID-19 guidelines. Apart from the Paul et al. (2021) study, the other aforementioned studies found willingness to take the COVID-19 vaccine was closely related to one's sense of collective responsibility and campaigning for the 'greater good'. Furthermore, these studies highlighted a need for better and more transparent information, the role of anti-vaccination campaigns, and a lack of trust in the government. Interestingly, it was found that low rates of COVID-19 vaccine acceptance were reported in the Middle East, Russia, Africa and several European countries.

Our study uses Big Data to construct a Vaccine Positive Attitude Index (VPAI); therefore, the rest of the literature review will focus on those that also use Big Data, with special attention to three studies closest to ours in spirit. We note a burgeoning of literature using Big Data in the form of Twitter to analyse vaccine-related topics. Therefore, we cannot possibly discuss all of them.

For example, Yousefinaghani et al. (2021) used vaccine-related tweets to track frequent hashtags, frequent mentions, main keywords, and main themes with positive and negative sentiments in the tweets. Hussain et al. (2021) used Facebook and Twitter to study people's hesitancy, perceptions and sentiment towards the COVID-19 vaccine. Küçükali et al. (2021), Nuzhath et al. (2020), Bonnevie et al. (2021) and Thelwall et al. (2021) all identified prominent themes about vaccine hesitancy and refusal on social media during the COVID-19 pandemic. These studies found that the most frequent themes that elicit a negative sentiment are anti-vaccination, poor scientific processes, conspiracy theories, mistrust of scientists and governments, lack of intent to get a COVID-19 vaccine, freedom of choice, and religious beliefs.

Sharma et al. (2021) and Bonnevie et al. (2020) focused on using Twitter to identify suspicious coordinated accounts in the dataset to find misinformation campaigns that drive the conversation against getting the COVID-19 vaccine. Based on an analysis of the collective behaviours and activities of accounts, they found that they correspond to a 'Great Reset' conspiracy theory and ten additional themes, such as research and clinical trials and vaccine ingredients.

Three studies that come the closest to ours in spirit are Lyu et al. (2021), Xue et al. (2021) and Chopra et al. (2021). Lyu et al. (2021) used 1.5 million English vaccine-related tweets collected between March 2020 and January 2021 and categorised the tweets into 16 topics grouped into five overarching themes. Their results showed that under their first theme, called "Opinions and Emotions Around Vaccines and Vaccination", the topic out of all 16 topics that were mostly tweeted was opinions about vaccination. In terms of their sentiment analysis (using the Syuzhet lexicon), they found that, apart from fluctuations throughout the period, the sentiment increased regarding the COVID-19 vaccine. Their emotions analysis (using the NRC lexicon) found trust was the most prevalent emotion, followed by anticipation and fear. They found fear was the most prevalent emotion before Moderna, one of the first to test their COVID-19 vaccine on humans in April 2020.

Xue et al. (2021) analysed four million English vaccine-related tweets using a list of 20 hashtags from 7 March to 21 April 2020. Their main aim was to identify popular unigrams (one word) and bigrams (two words), salient topics and themes, and sentiments in the collected tweets. In terms of unigrams, they found "virus", "lockdown", and "quarantine" to be the most popular. Bigrams "COVID-19", "stay home", "corona virus", "social distancing", and "new cases" were the most popular. Furthermore, they identified 13 discussion topics from the tweets and categorised them into five different themes. For example, theme 1, "Public health measures to slow the spread of COVID-19", included topics such as face masks, quarantine, test kits, lockdown, safety, vaccine and US shelter-in-place. Their emotions analysis (using the NRC lexicon) showed that anticipation followed by fear, trust, and anger were prevalent across 12 of the 13 topics.

Chopra et al. (2021) collected 1.8 million English vaccine-related tweets across India, the United States, Great Britain, Brazil, and Australia from June 2020 to April 2021. They aimed to create ten lexical categories, split between two classes, namely emotions (six categories) and influencing factors (four categories) and study the temporal evolution of these categories across time. The lexical emotions category includes hesitation, sorrow, faith, contentment, anticipation and rage, while their influencing factors are misinformation, vaccine rollout, inequities, and health effects. The authors used the word-count approach to measure each category's strength in a given tweet. They calculated the strength of the categories monthly and split their period under investigation in two: Before and After the date when each country's government approved the first COVID-19 vaccine. Their results differed across countries, with, for example, India experiencing a decrease in the strength of hesitation experienced after vaccine approval, with mentions of health effects contributing the most in tweets with a positive hesitation score. The United States experienced a significant increase in contentment after their vaccine approval. Rage and discussions on misinformation became significantly higher after vaccine approval in India, whereas the opposite was true for the United States.

Given the above literature review, it is clear that no other study has done what we did. Ours was the first study to use Big Data to determine the sentiment and emotions related to COVID-19 vaccines through a vaccine positive attitude index. Additionally, no other study had followed the trends in attitudes over time and derived emotion and sentiment time-series data across countries to determine the variables that significantly influence a positive attitude towards the COVID-19 vaccine.

7.4 Measuring COVID-19 Vaccine Hesitancy Using Big Data

To derive our time-series data used in Chaps. 8 and 9, which capture sentiment and emotions, we construct variables using Big Data by extracting tweets from Twitter. In our analysis, we extracted two sets of tweets based on keywords, one related to COVID-19 vaccines and the other to the government. The tweets containing these words amounted to 1,047,000 tweets. We extracted all tweets according to specific geographical areas (countries).

The first step in our analysis is determining the tweets' language (we detected 64 different languages), and all non-English tweets were translated into English. After translation, we use Natural Language Processing to extract the tweets' sentiment and underlying emotions. To test the robustness of coding the sentiment of the translated tweets, we use lexicons in the original language, if available, and repeat the process. We compared the coded sentiment of the translated and original text and found the results strongly correlated.

We make use of a suite of lexicons. Each of them differs slightly, but the primary aim is to determine the sentiment of unstructured text data. The two lexicons mostly used in our analysis are Sentiment140 and NRC (National Research Council of Canada Emotion Lexicon developed by Turney and Mohammad (2010)). The other lexicons are used for robustness purposes and are part of the Syuzhet package. The lexicons include Syuzhet, AFINN and Bing. The sentiment is determined by identifying the tweeter's attitude towards an event using variables such as context, tone, etc. It helps one form an entire opinion of the text. Depending on the lexicon used, the text (tweet) is coded. For example, if a tweet is positive, it is coded as 0; if neutral, 2; and if negative, 4.

We use the NRC lexicon to code the sentiment (as explained above) and analyse the underlying tweets' emotions. It distinguishes between eight basic emotions: anger, fear, anticipation, trust, surprise, sadness, joy and disgust (the so-called Plutchik (1980) wheel of emotions). NRC codes words with different values, ranging from 0 (low) to 8 (the highest score in our data), expressing the intensity of an emotion or sentiment.

To construct the time-series data, we use the coding of the tweets and derive daily averages. In this manner, we derive a positive sentiment, a negative sentiment and eight emotion time series. We derived the sentiment time series using different lexicons as a robustness test and compared these results using correlation analyses. We perform various additional robustness tests, for example, to determine whether the sampling frequency significantly influences the results.

To test the robustness of the *frequency,* we construct the relevant index (time series) per day (the norm); we repeat the exercise but construct the time series per hour. We found similar trends in our hourly and daily time series, indicating that the timescale at which sampling occurs does not significantly influence the observed trend.

To test whether the *volume* of tweets affects the derived time-series data, we extract random samples of differing sizes from the daily text corpus of tweets. The time series based on these smaller samples (50% and 80% of the daily extracted tweets) are highly correlated to the original time series.

7.5   Topic Modelling and Word Clouds

Artificial intelligence-powered word clouds are a powerful data analysis tool that can help identify patterns, trends, and key themes in large data sets. Visualising data in this way makes it easier to communicate complex data sets to a wider audience and supports data-driven decision-making. A word cloud is a visual representation of text data where words are arranged in a cloud-like shape, with the size of each word representing its frequency or importance in the text. Therefore, we constructed word clouds per country to ensure that the extracted vaccine-related tweets discussed attitudes related to receiving the COVID-19 vaccine (refer to Chap. 8 for the results).

To explain the trends we see regarding the positive attitude towards vaccines in Chap. 8, we rely on existing literature and topic modelling, which helps us understand the narrative behind the trend.

Topic modelling can help organise an extensive collection of unstructured text into different themes. Topic modelling is often referred to as probabilistic clustering. It is more robust and usually provides more realistic results than hard clustering (e.g., k-mean clustering) (Blum et al., 2020). A typical clustering algorithm assumes a distance measure between topics. It assigns one topic to each document, whereas topic modelling assigns a document to a collection of topics with different weights or probabilities without assuming the distance measured between topics. Many topic models are available, of which we prefer the most widely used Latent Dirichlet Allocation (LDA) model (Blum et al., 2020), developed by Blei et al. (2003).

7.6   Summary

This chapter laid the groundwork for our research objectives to be addressed in Chaps. 8 and 9 by providing an extensive literature review regarding COVID-19 vaccine hesitancy. Particular focus was paid to studies that used Big Data since they were the closest to ours in spirit.

This chapter also explained in-depth the construction of our time series data by extracting tweets in real-time from the social media platform Twitter and discussed the role of Natural Language Processing in measuring sentiment and emotions pertaining to the COVID-19 vaccine.

Furthermore, this chapter introduced the reader to the two lexicons mostly used in our analysis in Chaps. 8 and 9, Sentiment140 and NRC and informed our audience how we use topic modelling and word clouds to gain insights pertaining to attitudes regarding the COVID-19 vaccine.

As we conclude this Chapter and continue with Chap. 8, where we discuss the construction of our COVID-19 vaccine positive attitude index and analyse the trend over time, it is important to recognise our cumulative efforts thus far. We have gained valuable insights from the COVID-19 vaccine hesitancy literature and the intricacies of data acquisition. Additionally, we highlighted the power of NLP and related techniques to foster a more in-depth understanding of COVID-19 vaccine hesitancy.

With this Chapter foundation in place, we are better equipped to address our research questions and provide valuable insights for policymakers.

References

Akarsu, B., Canbay, Ö. D., Ayhan Baser, D., Aksoy, H., Fidancı, İ., & Cankurtaran, M. (2020). While studies on COVID-19 vaccine is ongoing, the public's thoughts and attitudes to the future COVID-19 vaccine. *The International Journal of Clinical Practice*, e13891.

Blei, D., Ng, A., & Jordan, M. (2003). Latent Dirichlet allocation. *Journal of Machine Learning Research, 3*, 993–1022.

Blum, A., Hopcroft, J., & Kannan, R. (2020). *Foundations of data science.* Cambridge University Press.

Bonnevie, E., Goldbarg, J., Gallegos-Jeffrey, A. K., Rosenberg, S. D., Wartella, E., & Smyser, J. (2020). Content themes and influential voices within vaccine opposition on twitter, 2019. *American Journal of Public Health, 110*, S326–S330.

Bonnevie, E., Gallegos-Jeffrey, A., Goldbarg, J., Byrd, B., & Smyser, J. (2021). Quantifying the rise of vaccine opposition on twitter during the COVID-19 pandemic. *Journal of Communication in Healthcare, 14*(1), 12–19.

Chopra, H., Vashishtha, A., Pal, R., Ashima, A., Tyagi, A., & Sethi, T. (2021). Mining trends of COVID-19 vaccine beliefs on twitter with lexical Embeddings. *arXiv*, 2104.01131.

Fisher, K. A., Bloomstone, S. J., Walder, J., Crawford, S., Fouayzi, H., & Mazor, K. M. (2020). Attitudes toward a potential SARS-CoV-2 vaccine: A survey of US adults. *Annals of Internal Medicine, 173*(12), 964–973.

Freeman, D., Loe, B. S., Chadwick, A., Vaccari, C., Waite, F., Rosebrock, L., et al. (2020). COVID-19 vaccine hesitancy in the UK: The Oxford coronavirus explanations, attitudes, and narratives survey (oceans) II. *Psychological Medicine, 11*, 1–15.

Google. (2020). Google COVID-19 Community Mobility Reports. https://www.google.com/covid19/mobility/. Accessed 01.08.21.

Google. (2021). Google COVID-19 Community Mobility Reports. https://www.google.com/covid19/mobility/. Accessed 1.08.21.

Greyling, T., Rossouw, S., & Afstereo. (2019). Gross National Happiness. Today Index. http://gnh.today. Accessed 01.08.21.

Hale, T., Angrist, N., Cameron-Blake, E., Hallas, L., Kira, B., Majumdar, S., et al. (2020). Oxford COVID-19 government response tracker. https://www.bsg.ox.ac.uk/research/research-projects/covid-19-government-response-tracker. Accessed 28.07.21.

Hussain, A., Tahir, A., Hussain, Z., Sheikh, Z., Gogate, M., Dashtipour, K., Ali, A., Sheikh, A. (2021). Artificial Intelligence–Enabled Analysis of Public Attitudes on Facebook and Twitter Toward COVID-19 Vaccines in the United Kingdom and the United States: Observational Study. *Journal of Medical Internet Research, 23*(4), e26627.

Küçükali, H., Ataç, O., Palteki, A. S., Tokaç, A. Z., & Hayran, O. E. (2021). Vaccine hesitancy and anti-vaccination attitudes during the start of COVID-19 vaccination program: A content analysis on Twitter data. *medRxiv preprint medRxiv:2021.*

Lyu, J. C., Han, E. L., & Luli, G. K. (2021). COVID-19 vaccine–related discussion on twitter: Topic modeling and sentiment analysis. *Journal of Medical Internet Research, 23*(6), e24435.

Mathieu, E., Ritchie, H., Ortiz-Ospina, E., Roser, M., Hasell, J., Appel, C., et al. (2021). A global database of COVID-19 vaccinations. *Nature Human Behaviour.* https://www.nature.com/articles/s41562-021-01122-8. Accessed 01.02.2022.

Nuzhath, T., Tasnim, S., Sanjwal, R. K., Trisha, N. F., Rahman, M., Mahmud, S., et al. (2020). COVID-19 vaccination hesitancy, misinformation and conspiracy theories on social media: A content analysis of Twitter data. https://doi.org/10.31235/osf.io/vc9jb. Accessed 10.08.21.

Paul, E., Steptoe, A., & Fancourt, D. (2021). Attitudes towards vaccines and intention to vaccinate against COVID-19: Implications for public health communications. *The Lancet Regional Health-Europe, 1*(100012), 1–10.

Plutchik, R. (1980). A general psychoevolutionary theory of emotion. In P. Robert & K. Henry (Eds.), *Theories of emotion* (pp. 3–33). Academic.

Roser, M., Ritchie, H., Ortiz-Ospina, E., & Hasell, J. (2020). Coronavirus Pandemic (COVID-19). https://ourworldindata.org/coronavirus. Accessed 10.08.21.

Sallam, M. (2021). COVID-19 vaccine hesitancy worldwide: A systematic review of vaccine acceptance rates. *Vaccine, 9*(160), 1–14.

Seale, H., Heywood, A. E., Leask, J., Sheel, M., Durrheim, D. N., Bolsewicz, K., et al. (2021). Examining Australian public perceptions and behaviors towards a future COVID-19 vaccine. *BMC Infectious Diseases, 21*(1), 1–9.

Sharma, K., Zhang, Y., & Liu, Y. (2021). COVID-19 vaccines: Characterizing misinformation campaigns and vaccine hesitancy on twitter. *arXiv*, 2106.0842.

Thelwall, M., Kayvan, K., & Thelwall, S. (2021). Covid-19 vaccine hesitancy on English-language twitter. *Profesional de la Información, 30*(2), e300212.

Turney, P., & Mohammad, S. (2010). Emotions evoked by common words and phrases: using Mechanical Turk to create an emotion lexicon. In: Proceedings of the NAACL HLT 2010 Workshop on Computational Approaches to Analysis and Generation of Emotion in Text. 2010 Jun Presented at NAACL HLT 2010 Workshop on Computational Approaches to Analysis and Generation of Emotion in Text; June 2010; Los Angeles, CA. pp. 26–34.

Ward, J. K., Alleaume, C., Peretti-Watel, P., Seror, V., Cortaredona, S., Launay, O., et al. (2020). The French public's attitudes to a future COVID-19 vaccine: The politicisation of a public health issue. *Social Science & Medicine, 265*, 113414.

Xue, J., Chen, J., Hu, R., Chen, C., Zheng, C., Su, Y., et al. (2021). Twitter discussions and emotions about the COVID-19 pandemic: Machine learning approach. *Journal of Medical Internet Research, 22*(11), e20550.

Yousefinaghani, S., Daraa, R., Mubareka, S., Papadopoulos, A., & Sharif, S. (2021). An analysis of COVID-19 vaccine sentiments and opinions on twitter. *International Journal of Infectious Diseases, 108*, 256–262.

Chapter 8
Measuring Attitudes About the COVID-19 Vaccine: A Cross-Country Analysis

Abstract In this chapter, we extend the groundwork laid in Chap. 7 to delve deeper into our research methodology and preliminary findings regarding attitudes toward the COVID-19 vaccine. Building upon our COVID-19 Vaccine Positive Attitude Index (VPAI), constructed from real-time Twitter data, we offer insights into the evolving landscape of public sentiment surrounding COVID-19 vaccines.

Firstly, we explain the process of creating the VPAI, emphasising our commitment to harnessing Big Data to gauge public attitudes. Our descriptive findings, spanning from 1 February 2021 to 31 July 2021, across ten countries (refer to Chaps. 4 and 5), highlight temporal trends in vaccine attitudes, distinguishing between the Northern and Southern Hemispheres and individual countries. We highlight successful government policy initiatives that have influenced these trends while also addressing instances where governmental failures have fuelled vaccine hesitancy, especially among ethnic minorities and the most vulnerable communities.

Our analysis reveals varying trends in vaccine attitudes across countries, with notable successes observed in Belgium and the Netherlands. Belgium's proactive governmental measures to address logistical challenges resulted in a positive trend in the VPAI, showcasing the impact of policy interventions on public sentiment. Conversely, the Netherlands' successful information campaigns transformed their initially sluggish vaccination programme into a success story, significantly increasing vaccination numbers.

This chapter serves as a critical phase in our investigation, setting the stage for Chap. 9, where we will identify variables significantly related to the VPAI and propose policy measures to enhance vaccine acceptance. By delving into the factors influencing positive attitudes toward COVID-19 vaccines, our research aims to contribute meaningfully to the discourse on public health and vaccination attitudes amidst a global pandemic.

Keywords Vaccine positive attitude · Twitter · Public sentiment · Government · Policymaking · Trust

© The Author(s), under exclusive license to Springer Nature
Switzerland AG 2024
S. Rossouw, T. Greyling, *Resistance to COVID-19 Vaccination*, Human
Well-Being Research and Policy Making,
https://doi.org/10.1007/978-3-031-56529-8_8

8.1 Introduction

This chapter is a natural extension of the groundwork in Chap. 7. Here, we build upon the foundation established in the preceding chapter to offer readers a deeper understanding of our research methodology and initial findings.

First and foremost, we explain the process by which we created our COVID-19 vaccine positive attitude index (VPAI). This key metric takes shape by utilising Big Data collected from real-time Twitter feeds, as previously discussed in Chap. 7. This index stands as a testament to our commitment to harnessing the power of digital discourse to gauge public sentiment regarding COVID-19 vaccines.

Subsequently, we present our descriptive findings, illustrating the trend in attitudes toward COVID-19 vaccines over a specific period, from 1 February 2021 to 31 July 2021. This temporal analysis encompasses ten countries (refer to Chaps. 4 and 5), providing insights into the emerging trends during this time frame. Our findings cover the entire sample, with a distinction between the Northern and Southern Hemispheres and an in-depth discussion about the prevailing attitudes in individual countries. Notably, we highlight successful government policy initiatives that have influenced these trends, emphasising the critical role of policy in shaping public sentiment. However, we will also show readers how, for example, a lack of trust in governments after failing in their COVID-19 vaccine rollout by not reaching the most marginalised first was the catalyst needed for the spread of misinformation to take hold, especially among ethnic minorities and the most vulnerable communities.

In essence, this chapter marks the initial phase of our investigation into positive attitudes towards COVID-19 vaccines. It lays the groundwork, offering valuable insights into the evolving landscape, which will be further scrutinised and enriched in Chap. 9. In the subsequent chapter, we will delve into identifying those factors that hold the potential to enhance and improve these positive attitudes toward COVID-19 vaccines, marking a pivotal step in our research journey.

8.2 Vaccine Positive Attitude Index (VPAI)

To construct the VPAI index, we follow the method explained in Sect. 7.4 and extract COVID-19-related tweets using the keywords: *vaccinate, vacc, vaccine, Sputnik V, Sputnik, Sinopharm, Astrazeneca, Pfizer (if NEAR) vaccine, Pfizer-BioNTech, Johnson & Johnson,* and *Moderna.*

To ensure that the extracted vaccine-related tweets discuss attitudes related to receiving the COVID-19 vaccine, we first constructed word clouds per country (refer to Sect. 7.5 for a discussion on word clouds). For example, Fig. 8.1 illustrates the word cloud generated for Great Britain. After generating word clouds for all countries, we returned to the original tweets and confirmed the context of the words with high frequencies. We determined that these vaccine-related tweets are indeed related to receiving the vaccine and expressed that "it's good to receive a vaccine"

Fig. 8.1 Word cloud based on positive sentiment for vaccine-related tweets, Great Britain. *Source*: Authors' own compilation using Word Cloud software

and that people are happy after receiving their second vaccination. For example, tweets that generated the word cloud for Great Britain included[1]:

> Here it is, worth its weight in gold. My consent form for the covid vaccine next week, normality on the horizon hope
> So excited to hear my mum, an NHS nurse, will be receiving the Pfizer Covid-19 vaccine today - a glimmer of hope af
> Grandmother the vaccine, as you can see, absolutely delighted?? (all credit to my younger brother for this absolute

From the positive sentiment vaccine-related tweets, we determined that more than 90% were directly related to receiving the COVID-19 vaccine. We realise that the data carries limited noise, but we believe that this noise does not affect our results, especially considering the large number of tweets analysed.

We use the NRC lexicon (discussed in Sect. 7.4) to calculate our VPAI by deriving the mean value of the positive sentiment-coded tweets per day and standardising these values using the minimum-maximum method. The index is measured on a scale from 0 to 1, with 0 being the lowest positive sentiment and 1 the highest. As a robustness test for the VPAI, we derive a similar index using Sentiment140. However, in this instance, we calculate the VPAI by expressing the number of positive tweets per day as a percentage of the sum of the number of positive and negative sentiment tweets (see Figs. 8.5, 8.6 and 8.7 in the Supplementary Information section for the graphs on the trends in positive attitudes using the VPAI based on Sentiment140).

---

[1] Please note the above tweets were taken directly from Twitter and do not represent the views of the authors, their institutions or Springer.

8.3   Methodology

In this chapter, we use descriptive statistics and graphs to analyse the trend in the VPAI over time and compare the results for the Northern and Southern Hemispheres and across the ten countries in our sample. Our descriptive analysis includes topic modelling of the tweets per country. We explore the text corpus by applying NLP and statistical analysis. The main statistical procedure we use in the topic modelling is factor analysis. This method attempts to uncover the text corpus's hidden thematic structure (topics).

8.4   Results of the Trend in the VPAI

We first focus on our descriptive analysis (graphs) to explain the trends in the VPAI towards the COVID-19 vaccines for the period 1 February 2021 to 31 July 2021. We describe the trends in our overall sample, the different Hemispheres, and each country. In all instances, we report the findings on the VPAI using NRC, and as a robustness test, we repeat the analyses using Sentiment140. In the Supplementary Information section, we report the results using Sentiment140 in Figs. 8.5, 8.6 and 8.7.

8.4.1   Trends in the VPAI

When we consider Fig. 8.2, we see that the trend in the VPAI towards the COVID-19 vaccines across all countries is downwards; we note an almost 8% decrease over time. Section 8.4.2 discusses possible explanations for this downward trend.

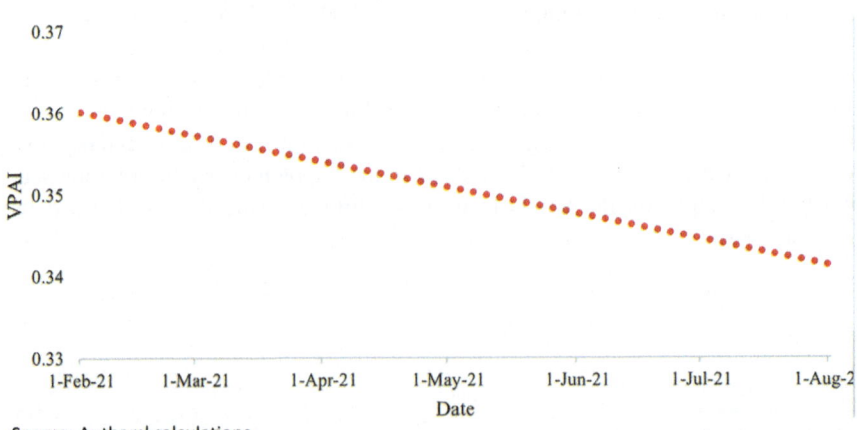

Source: Authors' calculations.

Fig. 8.2 Trend in positive attitude from February 2021 to the end of July 2021 for the whole sample. *Source*: Authors' calculations

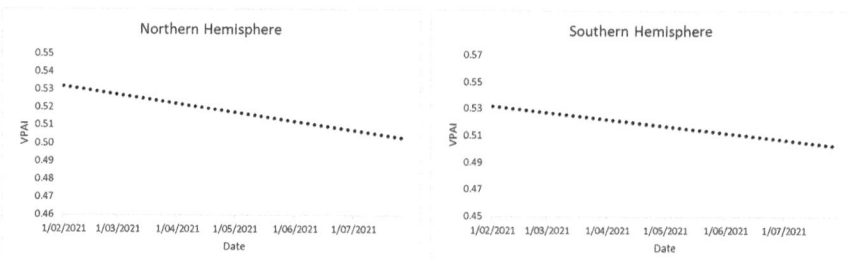

Fig. 8.3 Trend in positive attitude across the Northern and Southern Hemispheres from February 2021 to the end of July 2021. *Source*: Authors' calculations

Additionally, we note from Fig. 8.3 that the downward trend in positive attitude holds across both the Northern and Southern Hemispheres. However, the downward trend seems stronger in the Southern Hemisphere than in the Northern Hemisphere.

8.4.2   Trends in Positive Attitude Per Country

If we consider the individual countries, Fig. 8.4 shows the trend in the VPAI towards the COVID-19 vaccines for each of the ten countries and indicates that the attitude improved in only two countries, namely Belgium and the Netherlands. For the remaining eight countries, the trend was negative over time.

To explain the trends in the VPAI for our individual countries, we relied on existing literature and our topic modelling.

Upon further investigation into Belgium, we found that the positive trend in the VPAI in Belgium was likely due to the steps taken to correct government failure that plagued the country in 2020. In 2020 (Villani et al., 2020), Belgium was the European country with the highest loss of life and hospitalisation rate relative to the size of the population in Europe. According to Vanham (2021), Belgium was also hit with capacity issues, struggling to get vaccination centres up and running because of vaccine delivery delays. It seems that the Belgian people did not trust information coming from their government after reports of political favouritism in deciding who would get what little vaccine stock was available were leaked (Vanham, 2021). The above events led to widespread anger towards the politicians for making COVID-19 a political game.

However, the government took many steps to correct the situation, likely positively changing the attitude towards the COVID-19 vaccine. The Belgian government set up a COVID-19 task force responsible for addressing logistics and capacity issues. According to Vanham (2021), the high uptake of vaccinations could also result from lockdown regulation policies being relaxed during spring, which would depend on the vaccination rates rather than case numbers or hospitalisation rates. People wanting to return to 'normal' reacted positively to the policy. Our topic modelling also revealed that Belgians were found to be optimistic about the effectiveness of the COVID-19 vaccines, including AstraZeneca. However, they were pleased that younger people could receive the Janssen vaccine.

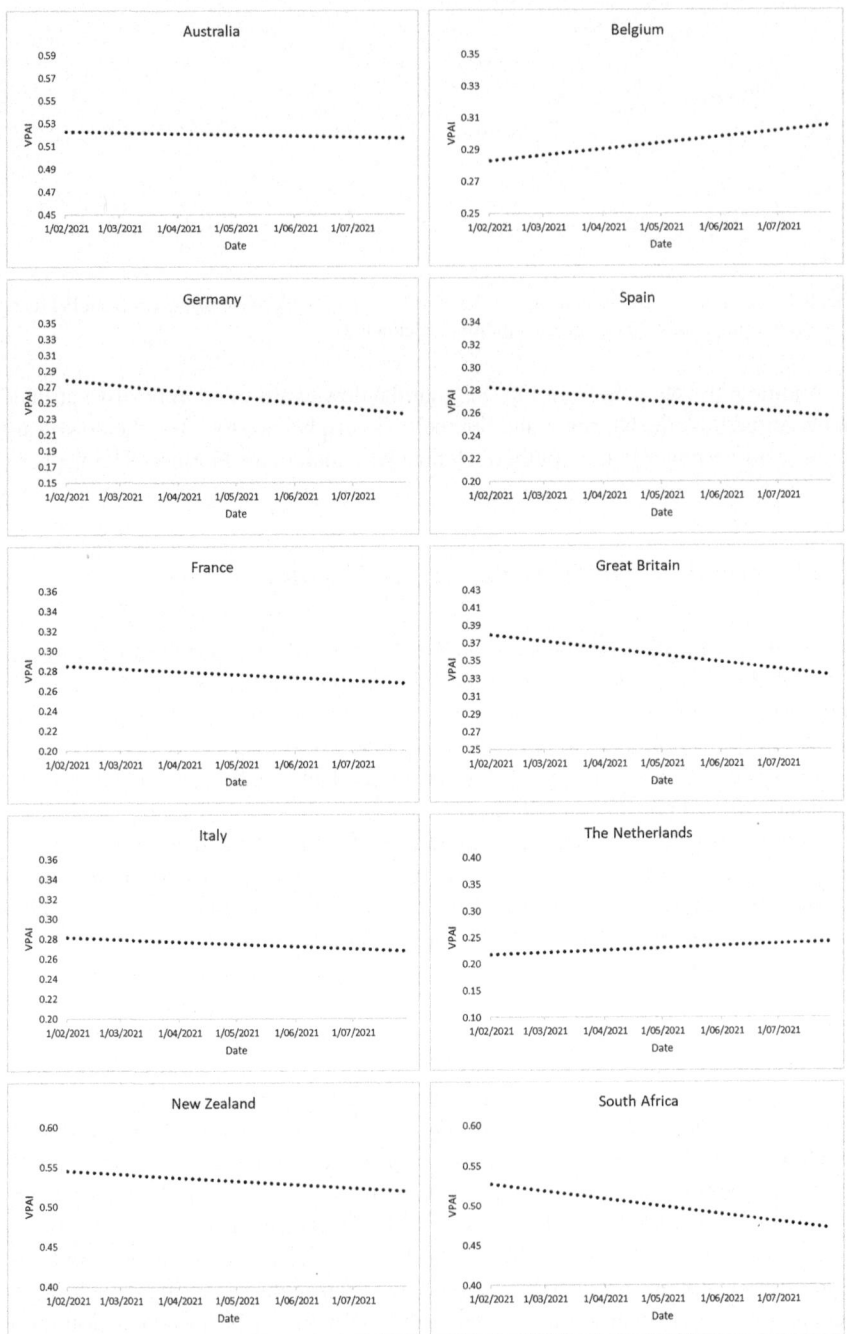

Fig. 8.4 Trend in the positive attitude for each of the ten countries. *Source*: Authors' calculations

The Netherlands was the last European country to start their vaccine rollout on 6 January 2021. Their rollout was hampered by a poor vaccination policy and a conservative strategy that kept more than 40 per cent of its vaccines from being used (Bahceli, 2021). Additionally, during the beginning phase of the vaccine rollout, young Dutch adults (18–34 years, which constitutes approximately 25% of the total population) who were willing to receive the COVID-19 vaccine constantly lagged about ten percentage points after the average percentage of the whole population (Vollmann & Salewski, 2021). To encourage a positive attitude towards vaccines, the Dutch government spent around €6 million (at the time of the study) on information campaigns to increase vaccine uptake by informing the public about the safety of the various COVID-19 vaccines (Bahceli, 2021). Vollmann and Salewski' (2021) results show that the relationship between information campaigns and a positive attitude towards vaccines leads to higher vaccine uptake. The Netherlands' fully vaccinated population increased significantly from 2430 people on 31 January 2021 to 9,288,187 by 1 August 2021 (Mathieu et al., 2021). We also found (from topic modelling) that the Dutch believed the benefits of getting the COVID-19 vaccine outweigh any potential costs, which is why they expressed support for the elderly and the vulnerable to be prioritised and getting the younger generation vaccinated as soon as possible.

Literature and topic modelling revealed the following likely explanations for those countries that experienced downward trends in positive attitudes over time.

Australia follows a federal system of government, and contradictory government-implemented regulations across the different states led to widespread confusion regarding COVID-19 vaccines and caused a downtrend in attitudes (Attwell et al., 2021). This was confirmed by our topic modelling as well. New South Wales (NSW) (Greater Sydney region), home to 32.33% of the total Australian population, was in lockdown at the time of conducting this study (August 2021), while other regions were not, regardless of case numbers. These discrepancies in COVID-19 regulations resulted in a significant proportion of people living within NSW refusing to comply with government-imposed regulations. Topic modelling illustrated that there was anger over government-mandated lockdowns, a perceived incompetent government and fear of side effects. In July 2021, approximately 15,000 people (most not wearing masks) protested against the lockdowns, and they demanded their liberties be restored (Swain, 2021). Figure 8.4 shows the downward trend in positive attitudes towards the COVID-19 vaccine.

Spain shows a downward trend in the VPAI. A possible explanation could be that the government delayed action and did not have workable contingency plans in place. This led to a failure to contain the virus early on, nearly overwhelming the health system and causing Spain to experience one of the highest death rates attributable to COVID-19 (Casasnovas et al., 2021). This lack of action caused during the first 5 months of 2021, Spain's COVID-19 vaccination campaign progressed slowly and failed to reach marginalised populations (Lazarus et al., 2021). In mid-April, when 13% of Great Britain's citizens were fully vaccinated, only about 7% of Spaniards were similarly protected (Mathieu et al., 2021). The above rhetoric was echoed through our topic modelling, where Spaniards expressed anger towards their government for failing to roll out the COVID-19 vaccine efficiently while at the same time expressing fear for the unknown long-term side effects of the vaccine.

According to Sprengholz et al. (2021), the Germans responded with anger towards their government's proposed policy to contain COVID-19. The policy stated that only vaccinated people would be allowed to enter venues like sports stadiums, movie theatres or restaurants because they deemed the residual risk high in such places. In July 2021, Chief of Staff Helge Braun announced he did not expect another COVID-19-related lockdown in Germany (Schultheis, 2021). However, this would mean that if there were a future outbreak, the liberties of the unvaccinated would be taken away with immediate effect. Additionally, according to Mario Czaja, head of the Berlin Red Cross, Germany has seen an increase in people not showing up for their vaccination appointments, with 5–10% missing appointments daily since July 2021 (Reuters, 2021).

The results of the topic modelling of tweets showed that the Germans were angry as they had to wait in queues at the vaccine centres. Furthermore, they were unhappy to receive AstraZeneca due to the news of potential blood clotting. They also mentioned concerns about side effects, but many tweets reassured that these were only mild. Lastly, Germany's anti-lockdown movement, the Querdenken, has been very active in spreading conspiracy theories ranging from the idea that "masks are deadly" to "vaccines can alter your DNA" (BBC Trending, 2021). These could all have contributed to the decreasing trend in the VPAI.

In Great Britain, the government faced criticism because of their vaccination policy, which, when writing this study, was yet to approve the COVID-19 vaccine for 12–15-year-olds (Mason & Elgot, 2021). This meant sending children back to schools with inadequate mitigations for COVID-19 in place, which could lead to widespread infections and more disruptions to learning. Additionally, trust in the ability of the government to see this pandemic through has decreased since the announcement of their so-called 'Freedom Day' (Donovan, 2021). Freedom Day brought with it a lifting of any remaining COVID-19 restrictions and came amidst 47,000 new cases of COVID-19 being reported in the previous 24 hours (Donovan, 2021). The decision of Freedom Day brought with it 1200 scientists worldwide criticising the decision to open up, saying it could pose a threat to the entire world if daily cases increased exponentially and vaccine-resistant mutations of the virus were allowed to develop (Ball, 2021). Our topic modelling found that people were concerned about Freedom Day and not wearing masks or applying social distancing rules. They were also concerned about the increasing number of COVID-19 cases and the blood-clotting side effect from AstraZeneca. The downward trend in the VPAI is likely (Fig. 8.4) a product of all the accumulated issues.

In France, introducing a stringent vaccination policy known as 'COVID-19 vaccine passports' has decreased the positive attitude towards the COVID-19 vaccine (The Economist, 2021). The news that movie theatres, museums and sports venues have begun asking visitors to provide proof of a COVID-19 vaccination or a negative test has many French nationals angry but willing to take the vaccine simply to return to their once normal way of living (The Economist, 2021). The topic modelling of tweets supported the abovementioned and highlighted the reluctance to accept the health pass and scan QR codes. They were also concerned about the side effects and mentioned that the "Covidliste" has a long waiting list. "Covidliste" is a voluntary and civic initiative allowing the connection between vaccination volunteers and health professionals who have vaccine doses.

Italy, the second-worst Northern Hemisphere country concerning people not fully vaccinated (52% at the time of conducting this study in August 2021), has faced an uphill battle to increase the COVID-19 vaccine uptake since the start of their vaccine rollout on 27 December 2020 (Roberts, 2021). They decided to take a tough stance, approving emergency legislation to make COVID-19 vaccines mandatory for all healthcare workers, including pharmacy staff (Roberts, 2021). Individuals working in this industry who refused the COVID-19 vaccine would be transferred to another job or suspended without pay for up to a year. In addition, they introduced vaccine passports. From both the topic modelling and Paterlini (2021), we saw that Italians demonstrated and protested against Italy's use of these passports and the subsequent green passes.

Furthermore, the emergency legislation faced fierce resistance from Italy's deeply rooted anti-vaccine movement, partly fostered by populist political forces (Roberts, 2021). These included the 5 Star Movement, which entered government in 2018, promoting vaccine hesitancy. Public trust in the vaccine has also taken a hit after the country temporarily decided to suspend the use of the Oxford/AstraZeneca vaccine after several deaths (Roberts, 2021).

The Aged Care Association (Wallis, 2021) described the COVID-19 rollout as a 'shambles' in New Zealand. This is due to the government of the day being responsible for a slow rollout of the vaccine because they and the country as a whole became complacent (Thaker & Floyd, 2021; Vance, 2021). At the time of conducting this study (August 2021), New Zealand found itself in a level-4 lockdown (the most stringent level of lockdown), even though it did not have a positive COVID-19 case during the previous 6 months. New Zealand's zero COVID-19 strategies were successful until the first Delta-variant positive case was announced. Soon, the government realised they did not have enough vaccines to vaccinate everyone, as previously promised. This was partly because of the government's strategy early in 2021 to reject the cheaper but potentially less effective vaccines like those made by AstraZeneca in favour of the high-performing vaccine made by Pfizer/BioNTech (Satherley, 2021).

Additionally, the increased spread of misinformation about the COVID-19 vaccine has increased distrust towards the vaccine (Thaker & Subramanian, 2021). Unfortunately for New Zealand, the spread of misinformation and conspiracy theories is rampant among its ethnic minority and most vulnerable communities (Tukuitonga, 2021). The lack of trust in the government after failing in their vaccine rollout by not reaching the most marginalised first (topic modelling) is precisely what was needed for the spread of misinformation to take hold. Our results confirm the study done by Paul et al. (2021), who found that distrustful attitudes towards vaccination were higher amongst individuals from ethnic minority backgrounds, which isn't a surprise since many minority groups have good reason not to trust the government given their historical mistreatment. All of the abovementioned likely contributed to the downtrend in the VPAI.

South Africa' has faced problems such as capacity issues, mistrust in the government and anti-vaccination campaigns (Cocks, 2021), which contributed to the decrease in a positive attitude towards the COVID-19 vaccines (see Fig. 8.4). From as early as December 2020, it seemed that the COVID-19 strategy was haphazard apart from its dependency on its fragile COVAX arrangement. After receiving their first delivery of the AstraZeneca vaccine on 1 February 2021, the government did not seem to have a clear vaccination policy (van den Heever et al., 2021). The Health Minister created confusion in the public arena when he announced that the AstraZeneca vaccine did not demonstrate efficacy against mild to moderate COVID-19 and placed the rollout of the vaccine on hold. The announcement by the Health Minister caused a decrease in trust in the COVID-19 vaccine and likely contributed to the downward trend in the VPAI. Local scientists criticised the decision, and the World Health Organization did not support it (van den Heever et al., 2021). This decision left approximately 17 million high-risk people unvaccinated (van den Heever et al., 2021). During the winter months from June to September 2021, South Africa lost 25,660 lives to COVID-19 (Roser et al., 2020). According to van den Heever et al. (2021), this probably could have been avoided if the South African government had not been plagued by corruption and mismanagement during its response to the pandemic. By August 2021, South Africa saw 'vaccine apathy' or 'vaccine fatigue', with the number of people coming forward to be vaccinated dropping below 200,000 a day, falling short of the set target of 300,000. According to a study conducted by the Human Sciences Research Council and the University of Johannesburg (Cooper et al., 2021), the vaccine-hesitant cite three primary concerns which could contribute to the downtrend in positive attitudes: side effects, effectiveness, and distrust of the vaccine and institutions.

To summarise, the downward trend in positive attitudes is partly due to a fear of the side effects, but many other factors also contribute. These include dissatisfaction with governments' rollout plan, procurement, corruption, resistance to mandatory vaccination and the use of COVID-19 passports.

In Chap. 9, we will continue investigating the attitude towards vaccines and determine those variables that can potentially improve the positive attitude towards the COVID-19 vaccine and inform policymakers.

8.5   Summary

This chapter discussed the construction of our COVID-19 Vaccine Positive Attitude Index (VPAI) by extracting COVID-19-related tweets using the keywords: *vaccinate, vacc, vaccine, Sputnik V, Sputnik, Sinopharm, Astrazeneca, Pfizer (if NEAR) vaccine, Pfizer-BioNTech, Johnson & Johnson,* and *Moderna.*

This first-of-a-kind metric represents a testament to our dedication and showcases the power of Big Data through the use of social media platforms such as Twitter. The VPAI allowed us to quantify and determine the trend in positive attitudes toward COVID-19 vaccines.

Our descriptive findings, from 1 February 2021 to 31 July 2021, for the ten countries under analysis, showed that apart from Belgium and the Netherlands, all countries experienced a negative trend in the VPAI towards the COVID-19 vaccine. Upon further investigation, we determined that the positive trend in the VPAI in Belgium was most likely due to the government proactively taking corrective steps to address logistics and capacity issues that initially plagued their vaccine rollout. For the Netherlands, we saw the power of successful information campaigns as the Dutch government turned their initial sluggish vaccination programme into a success story by increasing vaccination numbers from 31 January 2021 to 1 August 2021 by 157%.

Moving on to Chap. 9, we will identify variables significantly related to the VPAI and, therefore, could increase the uptake of COVID-19 vaccines if addressed by policy measures. This upcoming chapter represents a pivotal step in our research journey, promising to enrich our understanding and contribute meaningfully to the discourse on public health and vaccination attitudes in the face of a global pandemic.

Supplementary Information

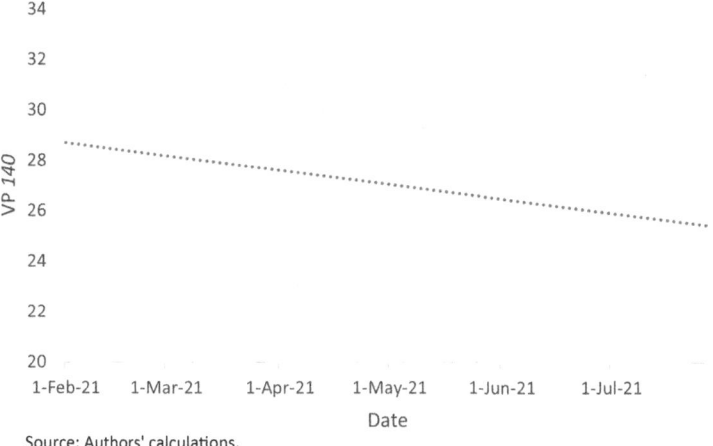

Source: Authors' calculations.

Fig. 8.5 Trend in positive attitude from February 2021 to the end of July 2021 for the whole sample, using Sentiment140

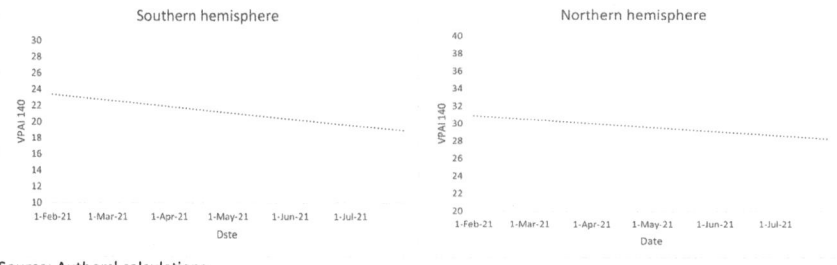

Source: Authors' calculations.

Fig. 8.6 Trend in positive attitude from February 2021 to the end of July 2021 per Hemisphere, using Sentiment140. *Source*: Authors' calculations

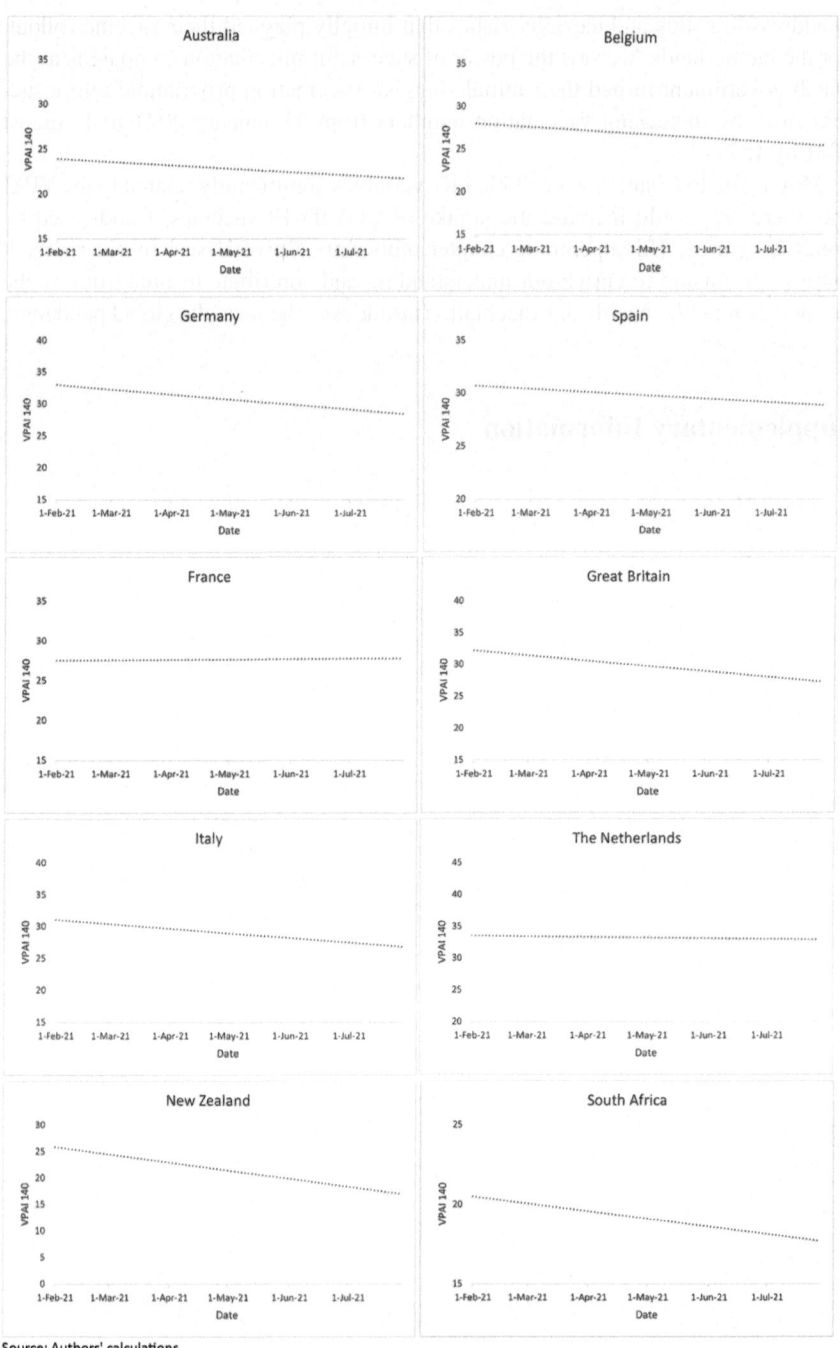

Source: Authors' calculations.

Fig. 8.7 Trend in positive attitude from February 2021 to the end of July 2021 per individual country, using Sentiment140. *Source*: Authors' calculations

References

Attwell, K., Rizzi, M., McKenzie, L., Carlson, S. J., Roberts, L., Tomkinson, S., et al. (2021). COVID-19 vaccine mandates: An Australian attitudinal study. *Vaccine*. https://www.sciencedirect.com/science/article/pii/S0264410X21015309. Accessed 01.02.22

Bahceli, Y. (2021). Wealthy, efficient Dutch play catch-up in vaccine rollout. *Health News*. https://www.reuters.com/article/us-health-coronavirus-netherlands-vaccinidUKKBN2AH1CC. Accessed 15.08.21.

Ball, P. (2021). Why England's COVID 'freedom day' alarms researchers. *Nature*. https://www.nature.com/articles/d41586-021-01938-4. Accessed 15.08.21

BBC Trending. (2021). The anti-vax movement targeting German children. https://www.bbc.com/news/blogs-trending-56675874. Accessed 15.08.21.

Casasnovas, J. L., Seguí, F. L., & Goset, A. A. (2021). *Sustainability and resilience in the Spanish health system. London School of Economics and Political Science (LSE) in partnership with health system sustainability and resilience (PHSSR)*. LSE Consulting.

Cocks, T. (2021). As vaccines arrive, South Africa faces widespread scepticism over safety. https://www.reuters.com/article/uk-health-coronavirus-safrica-anti-vacciidUSKBN2A90YT. Accessed 04.02.22.

Cooper, S., Van Rooyen, H., & Wiysonge, C. S. (2021). COVID-19 vaccine hesitancy in South Africa: how can we maximize uptake of COVID-19 vaccines? https://repository.hsrc.ac.za/handle/20.500.11910/16386 Accessed 15.08.21.

Donovan, E. T. (2021). The Detail: UK's 'Freedom Day' comes amid soaring Covid-19 cases. https://www.stuff.co.nz/national/the-detail/300362357/the-detail-uks-freedom-day-comes-amid-soaring-covid19-cases. Accessed 15.08.21.

Lazarus, J. V., Bassat, Q., Crespo, J., Fanjul, G., Hoyos, M. L., Mateos, C., et al. (2021). Vaccinate fast but leave no one behind: A call to action for COVID-19 vaccination in Spain. *Communications Medicine, 1*(1), 1–4.

Mason, R., & Elgot, J. (2021). JCVI 'largely opposed' to Covid vaccination for children under 16. The Guardian. https://www.theguardian.com/society/2021/aug/07/jcvi-largely-opposed-to-covid-vaccination-for-children-under-16. Accessed 04.02.22.

Mathieu, E., Ritchie, H., Ortiz-Ospina, E., Roser, M., Hasell, J., Appel, C., et al. (2021). A global database of COVID-19 vaccinations. *Nature Human Behaviour*. https://www.nature.com/articles/s41562-021-01122-8. Accessed 01.02.22

Paterlini, M. (2021). Covid-19: Italy sees protests against mandatory health passports for workplaces. *BMJ*. https://www.bmj.com/content/375/bmj.n2575. Accessed 01.02.22

Paul, E., Steptoe, A., & Fancourt, D. (2021). Attitudes towards vaccines and intention to vaccinate against COVID-19: Implications for public health communications. *The Lancet Regional Health-Europe, 1*(100012), 1–10.

Reuters. (2021). Germany Worried About COVID-19 Vaccination 'No Shows'. https://www.usnews.com/news/world/articles/2021-07-05/germany-worried-about-covid-19-vaccination-no-shows. Accessed 04.02.22.

Roberts, H. (2021). Italy's uphill battle to force health workers to get vaccinated. Politico. https://www.politico.eu/article/italy-health-workers-coronavirus-vaccinations/. Accessed 15.08.21.

Roser, M., Ritchie, H., Ortiz-Ospina, E., & Hasell, J. (2020). Coronavirus Pandemic (COVID-19). https://ourworldindata.org/coronavirus. Accessed 10.08.21.

Satherley, D. (2021). Coronavirus: Almost everyone in NZ will need a vaccine to stop Delta variant spreading—study. https://www.newshub.co.nz/home/new-zealand/2021/06/coronavirus-almost-everyone-in-nz-will-need-a-vaccine-to-stop-delta-variant-spreading-study.html. Accessed 04.02.22.

Schultheis, E. (2021). Germans divided over restrictions for the unvaccinated. https://apnews.com/article/europe-business-health-government-and-politics-germany-a46d18ff239dcbc71973cd1052c3866b. Accessed 15.08.21.

Sprengholz, P., Betsch, C., & Böhm, R. (2021). Reactance revisited: Consequences of mandatory and scarce vaccination in the case of COVID-19. *Applied Psychology, Health and Well-Being, 13*, 986–995.

Swain, S. (2021). More than 250 fined and 47 arrests made at Sydney protests. https://www.9news.com.au/national/coronavirus-nsw-updates-sydney-lockdown-protest-cbd-rally-police-taxi-uber-ban/955af903-002a-42a1-a269-0c55a6fb5ff0. Accessed 15.08.21.

Thaker, J., & Floyd, B. (2021). Shifting COVID-19 vaccine intentions in New Zealand: Next steps in the vaccination campaign. *The Lancet Regional Health, 15*(100278).

Thaker, J., & Subramanian, A. (2021). Exposure to COVID-19 vaccine hesitancy is as impactful as vaccine misinformation in inducing a decline in vaccination intentions in New Zealand: Results from pre-post between-groups randomized block experiment. *Frontiers in Communication, 6*.

The Economist. (2021). Why vaccine-shy French are suddenly rushing to get jabbed. https://www.economist.com/graphic-detail/2021/07/14/why-vaccine-shy-french-are-suddenly-rushing-to-get-jabbed. Accessed 15.08.21.

Tukuitonga, C. (2021). COVID-19 in Pacific Islands people of Aotearoa/New Zealand: Communities taking control. In Y. Campbell & J. Connell (Eds.), *COVID in the islands: A comparative perspective on the Caribbean and the Pacific*. Palgrave Macmillan.

Van den Heever, A., Valodia, I., Veller, M., Madhi, S. A., & Venter, W. D. F. (2021). South Africa's vaccine quagmire, and what needs to be done now. *The Conversation..* https://theconversation.com/south-africas-vaccine-quagmire-and-what-needs-to-be-done-now-163784. Accessed 15.08.21

Vance, A. (2021). We've been patient, but the vaccination rollout is not going to plan. https://www.stuff.co.nz/national/politics/opinion/300358215/weve-been-patient-but-the-vaccination-rollout-is-not-going-to-plan. Accessed 15.08.21.

Vanham, P. (2021). Belgium's COVID-19 comeback is a model for the World. https://foreignpolicy.com/2021/08/15/belgium-covid-19-pandemic-vaccination-campaign-model-europe-eu/. Accessed 15.08.21.

Villani, L., McKee, M., Cascini, F., Ricciardi, W., & Boccia, S. (2020). Comparison of deaths rates for COVID-19 across Europe during the first wave of the COVID-19 pandemic. *Frontiers in Public Health, 8*.

Vollmann, M., & Salewski, C. (2021). To get vaccinated, or not to get vaccinated, that is the question: Illness representations about COVID-19 and perceptions about COVID-19 vaccination as predictors of COVID-19 vaccination willingness among young adults in The Netherlands. *Vaccine, 9*(9), 941.

Wallis, S. (2021). Rest homes still waiting for Covid-19 vaccination start date. https://www.rnz.co.nz/national/programmes/checkpoint/audio/2018790783/rest-homes-still-waiting-for-covid-19-vaccination-start-date. Accessed 08.02.22.

Chapter 9
Drivers of COVID-19 Vaccine Hesitancy

Abstract This chapter is the second most technical chapter of the book and follows from Chap. 8, intending to identify the drivers of COVID-19 vaccine hesitancy. Employing a range of econometric techniques, including Pooled Ordinary Least Squares, Panel Fixed Effects, and Instrumental Variables regressions, we determine the variables significantly associated with the Vaccine Positive Attitude Index (VPAI) across ten countries (refer to Chap. 8) from 1 February 2021 to 31 July 2021.

Our analysis offers valuable insights into the factors influencing attitudes toward COVID-19 vaccines, addressing potential endogeneity and reverse causality to enhance the robustness of our findings. We aim to provide policymakers with actionable information to bolster vaccine uptake globally by explaining the relationships between various factors and vaccine acceptance.

Drawing from Chaps. 7 and 8, we highlight a decline in the VPAI trend over the study period, with Belgium and the Netherlands as notable exceptions, experiencing positive trends. Our regression models reveal significant associations between positive attitudes toward vaccines and factors such as information about vaccine safety and side effects, trust in government vaccine rollout procedures, and the role of social media in disseminating vaccine-related information.

Based on our findings, we propose policy measures to improve vaccine acceptance, emphasising the need for transparent and accessible communication, community engagement, and encouraging positive emotions toward vaccination. Additionally, we acknowledge the limitations of our study, including the reliance on Twitter data and the temporal constraints inherent in pandemic research. Nonetheless, our insights contribute to informed decision-making and pave the way for future research to expand and refine our understanding of vaccine hesitancy on a global scale.

Keywords Pooled ordinary least square · Panel fixed effects · Instrumental variables · Policymaking · Vaccine acceptance

9.1   Introduction

This chapter follows on from Chap. 8 and is the second most technical chapter of the book. However, all empirical modelling is discussed in layman's terms to ensure that readers from all interested parties can follow and duplicate if necessary.

This chapter uses Pooled Ordinary Least Squares as our base model and extends our investigations to incorporate Panel Fixed Effects and Instrumental Variables regressions. Our results shed light on those variables significantly related to the Vaccine Positive Attitude Index from 1 February 2021 to 31 July 2021 for the ten countries analysed (refer to Chap. 8). However, to mitigate the influence of confounding factors and enhance the robustness of our analysis, we introduce a range of estimation techniques designed to address potential endogeneity and reverse causality.

Through this comprehensive investigation, we hope to contribute valuable insights that can inform policymakers and guide efforts to bolster COVID-19 vaccine acceptance globally.

9.2   Selection of Variables

9.2.1   The Outcome Variable: Vaccine Positive Attitude Index (VPAI)

The construction of our outcome variable, the VPAI index, was discussed in-depth in Sects. 7.4 and 8.2. Please refer to these sections. However, we remind the reader that we extracted COVID-19-related tweets using the keywords: *vaccinate, vacc, vaccine, Sputnik V, Sputnik, Sinopharm, Astrazeneca, Pfizer (if NEAR) vaccine, Pfizer-BioNTech, Johnson & Johnson,* and *Moderna.*

9.2.2   Selection of Covariates

To select the covariates used to identify the drivers of positive attitudes towards the COVID-19 vaccine in subsequent analyses, we used several methods, including relevant literature (refer to Sect. 7.3.2), theoretical models, topic modelling (refer to Sect. 8.2) and the analysis of negative sentiment and negative emotion tweets.

By analysing the latter, we can determine the major issues that limit the uptake of vaccines and which are likely related to decreased positive attitudes. The reader should note that the negative sentiment associated with vaccine tweets is not the inverse of the positive sentiment. Our analyses find that negatively coded tweets primarily relate to anger, fear or sadness due to the procurement, the efficiency of the vaccine rollout, and a lack of information about the side effects (refer to Sect.

8.4.2). Additionally, our topic modelling revealed that people are dissatisfied with vaccine passports and QR scanning. Concerns were expressed about the Delta variant and misinformation (COVID-19 vaccines and the virus being fake), and various conspiracy theories also came to light, especially for New Zealand. People also express their discontent with social distancing and wearing masks.

In terms of theoretical framework, we use a measure that captures relevant predictors of vaccination behaviour called the 5C scale. The 5C scale measures the "psychological antecedents of vaccination" as designed by Betsch et al. (2018). It is grounded in established theoretical models of vaccine hesitancy and acceptance (Larson et al., 2014; MacDonald, 2015; Thomson et al., 2016) and relates these predictors to psychological models to explain health behaviour (Betsch et al., 2017). We note from the 5C that confidence, constraints, collective responsibility, complacency, and calculation are important when investigating vaccination behaviour.

For the analysis of the negative sentiment and negative emotion in vaccine-related tweets, we follow the same process as described in Sect. 8.2. For an example of the issues that cause negative sentiment and emotions in people, see the word cloud in Fig. 9.1 generated from tweets extracted for South Africa.

Sample tweets that generated the word cloud for South Africa's negative sentiment include, for example[1]:

With an incompetent government, a Minister of Health without a medical degree, NDZs dictatorial tendencies; a rural population still totally unaware of what a pandemic is added to a vaccine shortage, we are doomed

Fig. 9.1 Word cloud based on negative sentiment for vaccine-related tweets, South Africa. *Source:* Authors' own compilation using Word Cloud software

---

[1] Please note that the above tweets were taken directly from Twitter and do not represent the views of the authors, their institutions or Springer.

We are bored about 1) corruption 2) poor vaccine strategy 3) terrible national government 4) incompetent cabinet 5) stealing during a pandemic!

This vaccine rollout has been disastrous from the government, has cost lives, now another lockdown killing our already hurt economy. Massive change is needed in the running of this country

The rate with which people are dying every day should get SAHPRA concerned and energised to approve more vaccine even on trial basis, this apparent incompetence is really killing and destroying families.

After conducting an in-depth analysis of the negative sentiment in vaccine-related tweets for all ten countries, we discovered that the negative sentiment was mainly related to anger towards governments' incompetence in procurement, the lack of procuring a sufficient number of (or wrong) vaccines and the execution of the vaccine rollout, fear regarding side effects, fear of people dying because they cannot get access to vaccines and people refusing to be vaccinated. Interestingly, the words prominent in the word cloud, such as 'death', 'die', and 'killing', are related to not receiving the vaccine rather than fearing the side effects.

In analysing the negative sentiment tweets, we found that tweets expressing dissatisfaction with governments are false negatives. This means that, in reality, people have positive attitudes towards vaccines. However, they are negative about government incompetence related to issues such as the rollout process, the procurement and accessibility of vaccines, etc., hence the negative sentiment of the tweets. To test this hypothesis, we also create a VPAI in which we add the tweets coded as false negatives to the tweets coded as positive. We name the index VPAI2. See the trends in the Supplementary Information section, where Figs. 9.2, 9.3 and 9.4 indicate a predominant upward trend. This suggests that if policymakers address people's grievances related to the abovementioned government incompetence, they can turn around the downward trend in the VPAI.

Therefore, the selected covariates included in the regression analyses are:

1. Trust in the COVID-19 vaccine: as a proxy for how people perceive the vaccine's safety. We follow the method explained in Sect. 7.4 to construct this variable. We use the *NRC lexicon* to return the emotion score for each COVID-19 vaccine-related tweet for 'trust'. We construct a daily time series by averaging the measured value of 'trust' per tweet per day (Betsch et al., 2018; Greyling et al., 2019). We lag the variable to address possible endogeneity that might spread from confounding factors.

2. Anger towards the government: is included in our interaction variable (see point 8). However, to construct the 'anger towards the government' variable, we first extracted all tweets that included the following keywords: *government, parliament, ministry, minister, senator, MPs, legislator, political, politics, prime minister*. We use the same method to construct the time series as for the 'trust in the COVID-19 vaccine' variable (Betsch et al., 2018; Greyling et al., 2019). We use the emotion anger as a proxy for dissatisfaction with the government. We also lag the variable.

3. Compliance: as a proxy for collective responsibility. We follow Sarracino et al. (2022) and define compliance as the degree of association between people's behaviours and COVID-19 containment policies to construct the compliance

variable. We use information gathered from Google Mobility Reports (the change in duration from the residential category) (Google (2020, 2021)) and the Stringency Index, which consists of the following nine indicators: school closing, workplace closing, events cancelled, restriction of gatherings, closed public transport, staying at home requirements, restrictions of internal movements, international travel controls, and public information campaigns. The Stringency Index ranges from 0 to 100, with 100 being the most stringent, and we sourced it from Oxford's COVID-19 Government Response Tracker (Hale et al., 2020). Therefore, we estimate the following equation:

$$\text{res}_{ct} = \alpha + \beta_{ct} \bullet \text{Country}_c \bullet \text{Day}_t \bullet \text{Policy}_{ct} + \delta_c \bullet \text{Country}_c + \lambda_{ms} + \varepsilon_{ct} \qquad (9.1)$$

where res_{ct} is residential mobility in country c on day t; Country is a vector of dummies for each country included in the dataset; Day is a vector of dummies for the days from 1 February 2021 to 31 July 2021. We focus on this period because prior to February 2021, the vaccine rollout did not occur in all countries under investigation. Policy_{ct} represents the stringency of containment policies in country c on day t. A vector of dummies is depicted by λ for each combination of month m and Hemisphere s, to account for the different seasons and evolution of the pandemic among the Northern and Southern Hemispheres. The coefficient β_{ct} is our measure of compliance. It provides the correlation between policy stringency and mobility by country and day. We are aware that creating a daily compliance measure risks introducing noise in the correlation. However, to fulfil our aim of determining the daily evolution of positive attitudes towards vaccines, we need to assess daily changes in compliance.

4. All tweets related to vaccines (Greyling et al., 2019): this is a proxy for the prominence of vaccines as a conversation topic.
5. Daily COVID-19 vaccine doses administered per million people (Betsch et al., 2018; Mathieu et al., 2021): a proxy for how well a country handles the vaccine rollout. We lag this variable to address possible endogeneity that might spread from confounding factors. The rollout or lack thereof also proxies various constraints, such as problems with the physical availability of the COVID-19 vaccine, lack of geographical accessibility, or signalling a less than adequate appeal for vaccination services uptake. We find that the VPAI and the daily vaccines have an inversely proportional relationship; therefore, we transformed this variable using a hyperbolic function.
6. Daily total new cases: a proxy for the evolution of the COVID-19 pandemic across all ten countries (Hale et al., 2020). In our models, we lag new cases to capture people's expectations of the trend of the pandemic.
7. Vaccine policy: we control for the vaccination policy across our ten countries. According to Hale et al. (2020), a vaccination policy is classified as follows: 0—no vaccine available; 1—vaccine available for one of the following groups: key workers /clinically vulnerable groups/elderly groups; 2—available for two of the abovementioned groups; 3—available for all the abovementioned groups; 4—available for all three groups plus partial addi-

Table 9.1 Descriptive statistics of the variables included in the estimations of attitudes against the COVID-19 vaccine

Variable	Observations	Mean/Frequency (%)	Std Dev.	Min	Max
VPAI	1780	0.35	0.12	0.10	0.91
Lagged trust in the COVID-19 vaccine	1780	0.37	0.09	0.16	0.91
Stringency index	1780	60.88	17.48	22.22	87.96
Residential mobility	1780	8.32	24.62	−29.67	50.85
Lagged compliance	1780	1.07	0.273	0.621	2.37
Lagged anger towards the government # daily vaccinations	1780	0.84	0.54	0.00	2.52
Vaccine tweets[a]	1780	106.32	108.20	6	690
Lagged new daily vaccinations[a]	1780	231776.60	219928.20	0	873,515
Lagged new daily cases[a]	1780	148	154	0	701
Vaccine policy					
0	605	25.80	–	–	–
1	119	5.88	–	–	–
2	444	21.13	–	–	–
3	574	22.08	–	–	–
4	353	13.98	–	–	–
5	305	11.13	–	–	–

Source: Authors' calculations
[a]Note: Vaccine tweets were logged, and the hyperbolic function of new daily vaccination was derived; the new daily cases were logged, and all variables were smoothed using a seven-day average

tional availability (select broad groups/ages) and 5—the vaccine is universally available.

8. To capture anger directed towards the government, we use an interaction variable, 'government anger' interacted with 'new daily vaccinations'. This variable captures the anger expressed towards the government, given the number of new vaccinations per day. We use the above as a proxy for people's dissatisfaction with the vaccination rollout, which also encapsulates procurement, capacity and corruption issues, and accessibility of the vaccines.

Table 9.1 provides summarised statistics for the variables included in this chapter.

9.3 Methodology

We use various econometric techniques to derive and test the robustness of the relationships between our selected covariates and the attitudes towards vaccines.

The correlation between the VPAI and the covariates over time is likely to be affected by confounding factors, such as the severity of the pandemic, exposure to different types of social media, emotional well-being (depression) of the people, accessibility of the vaccine, the prejudice built into the social-cultural environment and the seasons of the year. Therefore, we resort to various econometric techniques to address biases arising from the confounding effects of these variables.

Ideally, we would like to estimate the following equation:

$$VPAI_{ct} = \beta_0 + \beta_1 Vac\_Trust_{ct-1} + \beta_2 Gov\_Anger_{ct-1} + \beta_3 Compliance_{ct-1} \\ + \beta_z X_{ct} + \lambda_m + \mu_c + \varepsilon_{ct} \tag{9.2}$$

where $VPAI_{ct}$ is the vaccine positive attitude index as defined in Sect. 9.2.1 for country c on day t; Vac_Trust_{ct-1} (see Sect. 9.2.2) is the average level of trust related to the COVID-19 vaccine for country c on day $t-1$. Gov_Anger_{ct-1} is the average level of anger towards the government for country c on day $t-1$; $Compliance_{ct-1}$ is the average level of compliance as defined in Sect. 9.2.2 for country c on day $t-1$. X_{ct} is a vector of variables, λ_m are month effects capturing common effects across countries, such as seasonal effects (changes in seasons), the evolution of the pandemic and holiday seasons (July for the Northern Hemisphere means Summer holidays and for the Southern Hemisphere Winter holidays), while μ_c are country effects.

9.3.1 Pooled Ordinary Least Squares (POLS)

As a baseline model, we use a POLS estimation. To address the bias that might spread from reverse causality, we lag 'trust in the COVID-19 vaccines', 'anger towards government', 'compliance', 'the daily number of COVID-19 vaccinations' and 'cases'. To address heteroscedasticity, we use robust standard errors in the estimated models.

9.3.2 Fixed Effect (FE) Estimation

Having the benefit of a panel dataset allows us to control for additional biases, particularly unobserved confounding factors. Specifically, the FE approach reduces the impact of confounding by time-invariant factors, such as the unobserved and, in this instance, observed characteristics of the countries.

We use the Haussmann test to test if the FE model rather than the Random Effects (RE) model is the most efficient estimator in the current study. We reject the null hypothesis that there is "no correlation between the unique errors and the regressors in the model", confirming that the FE will give the most robust estimations.

The country (individual) FE included in the model addresses the unobserved time-invariant heterogeneity between countries, considerably reducing the risk of the confounding factors discussed above. Additionally, the FE model partly addresses bias originating from omitted observed variables (related to country characteristics). However, the FE model cannot address bias for unmeasured time-varying confounding factors or reverse causality. To address reverse causality further, we turn to Instrumental Variable regressions.

9.3.3   Instrumental Variable (IV) Regression

In addition to the lagged variables introduced in the POLS and the FE estimations, we also use an IV model to address possible endogeneity and reverse causality. We use the Generalised Method of Moments (GMM) estimation rather than the Two-Stage Least Square (2SLS) estimator due to the efficiency gains derived from using the optimal weighting matrix. The efficient GMM estimator is robust to heteroscedasticity of unknown form.

We instrument 'lagged trust in the COVID-19 vaccine' and 'lagged compliance', with 'lagged fear of the vaccines', 'lagged disgust with the vaccines' and a two-day lag in 'compliance'. We use Hansen's J statistic to test for over-identifying restrictions. The joint null hypothesis is that the excluded instruments are valid instruments, i.e. uncorrelated with the error term and correctly excluded from the estimated eq. A rejection casts doubt on the validity of the instruments. However, serial correlation is present in our specified model as the error term in one period is correlated with the errors in previous periods. This causes the estimated variances of the regression coefficients to be biased, leading to unreliable hypothesis testing. Therefore, we consider the IV estimations with the POLS and FE estimations.

9.4   POLS, FE and IV Regression Results

This section discusses the results of those covariates that are significantly related to the VPAI and, therefore, could improve attitudes and the uptake of COVID-19 vaccines when addressed.

In Table 9.2, the results of the POLS estimation controlling for month and country fixed effects are similar to the results of the FE model and the IV regression. The covariate 'trust in the COVID-19 vaccine' is statistically significant and positively related to the VPAI across all the estimated models.

The methods have different advantages; thus, the joint results confirm that trust in the COVID-19 vaccine is a robust correlate of VPAI. We assume that when trust in the vaccine increases, the fear of adverse side effects decreases and that the positive attitude towards vaccines improves. This finding is in line with the works done by Akarsu et al. (2020), Fisher et al. (2020), Freeman et al. (2020), Ward et al. (2020), Seale et al. (2021), Paul et al. (2021) and Sallam (2021) (refer to Sect. 7.3.2).

Compliance, the act of complying with government-mandated regulations to curb the spread of COVID-19, is statistically significant and negatively related to

Table 9.2 Results from POLS with FE and IV

Variable	POLS		FE		IV	
	Coefficient	SE	Coefficient	SE	Coefficient	SE
VPAI						
Lagged trust in the COVID-19 vaccine	0.2938***	(0.0281)	0.2938***	(0.0193)	0.3127***	(0.0999)
Lagged compliance	−0.0176***	(0.0060)	−0.0176***	(0.0037)	−0.0170***	(0.0064)
Lagged anger towards the government # daily vaccinations	−0.0274***	(0.0073)	−0.0274***	(0.0073)	−0.0273***	(0.0072)
Lagged new daily vaccinations	0.0055***	(0.0013)	0.0055***	(0.0014)	0.0055***	(0.0014)
Lagged new daily cases	−0.0032***	(0.0080)	−0.0032***	(0.0011)	−0.00324***	(0.0080)
Log vacc tweets	−0.0049*	(0.0029)	−0.0049*	(0.0029)	−0.0047*	(0.0029)
Vaccine policy (reference—Level 0)						
Level 1	0.0598***	−0.0125	0.0598**	−0.0232	0.0596***	(0.0123)
Level 2	0.0451***	−0.0091	0.0451**	−0.0227	0.0454***	(0.0105)
Level 3	0.0476**	−0.0088	0.0476**	−0.0228	0.0480***	(0.0092)
Level 4	0.0536**	−0.0092	0.0536**	−0.0227	0.0542***	(0.0103)
Level 5	0.0473***	−0.0102	0.0473**	−0.0233	0.0477***	(0.0109)
Country FE	Yes		Yes		Yes	
Month FE	Yes		Yes		Yes	
N	1727		1727		1727	
Adjusted R^2	0.867		0.422		0.866	
Hansen J-statistic of overidentification					$p = 0.6544$	
Prob > F = 0.0000					p	
F (9, 9) = 491.10						
Prob > F = 0.0000						

Source: Authors' calculations

Robust Standard errors in parentheses $^*p < 0.10$, $^{**}p < 0.05$, $^{***}p < 0.01$

the VPAI. We interpret this as when people are reluctant or unwilling (do not feel like it) to comply with orders such as mask-wearing, staying at home, etc., then those individuals would be more willing to receive the COVID-19 vaccine, hence a more positive attitude (thus an inverse relationship).

A study by Wright et al. (2022) investigated the relationship between vaccinated individuals' willingness to comply and the implemented behavioural regulations. The entire premise of the study is that vaccinated individuals believe they are less at risk because of their vaccination status. People think when vaccinated, they do not need to comply with, for example, mask-wearing, social distancing, etc., therefore creating a more positive attitude towards vaccines. This finding is informative to policymakers as a message of "less strict regulations" after vaccination can increase vaccine uptake.

The variable 'anger towards the government' interacted with the new daily vaccinations is statistically significant and negatively related to the VPAI. Therefore, positive attitudes decrease when people's dissatisfaction with the government increases. Analysing the tweets, we find that people are angry with governments due to the lack of procurement, the procurement of incorrect vaccines, the rollout of vaccination plans, and corruption within governments. This anger directed at governments due to a lack of access to vaccines sabotages the positive attitude towards vaccines and hinders the uptake of vaccines.

The relationship between the VPAI and the number of daily new vaccinations is inversely proportional, significant and positively related. This implies that the positive attitude is high when the daily number of vaccines administered is very low. Still, as the number of vaccines administered daily increases, the positive attitude starts to plateau. Also, using the vaccine rollout or the lack thereof, as a proxy for constraints in information campaigns, the physical availability of vaccines or a lack of geographical accessibility, we can see how important it is to overcome any barriers which might impede the intention to be vaccinated (Cylus & Papanicolas, 2015).

We find that daily new cases, a proxy for the evolution of the COVID-19 pandemic across all ten countries, are statistically significant and negative. If the daily cases are high, the positive attitude towards the vaccine is relatively low, but as the daily cases start decreasing, the positive attitude improves.

Controlling for the vaccination policy, thus the groups that can access the COVID-19 vaccine, we find that when more groups of people can access the vaccine, for example, all age groups compared to fewer groups, it is positively related to the VPAI. Once again, it shows that when more people have access to the COVID-19 vaccine, positivity towards the vaccine is enhanced.

The number of vaccine-related tweets is statistically significant and negatively related to the VPAI in all the estimated models. This implies that the positive attitude towards vaccines decreases as vaccine-related tweets increase. We found that the number of vaccine-related tweets increased over time; thus, vaccines became a "hot" topic of discussion. Topic modelling on the vaccine-related tweets indicates that negative sentiment is related to, among others, the long-term effects of the

COVID-19 vaccine, dissatisfaction with vaccine passports and QR code scanning, concerns about the Delta variant, anger about procurement, struggling to make appointments (vaccine rollout) and conspiracy theories. People also express their discontent with social distancing and wearing masks. Our topic modelling results are in line with studies such as Küçükali et al. (2021), Nuzhath et al. (2020), Bonnevie et al. (2021) and Thelwall et al. (2021).

All of the above leads us to believe that increased tweets with negative connotations to the COVID-19 vaccine decrease positive attitudes towards vaccines.

In summary, we see that those variables that can improve the positive attitude towards vaccines are related to information about the safety and side effects of the vaccines (increased trust in vaccines) and a balance between the strictness of regulations and access to vaccines. Additionally, increased trust in the government's capabilities, honesty, and dealing with capacity constraints can decrease dissatisfaction with governments and increase vaccine uptake. Precise information about the COVID-19 vaccines in general, also disseminated via social media, can increase positivity towards the COVID-19 vaccine. Misinformation about COVID-19 vaccines and social media should be monitored, and campaigns against this misinformation should be launched. Vaccines should also be made accessible to all groups of people.

9.5   Summary from Chaps 7 to This Chapter

In Chap. 7 to this chapter, we constructed a real-time Vaccine Positive Attitude Index (VPAI) derived from Big Data to illustrate the evolution of people's positive attitudes toward the COVID-19 vaccine across ten countries. Our descriptive analysis showed that the VPAI generally indicates a decline in attitude over the time period investigated. The trend is downward in the Northern and Southern Hemispheres when we consider the different Hemispheres. Furthermore, considering the ten individual countries, only Belgium and the Netherlands experienced a positive trend in the VPAI, whereas the other countries experienced a negative trend.

Using Pooled Ordinary Least Squares, Panel Fixed Effects and Instrumental Variables regression models, we determined which variables are significantly related to the VPAI and, therefore, could increase the uptake of COVID-19 vaccines if addressed by policy measures. We found that those variables that could improve people's attitudes towards vaccines were: (i) information related to the safety and side effects of the vaccines, (ii) increased trust in governments in conducting the vaccine rollout and handling procurement and capacity issues, (iii) cognisance of the compliance versus the vaccine up-take decision, and (iv) better information about the COVID-19 vaccines in general, but primarily disseminated via social media.

These results give policymakers the necessary information to increase positive attitudes towards the COVID-19 vaccine. Policymakers should focus on improving trust in the COVID-19 vaccines. They could more openly disseminate information regarding the vaccine, do it in layman's terms, and acknowledge people's fears, anger, and other negative emotions. They can emphasise the stringent safety and efficacy standards of the COVID-19 vaccine development process, thus fostering trust in the vaccine. All of this may increase vaccine confidence. Additionally, countries can overcome the lack of accessibility to vaccination clinics by following the example set by the United States of America of introducing mobile vaccination clinics to reach people in remote areas.

Furthermore, policymakers should implement policies to increase people's sense of collective responsibility. This can be done by raising awareness of emotional manipulations by anti-vaccine disinformation efforts and activating positive emotions such as altruism and hope as part of vaccine education endeavours. Another potential strategy is to elicit positive emotions toward helping one's community restore health and well-being when deciding to vaccinate against what is called the most consequential disease of our time.

Lastly, the analyses conducted in Chap. 7 to this chapter have limitations. We only used Twitter in our analyses as other social media platforms, for example, Facebook, is highly protected. In the future, additional social media platforms should be analysed. A drawback of social media data, including Twitter, is their lack of population representation. However, a case can be made that the sample sizes using Big Data contribute to robust results. When translating tweets from a non-English language, errors can occur at three levels: lexical, syntactical, and discursive. These errors inevitably can cause unintelligibility, which means the tweet will be disregarded. However, in this study, we used lexicons in the original languages (if available) and compared the results to the translated text corpus. We find the time-series trends using the original language and translated text well correlated.

Furthermore, we only examined the tweets for a specific time period. Therefore, we cannot examine the tweet's effects following the study. Another limitation is the timeline of research and the publication thereof. Publication rates cannot keep up with the tempo at which the pandemic evolves; therefore, new COVID-19 variants might have emerged by the time of publication, and research on vaccines would have progressed. Nonetheless, the knowledge gained in this research contributes to more informed decision-making in the future. Lastly, the countries used for this study are solely based on data availability, which can be considered a limitation, especially given a non-characterisation of how other countries could present attitudes towards vaccines. In future studies, with more resources, we can expand the text corpus to include more countries over a longer period with more sources of Big Data.

Supplementary Information for This Chapter

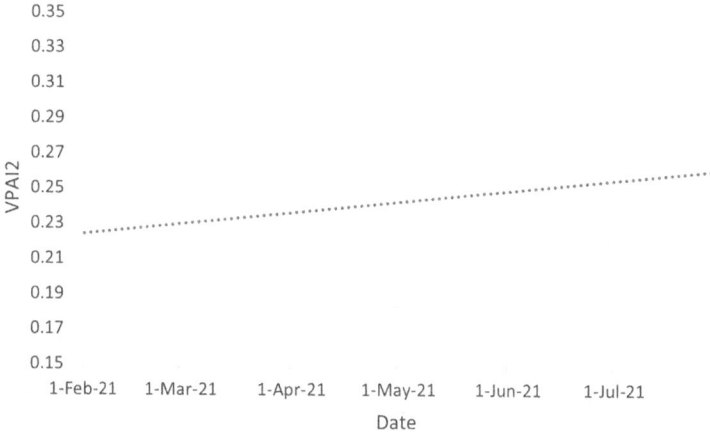

Source: Authors' calculations.

Fig. 9.2 Trend in positive attitude, including false negatives related to governments (VPAI2) for the whole sample from February 2021 to the end of July 2021. *Source*: Authors' calculations

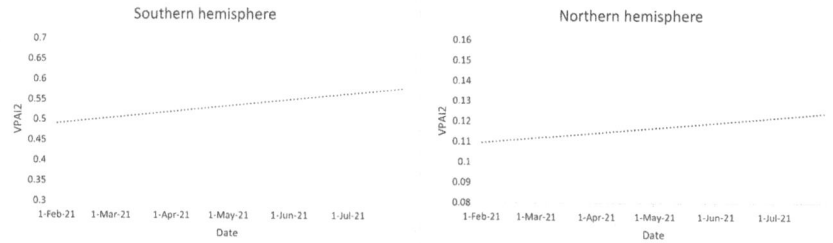

Source: Authors' calculations.

Fig. 9.3 Trend in positive attitude, including false negatives related to governments (VPAI2) for the different Hemispheres from February 2021 to the end of July 2021. *Source*: Authors' calculations

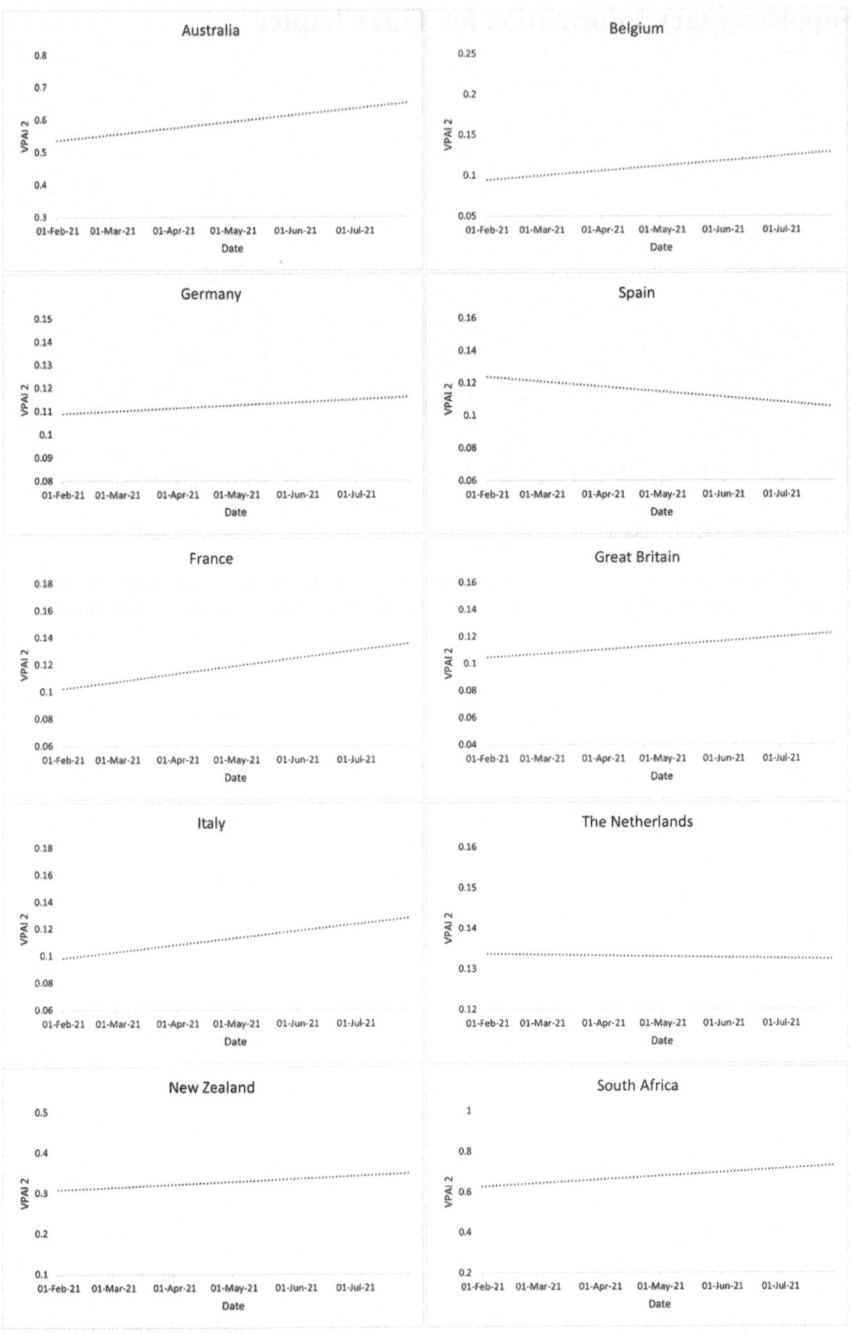

Source: Authors' calculations.

Fig. 9.4 Trend in positive attitude, including false negatives related to governments (VPAI2) for the individual countries from February 2021 to the end of July 2021. *Source*: Authors' calculations

References

Akarsu, B., Canbay, Ö. D., Ayhan Baser, D., Aksoy, H., Fidancı, İ., & Cankurtaran, M. (2020). While studies on COVID-19 vaccine is ongoing, the public's thoughts and attitudes to the future COVID-19 vaccine. *The International Journal of Clinical Practice*, e13891.

Betsch, C., Böhm, R., Korn, L., & Holtmann, C. (2017). On the benefits of explaining herd immunity in vaccine advocacy. *Nature Human Behaviour, 1*(56), 1–6.

Betsch, C., Schmid, P., Heinemeier, D., Korn, L., Holtmann, C., & Böhm, R. (2018). Beyond confidence: Development of a measure assessing the 5C psychological antecedents of vaccination. *PLoS One, 13*(12), e0208601.

Bonnevie, E., Gallegos-Jeffrey, A., Goldbarg, J., Byrd, B., & Smyser, J. (2021). Quantifying the rise of vaccine opposition on twitter during the COVID-19 pandemic. *Journal of Communication in Healthcare, 14*(1), 12–19.

Cylus, J., & Papanicolas, I. (2015). An analysis of perceived access to health care in Europe: How universal is universal coverage? *Health Policy, 119*(9), 1133–1144.

Fisher, K. A., Bloomstone, S. J., Walder, J., Crawford, S., Fouayzi, H., & Mazor, K. M. (2020). Attitudes toward a potential SARS-CoV-2 vaccine: A survey of US adults. *Annals of Internal Medicine, 173*(12), 964–973.

Freeman, D., Loe, B. S., Chadwick, A., Vaccari, C., Waite, F., Rosebrock, L., et al. (2020). COVID-19 vaccine hesitancy in the UK: The Oxford coronavirus explanations, attitudes, and narratives survey (oceans) II. *Psychological Medicine, 11*, 1–15.

Greyling, T., Rossouw, S., & Afstereo. (2019). Gross national happiness. Today Index. http://gnh. today. Accessed 01.08.21.

Google. (2020). Google COVID-19 Community Mobility Reports. https://www.google.com/covid19/mobility/. Accessed 01.08.21.

Google. (2021). Google COVID-19 Community Mobility Reports. https://www.google.com/covid19/mobility/. Accessed 01.08.21.

Hale, T., Angrist, N., Cameron-Blake, E., Hallas, L., Kira, B., Majumdar, S., et al. (2020). Oxford COVID-19 government response tracker. https://www.bsg.ox.ac.uk/research/research-projects/covid-19-government-response-tracker. Accessed 28.07.21.

Küçükali, H., Ataç, O., Palteki, A. S., Tokaç, A. Z., & Hayran, O. E. (2021). Vaccine hesitancy and anti-vaccination attitudes during the start of COVID-19 vaccination program: A content analysis on Twitter data. *medRxiv preprint medRxiv:2021*.

Larson, H. J., Jarrett, C., Eckersberger, E., Smith, D. M. D., & Paterson, P. (2014). Understanding vaccine hesitancy around vaccines and vaccination from a global perspective: A systematic review of published literature, 2007–2012. *Vaccine, 32*, 2150–2159.

MacDonald, N. E. (2015). SAGE working group on vaccine hesitancy. Vaccine hesitancy: Definition, scope and determinants. *Vaccine, 33*, 4161–4164.

Mathieu, E., Ritchie, H., Ortiz-Ospina, E., Roser, M., Hasell, J., Appel, C., et al. (2021). A global database of COVID-19 vaccinations. *Nature Human Behaviour*. https://www.nature.com/articles/s41562-021-01122-8. Accessed 01.02.22.

Nuzhath, T., Tasnim, S., Sanjwal, R. K., Trisha, N. F., Rahman, M., Mahmud, S., et al. (2020). COVID-19 vaccination hesitancy, misinformation and conspiracy theories on social media: A content analysis of Twitter data. https://doi.org/10.31235/osf.io/vc9jb. Accessed on 28.07.21.

Paul, E., Steptoe, A., & Fancourt, D. (2021). Attitudes towards vaccines and intention to vaccinate against COVID-19: Implications for public health communications. *The Lancet Regional Health-Europe, 1*(100012), 1–10.

Sallam, M. (2021). COVID-19 vaccine hesitancy worldwide: A systematic review of vaccine acceptance rates. *Vaccine, 9*(160), 1–14.

Sarracino, F., Greyling, T., O'Connor, K., Peroni, C., & Rossouw, S. (2022). Trust predicts compliance with COVID-19 containment policies: Evidence from ten countries using big data. Institute of Labour Economics (IZA). Discussion Paper No. 15171.

Seale, H., Heywood, A. E., Leask, J., Sheel, M., Durrheim, D. N., Bolsewicz, K., et al. (2021). Examining Australian public perceptions and behaviors towards a future COVID-19 vaccine. *BMC Infectious Diseases, 21*(1), 1–9.

Thelwall, M., Kayvan, K., & Thelwall, S. (2021). Covid-19 vaccine hesitancy on English-language twitter. *Profesional de la Información, 30*(2), e300212.

Thomson, A., Robinson, K., & Valle'e-Tourangeau, G. (2016). The 5As: A practical taxonomy for the determinants of vaccine uptake. *Vaccine, 34*, 1018–1024.

Ward, J. K., Alleaume, C., Peretti-Watel, P., Seror, V., Cortaredona, S., Launay, O., et al. (2020). The French public's attitudes to a future COVID-19 vaccine: The politicisation of a public health issue. *Social Science & Medicine, 265*, 113414.

Wright, L., Steptoe, A., Mak, H. W., & Fancourt, D. (2022). Do people reduce compliance with COVID-19 guidelines following vaccination? A longitudinal analysis of matched UK adults. *Journal of Epidemiology & Community Health, 76*, 109–115.

Chapter 10
Vaccination Uptake, Happiness and Emotions: Using a Supervised Machine Learning Approach

Abstract This chapter presents a retrospective evaluation of the COVID-19 pandemic, focusing on the factors influencing vaccination uptake to achieve herd immunity thresholds of 70% and 90% in ten countries (refer to Chaps. 4, 5, and 7 through 9). We identify the most important variables contributing to high vaccination rates by utilising supervised machine learning techniques, particularly the Extreme Gradient Boosting (XGBoost) algorithm.

Our analysis explores the relationship of factors within a global health crisis context by drawing from comprehensive datasets encompassing COVID-19-related information, population demographics, and sentiment analysis from social media. Special consideration is given to exploring whether subjective well-being measures played a role in the decision to get vaccinated since we know from Chap. 9 that negative emotions, such as fear of vaccine side effects, can sway people's attitudes towards vaccination and that happier people make better health-related decisions.

Our findings offer several significant contributions to the literature. Firstly, we conduct a pioneering post-COVID-19 cross-country analysis, identifying factors important for reaching different herd immunity levels. Secondly, we integrate subjective well-being measures into our estimations, providing insights into the influence of emotional states on vaccine uptake. Thirdly, we differentiate between factors impacting the achievement of various vaccination thresholds, shedding light on nuanced dynamics.

The XGBoost model is the most effective, delivering precise predictions and highlighting key factors such as vaccination policies, international travel controls, rural population percentages, and average temperature. Interestingly, happiness emerges as an important factor in attaining the 90% vaccination threshold, underscoring the importance of addressing emotional perceptions in vaccination strategies.

However, our study acknowledges limitations, including the focus on primarily developed countries and the inability to incorporate variables reflecting international support due to high missingness. Nonetheless, our insights offer actionable recommendations for policymakers to enhance vaccination rates and mitigate pandemics' health, economic, and political impacts.

S. Rossouw, T. Greyling, *Resistance to COVID-19 Vaccination*, Human Well-Being Research and Policy Making, https://doi.org/10.1007/978-3-031-56529-8_10

Keywords Subjective well-being · Emotions · XGBoost · Supervised machine
learning · Vaccination rate · Herd immunity

10.1 Introduction

Chaps. 3 through 5 and 7–9 stand witness to the fact that the COVID-19 pandemic
is an example of an immense global failure to curb the spread of a pathogen and
save lives. To indirectly protect people against a deadly virus, a population needs to
achieve herd immunity, which is attained either through vaccination or prior infection. However, achieving herd immunity by vaccination is preferable as it limits the
health risks of disease. As the coronavirus mutated, vaccination estimates for
achieving herd immunity went from 70% to 90%.

In this chapter, arguably the most technically demanding section of this book, we
embark on a meticulous retrospective evaluation of the COVID-19 pandemic. Our
goal is to ascertain the order of the importance of the variables to identify those factors that contribute most to achieving high vaccination rates. Specifically, we aim to
identify the factors most influential in achieving herd immunity at the 70% and 90%
vaccination thresholds. Furthermore, we aim to determine those factors that differ
between the 70% to 90% vaccination threshold to see which factors are responsible
for advancing a population's decision to reach a higher vaccination level.

Special consideration is given to exploring whether subjective well-being measures played a role in the decision to get vaccinated since we know from Chap. 9
that negative emotions, such as fear of vaccine side effects, can sway people's attitudes towards vaccination and that happier people make better health-related decisions (Anik et al., 2009; Lyubomirsky et al., 2005).

To facilitate our analysis, we employ an Extreme Gradient Boosting (XGBoost)
algorithm to build a model to determine the most important factors that can predict
reaching vaccination thresholds. We chose the XGBoost model since it is more efficient, computationally much lighter and has been shown to outperform most supervised algorithms (Abdurrahim et al., 2020; Nielsen, 2016). However, we construct
two other models using Random Forest and Decision Tree algorithms as robustness
tests. After the model is built, we test the precision of our model's predictions using
our test data and calculate the necessary test (fit) statistics, i.e., mean squared error,
mean absolute error and root mean square error. In line with expectations, the
XGBoost model gives the best-fit measures and delivers the best predictions compared to the other two methods. Consequently, we discuss the results of the XGBoost
model within this chapter. However, we also present the results of the other models
in Supplementary Information C.

The crux of our investigation revolves around the target output variable: the number of people vaccinated as a percentage of the population. We consider two thresholds of our output variable, the first at 70% of a country's population, corresponding

to the initial suggestions to achieve herd immunity, and the second with a threshold of 90%, suggested later due to the highly infectious virus.

Our dataset draws from various sources, encompassing the ten countries featured in Chaps. 4, 5, and 7 through 9. Notably, we draw from four datasets. The first dataset is extracted from Google COVID-19 Open Data.[1] It provides us with abundant information related to COVID-19 and information on population, geographical location, the economy, general health and climate. The other three time series datasets are derived from tweets and form part of the *Gross National Happiness.today* project.[2] These three unique datasets reflect (i) the general sentiment and emotions within countries, (ii) the sentiment and emotions towards vaccines and (iii) the sentiment and emotions towards government institutions.

This comprehensive exploration reveals the relative importance of various factors underpinning the achievement of high vaccination rates. Our findings shed light on the intricate interplay of variables within a global health crisis context. Consequently, this chapter contributes significantly to the existing literature in several ways. First, it is the first study conducting a post-COVID-19 cross-country analysis of the most important variables to increase vaccine uptake. Second, we are the first study to include subjective measures of well-being in our estimations, such as happiness levels, people's emotions and their perceptions towards vaccines and governments, to establish whether subjective measures play a role in increasing vaccination uptake. Third, we are the first to apply supervised machine learning models to determine which factors matter most to achieve different vaccination thresholds (please note that our dependent variable is continuous, thus different to models in which a binary (mostly a "yes-no") response is used). Our XGBoost model can be used as a benchmark for future research related to the most important factors for increasing vaccination uptake. Furthermore, this study offers some actionable insights for policymakers on increasing vaccination rates to curb pandemics' health, economic and political effects.

10.2   Background

The COVID-19 pandemic is an example of an immense global and national failure to curb the spread of the virus and save lives. As mentioned in Sect. 3.3, the sheer magnitude of this failure becomes evident when we consider the death toll due to COVID-19. As of 20 July 2023, the World Health Organisation (WHO) (2023) reported that there had been a total of 768,237,788 confirmed cases of COVID-19, including 6,951,677 deaths. Europe has been the hardest hit region, with 2,245,217

---

[1] Available from https://health.google.com/covid-19/open-data/explorer.

[2] Available from https://gnh.today/.

deaths, and Africa has the least recorded deaths, with 175,408 deaths (Africa faces doubts regarding the accuracy of its data). The enormity of this death toll (lagging only behind the Spanish flu and HIV/AIDS—refer to Table 2.1 in Chap. 2) and the economic damage to countries, industries and individuals are unmeasurable (Baldwin, 2020; Ludvigson et al., 2020; Lu et al., 2020; Fetzer et al., 2020).

Furthermore, COVID-19 not only affected health but also had a profound impact on family functioning and well-being. For example, New Zealand found a significant increase in family violence reports to police, which ranged from 345 to 645 a day, compared to 271 to 478 a day in the same period in 2019 (Mental Health and Wellbeing Commission, 2023). Andrade et al. (2022) note that the fear and uncertainty of health risks, the stress from restrictions and constraints on everyday life, and financial concerns impacted emotional well-being.

During a pandemic, the aim is to stop the spread of the disease and protect individuals against a specific pathogen. We know that globalisation, the geography of economic relations and international travelling pose significant challenges in stopping the spread of a virus. A population must achieve herd immunity to protect people from the disease indirectly. Herd immunity is achieved when a population is immune through vaccination or immunity developed through previous infection. However, the World Health Organisation (WHO) supports achieving herd immunity through vaccination rather than exposing them to the pathogen. To safely achieve herd immunity against COVID-19, it was estimated at the early stages of the pandemic that a vaccination threshold of 70% should be achieved (Randolph & Barreiro, 2020; Bartsch et al., 2020; Goldblatt et al., 2022). However, as COVID-19 evolved, the virus mutated and became more infectious, and the estimated vaccination threshold increased to 90% (Plans-Rubió, 2022). According to Bloom et al. (2021), high vaccination uptake yields sizable and diverse health, economic, and social benefits, including herd protection, increased work hours and productivity, and potentially improved social equity. In other words, the faster the uptake, the fewer lives are lost, and the potentially devastating economic and social impact is minimised.

As of 22 July 2023, a total of 13,474,265,907 vaccine doses have been administered. This translates into 64.8% of the world population being fully vaccinated[3] (WHO, 2023). However, when we disaggregate the data, we see the stark inequality between high-income countries, 74.32%, and low-income countries, 27.54% (Mathieu et al., 2021). These low vaccination rates in developing and underdeveloped countries, despite global partnerships like COVAX, highlight the lack of international support and cooperation. As Sheikh et al. (2021) noted, most developing nations lack the financial and technological resources to invest in vaccine development. Therefore, relying on developed nations through global cooperation was instrumental in vaccinating their people. Unfortunately, in a shameful show of 'indi-

---

[3] Total number of people who received all doses prescribed by the initial vaccination protocol, divided by the total population of the country.

viduality', developed nations, constituting only 16% of the world's population, bought more than half of the vaccines available at the start of 2021. This glaring absence of international support and cooperation is seen as one of the biggest failures of the COVID-19 pandemic.

Chapter 9 posited that this immense failure is partly due to the inability to distribute and administer vaccines efficiently globally and nationally. Furthermore, at the national level, governments and the public health care systems not only failed at stopping the spread of the virus and protecting human lives but also failed to adhere to basic norms of institutional rationality and transparency, breeding mistrust in governments (Paul et al., 2021; Sallam, 2021).

10.3 Literature Review

Since increasing the uptake of the COVID-19 vaccine was fundamentally important to decrease the harm caused to human lives and livelihoods, many studies have focused on predicting factors associated with the uptake. However, there are not many studies that used machine learning to determine those factors that contribute to higher levels of vaccine uptake. Therefore, the literature review mainly discusses studies that relied on survey data and traditional empirical analysis, which also informs our discussion in the results section. Studies that used machine learning in their approach conclude this section.

10.3.1 Factors Associated with Vaccination Uptake: Evidence From Survey Data

In the realm of individual European country studies, Bajos et al. (2022) and Ward et al. (2020) focused on France and used data from the EpiCov survey and self-collected data, respectively. In a similar vein, Gomes et al. (2022) conducted a study in Portugal using a community-based survey called the COVID-19 Barometer: Social Opinion. These three studies generally concluded that the COVID-19 vaccine uptake was positively associated with age, educational attainment and income. According to Bajos et al. (2022), the least educated, those with the lowest incomes, and racial minority groups were less likely to accept the vaccine, and these differences were maintained or increased over time. Additionally, people's lack of trust in the government and scientists to manage the health crisis remained the primary reason for refusing to vaccinate. Ward et al. (2020) pre-vaccine study also found that individuals feeling close to a Far-Right party would refuse the vaccine when it became available. The primary reason any individual would refuse the vaccine was that it would not be safe. Gomes et al. (2022) also concluded that higher odds of hesitancy were associated with low confidence in Portugal's health services response to COVID-19 and non-COVID-19 and perceived the measures implemented by the government as inadequate.

In the domain of cross-country analysis, Bergmann et al. (2022) and Pronkina and Rees (2022) used the 2021 summer SHARE Corona survey data (administered across 27 European countries). They confirmed the results of Bajos et al. (2022), Ward et al. (2020) and Gomes et al. (2022) by finding that the probability of being vaccinated increased with age, income, and educational attainment. Furthermore, Bergmann et al. (2022) concluded that prior illnesses were associated with a higher willingness to vaccinate. Interestingly, there was no clear and significant effect of subjective health and no strong effects with mental health issues were found. Pronkina and Rees (2022) argued that people who express trust in others are more likely to be vaccinated, while risk aversion and frequency of praying (a proxy for religiosity) were negatively correlated with the probability of being vaccinated against COVID-19. Furthermore, Europeans aged 50 and older did not base their decision to vaccinate against COVID-19 on case counts or excess mortality during the pandemic.

Turning to the American context, Corcoran et al. (2021), Czeisler et al. (2021), El-Mohandes et al. (2021) and Gatwood et al. (2021) found that Americans who express conservative political or religious beliefs are, on average, more vaccine-hesitant than those who do not although. However, the relationship between political beliefs and COVID-19 vaccination hesitancy appears to be considerably more nuanced in Europe than it is in the United States (Ward et al., 2020; Lindholt et al., 2021; Raciborski et al., 2021; Bíró-Nagy & Szászi, 2022; Wollebæk et al., 2022). COVID-19 vaccine hesitancy is especially prevalent among individuals who express distrust in the government and scientists (Kerr et al., 2021; Latkin et al., 2021; Lindholt et al., 2021; Rozek et al., 2021; Bajos et al., 2022).

10.3.2 Factors Associated with Vaccination Uptake: Evidence from Machine Learning

In terms of previous machine learning studies, Lincoln et al. (2022) used Random Forest to probe for the optimum prediction accuracy for vaccine hesitancy and to find an economical model based on a selection of common global predictors. They used SHapley Additive exPlanations (SHAP) and permutation feature importance to estimate the importance of each variable in their model across their sample of five advanced countries (UK, US, Australia, Germany and Hong Kong). The authors found that by using only 12 variables (the combined most important variables from permutation feature importance and SHAP), they could achieve an 82% accuracy in predicting vaccine hesitancy, with the most crucial factors being vaccination conspiracy beliefs and a lack of confidence in governments, companies, and organisations in handling the pandemic (i.e., pandemic conspiracy beliefs).

Previous studies have successfully used XGBoost-based predictive models to predict influenza vaccine uptake. Shaham et al. (2020) used primary data from 250,000 Israelis collected between 2007 and 2017 to predict whether a patient would get vaccinated in the future. Their XGBoost-based predictive model achieved an ROC-AUC[4] score of 0.91 with accuracy and recall rates of 90% on the test set. Prediction relied mainly on the patient's individual and household vaccination status in the past, age, number of encounters with the healthcare system, number of prescribed medications, and indicators of chronic illnesses. Using the XGBoost regressor, Cheong et al. (2021) used sociodemographic data to predict vaccine uptake across counties in the United States (US). Their model predicted COVID-19 vaccination uptake across US counties with 62% accuracy. The results from their permutation analysis and SHAP revealed the most important factors to drive their predictive model were geographic location (longitude, latitude), education level (per cent of adults with less than a high school diploma, per cent of adults with a bachelor's or higher), and online access (households with broadband internet).

Also focusing on the US, Osman and Sabit (2022) use state-level vaccination rates to identify the most critical features that predict which states will meet the vaccination threshold of 70%. Relying on a Chi-square Automatic Interaction Detector (CHAID), a decision tree algorithm, the authors include several variables that may influence the state-specific vaccination rate. They categorise the variables into four groups: economic indicators, COVID-19-related indicators, Google mobility data, and COVID-19-related policy measures. After using three different model specifications, they discovered that workplace travel, the political affiliation of the governor, and the vaccine mandate in schools were the top three features of achieving the vaccination threshold.

In the abovementioned studies on machine learning applications, the outcome variables were binary variables, for example—a person's decision to be vaccinated or whether a certain vaccination threshold would be reached. These studies determined the most important factors to reach success (yes) during COVID-19. Our study differs from the previous literature in that we benefit from hindsight. Therefore, we investigate the most important factors contributing to reaching herd immunity (at different levels of 70% or 90%) and how these factors change when higher herd immunity levels are to be reached. Our outcome variable is the percentage of the population vaccinated as a percentage of a country's population (thus, the measure used to determine herd immunity). It is a continuous variable representing a high level of variance and is not restricted to only a yes or no answer. Furthermore, our

---

[4] Area Under the Curve of the Receiver Operating Characteristic curve.

study includes a wide-reaching dataset including variables related to COVID-19 regulations, vaccination policies, country characteristics, and, very importantly, subjective measures of well-being. We are the first study to include subjective well-being measures to highlight the importance of moods and emotions when higher vaccination thresholds must be attained.

10.4 Data and Variables

10.4.1 Construction of Datasets

The timeframe under consideration is from 1 December 2020 to 16 September 2022. This period includes the first vaccine rollout and ends when new COVID-19 tests reach almost zero in all countries. Consequently, the primary data source related to COVID-19, the *COVID-19 Government Response Tracker* dataset (Mathieu et al., 2021), was discontinued on 31 December 2022. We consider the data to find a retrospective view of those factors that mattered most for higher vaccination rates.

We use a merged dataset, including the Google COVID-19 Open Data[5] and our three constructed time-series datasets derived from tweets.[6] The three Twitter datasets reflect (i) happiness levels and emotions of countries, (ii) happiness levels and emotions towards vaccines and (iii) happiness levels and emotions towards government institutions. The construction and validation of the Twitter datasets are explained in Supplementary Information A.

This section briefly explains the Twitter data with a more detailed explanation available in Supplementary Information A. Tweets are extracted in real-time based on a geographic bounding box corresponding to the country in question. Next, we use sentiment and emotion analysis to score the tweets. We aggregate the scores and derive indices for happiness and each of the eight emotions. For the Twitter datasets related to the government and COVID-19 vaccines, we used the same keywords as in Sects. 8.2 and 9.2.2 to identify those tweets directly related to the topic.

To derive the dataset related to the COVID-19 vaccines, we extracted tweets using the keywords: *vaccinate, vacc, vaccine, Sputnik V, Sputnik, Sinopharm, Astrazeneca, Pfizer (if NEAR) vaccine, Pfizer-BioNTech, Johnson & Johnson,* and *Moderna.*

For the dataset related to governments, we extracted tweets using the keywords: *government, parliament, ministry, minister, senator, MPs, legislator, political, politics, prime minister.*

---

[5] Available from https://health.google.com/covid-19/open-data/explorer.
[6] Available from https://gnh.today/.

After extraction, we analysed the text of the tweets to determine the noise captured in the tweets. Subsequently, we found that the noise was minimal in both instances.

The Google COVID-19 Open dataset is rich and includes variables related to COVID-19 cases, deaths, vaccinations, demographics, economics, geography, climate, health, health infrastructure, and health care.

10.4.2 Data Cleaning and Validation

Following the merger of datasets outlined in Sect. 10.4.1, we initially assembled a comprehensive merged dataset featuring a total of 145 variables.

As a first instance, we set about identifying missing data. If the data was randomly missing with less than 3% overall missingness, we imputed the data by either using the mean or the previous data point, for example, population size.

Secondly, we dropped variables from our dataset with high missingness levels. For example, international support (67% missingness), emergency investment in health care (68% missingness) and mobility regulations (74% missingness), which reflects the strong regulations implemented during the first lockdowns in countries, such as access to retail and recreation, grocery stores, pharmacies and parks, were dropped.

Thirdly, we removed highly correlated data so that only one of the variables remained in the dataset, for example, cumulative confirmed cases and cumulative tested cases; this eases the interpretation of the results.

Once the data was cleaned, we were left with 69 variables (including our outcome variable), which we classified into five categories (refer to Sect. 10.4.4). Subsequently, these variables were used in the supervised algorithms (refer to Sects. 10.5.1–10.5.3) to train the models. We have 6530 observations, which means we have 653 (just short of 2 years) observations per country in our sample.

In our study, the data comprising 69 variables are split into a training and testing dataset with an 80:20 split on all data, with the evaluation done on the unseen testing data.

10.4.3 Target/Outcome Variable

Our primary variable of interest is the country-level vaccination rate. We calculate vaccination rates as the percentage of the vaccinated population among those 18 and older as a percentage of the total population in the respective countries. This is in line with studies such as Randolph and Barreiro (2020), Bartsch et al. (2020) and Goldblatt et al. (2022).

Table 10.1 Maximum vaccination rates on 16 September 2022

Country	Percentage of the population vaccinated on 16 September 2022
Australia	85.35
Belgium	76.19
Germany	76,43
Spain	86.58
France	80.07
Great Britain	76.15
Italy	79.46
The Netherlands	69.19
New Zealand	85.67
South Africa	32.64

Source: Authors' own calculations

In our sample, nine out of the ten countries met the lower threshold of 70% (see Table 10.1); South Africa lagged behind, reaching a mere 32.6%. Therefore, our 70% threshold model was reachable for the countries in the developed world but not for our developing country, South Africa (likely to be the same in other developing and underdeveloped countries). However, none of the countries in our sample achieved the higher 90% threshold, with Spain coming closest with 87%.

10.4.4   Predictor Variables/Features

As discussed in Sect. 10.4.2, our models include 68 variables (apart from our outcome variable) to determine those factors most important for country-specific vaccination thresholds. We remind the reader that two variables, international support and emergency investment in health care, were not included as predictors in our models due to their high levels of missingness, 68 and 74%, respectively.

We acknowledge that these variables could have ranked among the most important variables and potentially have been included in the top ten. Therefore, when we report the results of our models, their absence should be kept in mind.

We categorise the variables into five groups: demographic, geographical, economic, COVID-19-related indicators and COVID-19-related policy measures. The COVID-19-related and policy data are high-frequency daily data, while the demographic, geographical and economic data are more stable over time. Table 10.2 gives an abbreviated list of the variables included in the models. For a complete list, see Supplementary Information B.

Table 10.2 An example of variables used

Variable	Description	Scale	Coding	Source
Vaccination policy	Policies for vaccine delivery for different groups	Ordinal scale	0—No availability *** 1—Availability for ONE of following: key workers/clinically vulnerable groups (non-elderly)/elderly groups 2—Availability for TWO of following: key workers/clinically vulnerable groups (non-elderly)/elderly groups 3—Availability for ALL of following: key workers/clinically vulnerable groups (non-elderly)/elderly groups 4—Availability for all three plus partial additional availability (select broad groups/ages) 5—Universal availability	Mathieu et al. (2021)
Average temperature	Average temperature in the country	Celsius		World Bank (2023a)
Population density	People per square kilometre of land area	Continuous		World Bank (2023b)
Restrictions on gatherings	Record limits on gatherings	Ordinal	0–no restrictions 1—restrictions on very large gatherings (the limit is above 1000 people) 2—restrictions on gatherings between 101–1000 people 3—restrictions on gatherings between 11 and 100 people 4—restrictions on gatherings of 10 people or less Blank—no data	Mathieu et al. (2021)
GNH	Happiness	Ordinal	Score per hour ranges from 0 to 10, with higher values indicating higher happiness. To generate daily data, the mean GNH per day is calculated.	Greyling et al. (2019)

10.5   Methodology

The methodology first explains the different machine-learning algorithms utilised and how we applied each algorithm to construct the models (training the models). We start with the XGBoost (our algorithm of choice) and include a Random Forest and Decision Tree algorithm as robustness measures. Next, we expound upon the fit statistics that were harnessed to evaluate and gauge the performance of the models.

10.5.1   Extreme Gradient Boosting (XGBoost)

To determine those factors most important in achieving our vaccination thresholds of 70% and 90%, we rely on the XGBoost method. It should be noted that traditionally, XGBoost models were used where only a binary outcome was considered (limiting the prediction to either an up or down or a yes and no option). However, we adjust the algorithm to consider a continuous dependent variable since our model's predictions are not limited to a binary outcome but to various rates.

XGBoost represents an end-to-end tree-boosting system (Chen & Guestrin, 2016) and is a powerful supervised learning approach to classification and regression tree models based on ensemble methods. The scalability of XGBoost allows for a system that runs ten times faster than existing popular solutions on a single machine. As it is a gradient-boosting algorithm, XGBoost combines predictions from decision trees. XGBoost creates a better overall model while boosting it, continuously rebuilding it by focusing on the previous models' weaker points.

More specifically, the XGBoost algorithm works by assigning weights to all the independent variables, which are then fed into the decision tree as a simple method to recursively split the data into smaller groups to predict the target variable. A single decision tree would not work well on complex problems, so through the boosting phase, the weights of variables predicted wrong by the first decision tree are increased, and these variables are then fed to the second decision tree. Therefore, an ensemble method combines multiple trees to build a single model sequentially, focusing on the decision trees that did not perform as well and combining these to create a stronger and more precise model. See Fig. 10.1 for a brief illustration of how gradient tree boosting works.

In all models, XGBoost minimises a regularised objective function consisting of two parts (see Eq. 10.1). The first part is a convex loss function (based on the predicted and target outputs) and measures how predictive our model is with respect to the training data. The training proceeds iteratively, adding new trees that predict the residuals or errors of prior trees that are then combined with previous trees to make the final prediction. In our model, gradient descent[7] optimisation is used to mini-

---

[7] Gradient descent is an iterative first-order optimisation algorithm used to find a local minimum/maximum of a given function. It trains machine learning models by minimising the loss incurred

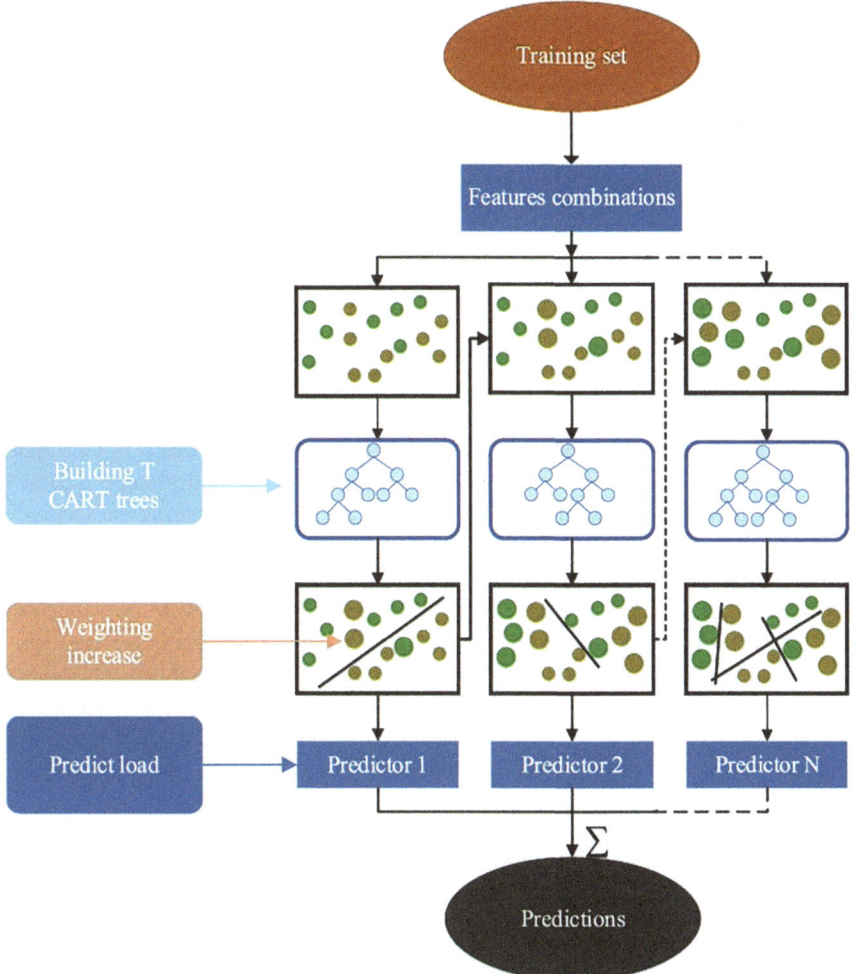

Fig. 10.1 Illustration of how gradient tree boosting works. *Source*: Geeks for Geeks (2023). In the public domain

mise the loss. The second part is a term inserted to reduce the risk of overfitting, which incorporates two steps: regularisation and pruning. The regularisation term for model complexity (in other words, the regression tree functions) penalises the model by adding extra terms (k times iteration) to the objective function, thus discouraging the model from becoming too complex. At the same time, pruning removes the nodes in decision trees that do not contribute significantly to the model's performance.

---

between predicted and actual results.

Therefore, following Liang et al. (2020), the objective function that is optimised in our model is specified in Eq. (10.1) as:

$$O(\theta) = \sum_i^n l\left(y_i, \widehat{y}_i\right) + \sum_1^k \lambda\left(f_k\right) + c \qquad (10.1)$$

Where $\sum_i^n l\left(y_i, \widehat{y}_i\right)$ is the loss function, $\sum_1^k \lambda\left(f_k\right)$ is the regularisation term, and c is the constant. In turn, the regularisation term can be further explained in Eq. (2):

$$\lambda\left(f_k\right) = \delta H + \frac{1}{2}\psi \sum_1^T w_j^2 \qquad (10.2)$$

Where T stands for the number of leaves, δ represents the complexity, and ψ is the penalty parameter (Liang et al., 2020).

Other than performance alone, XGBoost is computationally much lighter than, for example, the Random Forest method and has demonstrated greater accuracy over other methods. For example, Abdurrahim et al. (2020), comparing the accuracy of different predictive modelling algorithms, shows that XGBoost shows the highest accuracy score compared to other methods such as logistic regression, naive Bayes classifier, decision trees, and random forest. However, our study uses Random Forest and Decision Trees to see if they give us the same collection of relevant variables since this study mainly focuses on determining the significant drivers to attain a vaccination threshold (see Sects. 10.5.2 and 10.5.3). Furthermore, Nielsen (2016) demonstrated that XGBoost learns better tree structures over decision tree models that use gradient boosting since XGBoost uses Newton boosting instead.

Multiple combinations were tested for the XGBoost model in our study, and a tree depth of seven was selected since it delivered optimal results. Therefore, our XGBoost model is defined in Eq. (10.3) as:

$$F_M(x) = F_0 + v\beta_1 T_1(x) + v\beta_2 T_2(x) + \cdots + v\beta_M T_M(x) \qquad (10.3)$$

Where M is the number of iterations. The gradient boosting model is a weighted $(B_1...\beta_M)$ linear combination of simple models $(T_1...T_M)$. $F_M(x)$ is the vaccination threshold as described in Sect. 10.4.3.

10.5.1.1   Constructing the XGBoost Model

To build the model, we first started by using all the default settings of the XGBoost algorithm on the training data and refined the parameters afterwards. We started by refining the depth of the trees and tested depths between three and ten using the value with the lowest Root Mean Square Error (see Sect. 10.5.4.3).

After extensive experimentation, the final tree depth was selected as seven, resulting in the lowest RMSE. The number of iterations is set to 100, with a termination clause added to stop the algorithm if the RMSE does not decrease after five iterations. After completing the refining stage, the model reached the lowest RMSE at 16 iterations, ensuring we selected the most effective parameters for our analysis.

Our evaluation metrics rely on Mean Squared Error (MSE), Mean Absolute Error (MAE), and Root Mean Square Error (RMSE) for assessing model performance.

10.5.2   Random Forest

As mentioned in Sect. 10.5.1, we want to see if the XGBoost model's results related to the most important variables are resilient. Therefore, we use an alternative tree-based machine learning approach to see if it gives us the same collection of relevant variables since the main focus is determining the major factors associated with reaching a vaccination threshold (70% and 90%, respectively). We are more concerned with whether we acquire the same set of variables than with the order in which these variables are important.

For this purpose, we employ the Random Forest and Decision Tree (refer to Sect. 10.5.3) models. The Random Forest algorithm (Breiman, 2001) is an ensemble method using bootstrap aggregation to produce multiple independent models to be combined to finalise the predictions.

The Random Forest process uses subsets of the training data to build decision trees. The training data subsets are generated by sampling with replacement bootstrap samples from the training data. The decision tree created using the bootstrap sample can then only evaluate the parameters that are a part of the subset; this reduces the risk of overfitting. After training multiple decision trees, the predictions' averages are taken to get the final prediction output.

A critical characteristic of Random Forests is that they produce measures of variable importance that may be used to find the most important predictor variables (Hapfelmeier et al., 2014; Breiman, 2001). It also works well with small sample sizes and highly correlated sample features (Strobl et al., 2008). Random Forest ranks the variables in terms of a 'mean decrease in accuracy' (MDA). The MDA score indicates the accuracy lost when each variable is removed from the model. The variables are listed in order of decreasing relevance.

10.5.2.1   Constructing the Random Forest Model

Similar to the XGBoost model, we first started by using the default Random Forest algorithm on the training data and refined the parameters afterwards. We set the depth of the trees to seven to be consistent with the XGBoost model.

Initially, we used 20 trees, but after some investigation, the MSE (refer to Sect. 10.5.4.1) only started converging with 50 trees. We finally steeled on a total of 200 trees as it gives good results while not being overly computationally expensive. This configuration provides satisfactory results while remaining computationally efficient.

Our evaluation metrics also remain consistent, relying on MSE, MAE, and RMSE for assessing model performance.

10.5.3 Decision Trees

Our last robustness measure uses a Decision Tree algorithm, a non-parametric supervised learning algorithm for classification and regression tasks. It has a hierarchical tree structure consisting of a root node, branches, internal nodes and leaf nodes. Please see Fig. 10.2 for a brief illustration of how Decision Trees work.

Decision trees comprise many nodes that form a tree when put together; each of these nodes represents decisions made that split the data. The decision of which attribute to use for the split at each node is made by optimising some criteria; in our case, the mean square error is minimised.

As illustrated in Fig. 10.2, a decision tree starts with a root node with no incoming branches. The outgoing branches from the root node feed into the internal nodes, also known as decision nodes. Based on the available features, both node types conduct evaluations to form homogenous subsets denoted by leaf nodes or terminal nodes. The leaf nodes represent all the possible outcomes within the dataset.

Decision Tree learning employs a divide-and-conquer strategy by conducting a greedy search to identify the optimal split points within a tree. This process of splitting is then repeated in a top-down, recursive manner until all or the majority of records have been classified under specific class labels. Whether or not all data points are classified as homogenous sets largely depends on the decision tree's complexity. Smaller trees can more easily attain pure leaf nodes—i.e., data points in a single class. However, as a tree grows in size, it becomes increasingly difficult to maintain this purity, and it usually results in too little data falling within a given subtree. When this occurs, it is known as data fragmentation, which can often lead to overfitting.

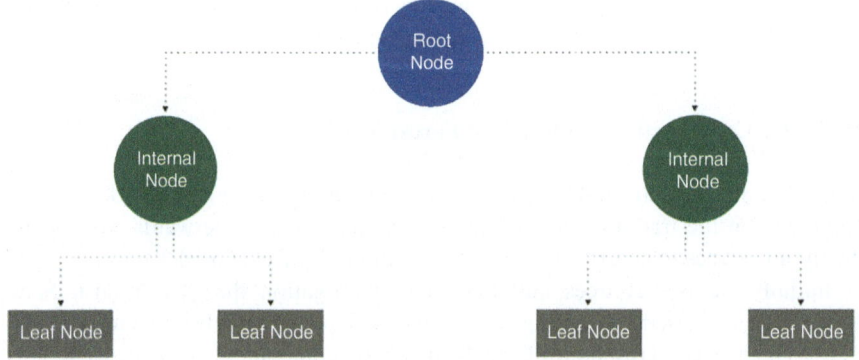

Fig. 10.2 Illustration of how Decision Trees work. *Source*: Geeks for Geeks (2023). In the public domain

As a result, decision trees prefer small trees, which is consistent with the principle of parsimony in Occam's Razor; that is, "entities should not be multiplied beyond necessity." Said differently, decision trees should add complexity only if necessary, as the simplest explanation is often the best. Pruning is usually employed to reduce complexity and prevent overfitting; this is a process that removes branches that split on features with low importance. The model's fit can then be evaluated through the process of cross-validation. Another way that decision trees can maintain their accuracy is by forming an ensemble via a random forest algorithm; this classifier predicts more accurate results, particularly when the individual trees are uncorrelated with each other.

10.5.3.1 Constructing the Decision Tree Model

We follow the specifications set out in Sects. 10.5.1 and 10.5.2 for the Decision Tree model in this chapter. The number of nodes in the decision tree is 8. We also rely on MSE, MAE and RMSE as evaluation metrics.

10.5.4 Evaluation

Model evaluation uses metrics to analyse the model's performance and, thus, how well the model generalises future predictions. One can use many metrics, including Accuracy, Precision, Recall, F1 score, Confusion Matrix, and various error calculations such as the Root Mean Square Error.

The first group applies to classification models and models in which the predicted outcome variable is discrete (or binary). However, our dependent variable (predicted variable) is a continuous variable (vaccinated population/total population). To evaluate the performance of the models, we consider different error calculation measures as they summarise how close the prediction is to the actual value.

We consider the Mean Absolute Error (MAE), the Mean Squared Error (MSE), and the Root Mean Square Error (RMSE).

10.5.4.1 Mean Squared Error

The mean squared error (MSE) evaluates the proximity of a regression line to a group of data points. It is a risk function that corresponds to the predicted squared error loss value. MSE is computed by calculating the average of the squared mistakes resulting from a function's data, especially the mean. From Eq. (10.4), we see that the MSE is calculated by taking the observed value (y_i), subtracting the expected value ($\hat{y_i}$), and then squaring. Repeat for every observation. Afterwards, divide the total by the total number of occurrences (n) by the sum of the squares of the values.

$$MSE = \frac{1}{n}\sum_{i=1}^{n}\left(y_i - \widehat{y}_i\right)^2$$

(10.4)

Therefore, the MSE measures the error in prediction algorithms. This statistic quantifies the average squared variance between observed and predicted values. Squaring the differences removes negative mean squared error differences and guarantees that the squared mean error is always larger than or equal to zero. The value is usually always positive. When there are no errors in a model, the MSE equals 0.

Moreover, squaring magnifies the effect of greater inaccuracies. These computations punish greater mistakes disproportionately more than smaller ones, i.e., a model's worth increases proportionally to its degree of error. This attribute is necessary if we want our model's mistakes to be fewer.

The MSE in regression, for instance, might indicate the average squared residual. The MSE decreases as the data points align with the regression line, indicating less error in the model. A model with fewer errors yields more accurate predictions.

If the MSE is high, the data points are spread out quite a bit from the centre moment, while a low value implies the opposite. When the data points cluster tightly around their mean, the MSE will be modest (mean). It shows that our data values are distributed normally, that there is no skewness, and, most importantly, that there are fewer errors, where errors are defined as how far our data points are from the mean.

10.5.4.2   Mean Absolute Error

In the context of machine learning, absolute error refers to the magnitude of difference between the prediction of an observation and the true value of that observation. Mean absolute error (MAE) takes the average of absolute errors for a group of predictions and observations to measure the magnitude of errors for the entire group. MAE can also be referred to as the loss function specified in Eq. (10.1).

As one of the most commonly used loss functions for regression problems, MAE (Eq. 10.5) helps formulate learning problems into optimisation problems. It also serves as an easy-to-understand quantifiable measurement of errors for regression problems.

$$MAE = \frac{1}{n}\sum_{i=1}^{n}\left|y_i - \widehat{y}_i\right|$$

(10.5)

10.5.4.3   Root Mean Square Error

The Root Mean Square Error (RMSE) represents the square root of the average squared differences between predicted and observed outcomes. It is a metric predominantly utilised in regression analysis and forecasting, where accuracy matters significantly. The lower the RMSE, the better the model's ability to predict accurately. Conversely, a higher RMSE signifies a greater discrepancy between the predicted and actual outcomes. RMSE initially computes the difference between each data point's observed and predicted value. This difference, known as the residual, is squared. The squared residuals are then summed up to obtain a cumulative figure divided by the number of data points to give the MSE. Finally, the square root of the MSE is calculated, resulting in the RMSE (see Eq. 10.6).

$$RMSE = \sqrt{\frac{1}{n}\sum_{i=1}^{n}\left(y_i - \hat{y}_i\right)^2} \qquad (10.6)$$

Where y_j is the true value of the dependent variable (vaccination rate), $\hat{y}_j$ is the predicted value of the dependent variable (vaccination rate), and n is the number of observations.

10.6 Results of the Training of the Models

In this section, we first discuss the results of the model construction. Second, we discuss the evaluation of the fit of the models. Lastly, we discuss the application of the models to address our research questions.

10.6.1 Results of Models Through Iterations

Figures 10.3 and 10.4 show the size of the RMSE and MSE over iterations for XGBoost and Random Forest, respectively. Please note there is no comparable figure for the Decision Tree since it does not employ an ensemble approach. Figure 10.3 shows how the RMSE decreases over the number of iterations. It reaches a minimum at 16 iterations and remains constant up to 20 iterations.

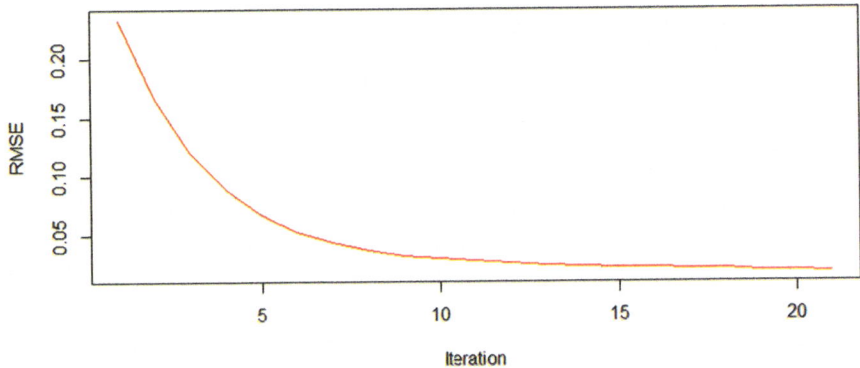

Fig. 10.3 RMSE over iterations for XGBoost. *Source*: Authors' calculations

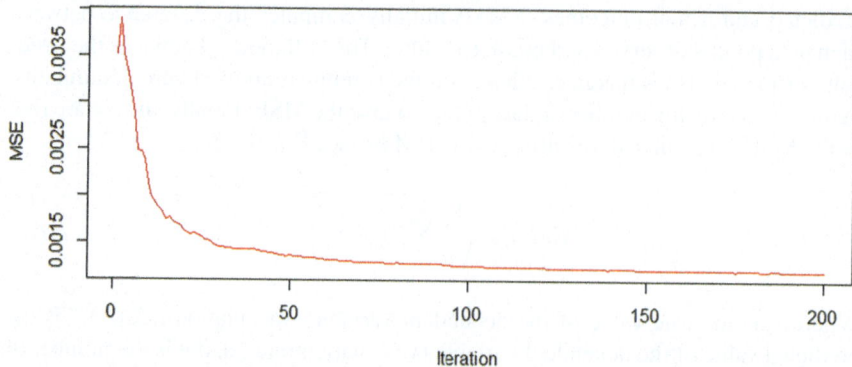

Fig. 10.4 MSE over iterations for Random Forest. *Source*: Authors' calculations

The Random Forest model (Sect. 10.5.2) took much longer to train compared to the effectiveness of the training of the XGBoost model. After 50 trees, it seemed as though the model converged, but upon further inspection, the results continued to improve with minute increments with each additional iteration. In Fig. 10.4, an illustration of the Random Forest algorithm training is given. The MSE decreases, and we can see that after 50 iterations, the MSE is relatively small. The MSE becomes smaller with each iteration but does not converge to a specific value.

10.6.2 Evaluation of the Fit of the Models

In this section, we discuss the evaluation of the three models that we built: XGBoost, Random Forest and Decision Tree. In Table 10.3, the fit statistics for the three models are given. We discuss the fit measures when constructing the model to reach a 90% threshold since this provides us with the largest possible test dataset (the fit measures are also available for the 70% level). Our test data includes all variables (obviously excluding the target output variable). We notice that all measures of fit reveal very small errors, indicating a good-fitting model. Across all three of the fit statistics, the XGBoost performs the best with the lowest values. For the XGBoost, the MSE is 0.0014, the MAE is 0.0227, and the RMSE is 0.0375.

Though the fit statistics indicate that the XGBoost model performed best when considering all models, a visual representation of all three models' predicted values is also provided in blue, with the true values of the dependent variable displayed in red. In Fig. 10.5, the XGBoost results are displayed. The predicted values (the blue line) are quite close to the true values (in red), reflecting a good fit.

As depicted in Fig. 10.6, we notice that using the Random Forest model, the predicted values (blue line) compared to the true values (red line) are not as good as in the case of the XGBoost model. This is also shown in the fit statistics (Table 10.3) with an MSE of 0.0018, an MAE of 0.0299 and an RMSE of 0.0431; thus, each fit statistic reveals bigger errors than in the case of the XGBoost model.

Observing Fig. 10.7, we notice that using the predicted values (blue line) compared to the true values (red line) in the Decision Tree model, we could not reach

Table 10.3 Evaluation metrics across models

Model	MSE	MAE	RMSE
XGBoost	0.001412552	0.022707714	0.0375839
Random Forest	0.001861686	0.029981258	0.043147264
Decision tree	0.01222601	0.07180425	0.11057130

Source: Author's own calculations

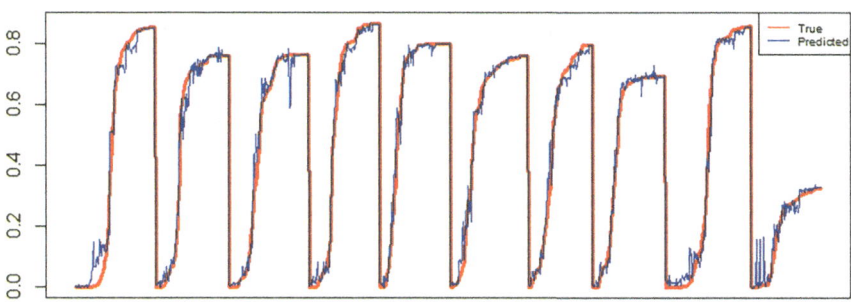

Fig. 10.5 XGBoost—predicted values of the output variable against the true values. *Source*: Authors' calculations

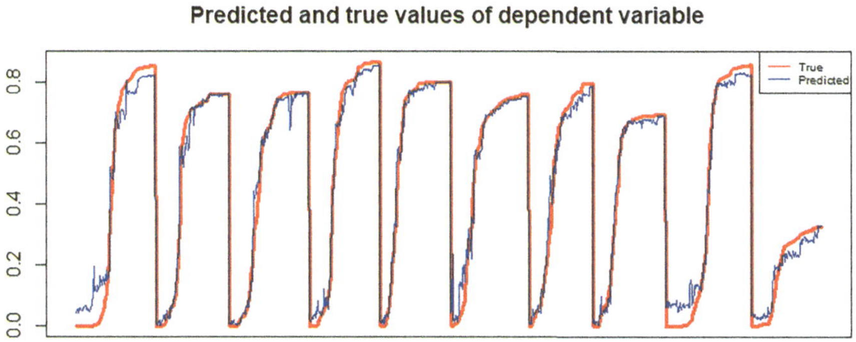

Fig. 10.6 Random Forest - predicted values of the output variable against the true values. *Source*: Authors' calculations

similar levels of prediction as we did with either the XGBoost or the Random Forrest models. The fit statistics also reveal larger errors compared to the other models. The MSE is 0.0122, the MAE is 0.0718, and the RMSE is 0.1105 (Table 10.3).

Figure 10.8 shows the predicted values of the outcome variable of all three models against the true value of the dependent variable. In Fig. 10.8, the true value of the dependent variable is represented in red, while the predictions for the three models are represented in blue, XGBoost, green, Random Forest, and magenta, the Decision Tree. Figure 10.8 supports the results in Table 10.3 and Figs. 10.5, 10.6 and 10.7, as the XGBoost predictions (blue line) are consistently closer to the true value (red

Predicted and true values of dependent variable

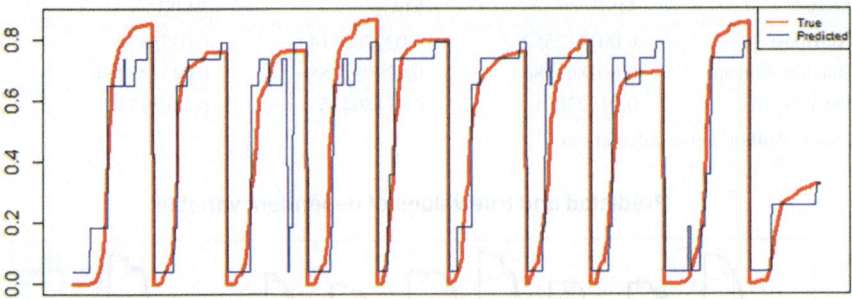

Fig. 10.7 Decision Tree—predicted output variable values against the true values. *Source*: Authors' calculations

True value with all model predictions

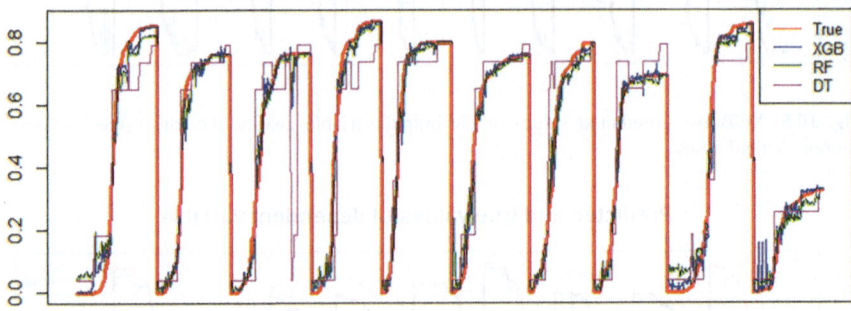

Fig. 10.8 True value with all model predictions. *Source*: Authors' calculations

line) than those using the other two models. This aligns with our expectations that the XGBoost model outperforms the other models.

As mentioned previously, the XGBoost model performs better and uses less computational power. Therefore, in discussing the application of the model to answer our research question, we interpret the XGBoost results.[8]

10.6.3   Results of the XGBoost Model on Variable Importance

Table 10.4 shows the results from our XGBoost model on ranking the importance of variables to reach a 70% and 90% vaccination threshold rate (see Supplementary Information C for the Random Forest and Decision Tree). We also consider a third model at the 80% vaccination threshold level for comparative analysis.

---

[8] The reader should note that although the XGBoost outperforms the other models and is computationally less expensive, the Random Forest and Decision Tree Models have the benefit that they are easier to understand and visualise.

Table 10.4 Results on the order of the importance of the variables predicting vaccination thresholds of 70, 80 and 90%, respectively

70% threshold	80% threshold	90% threshold
Vaccination policy	Vaccination policy	Vaccination policy
Population aged between 10 and 19	International travel controls	International travel controls
International travel controls	Percentage of population in rural areas	Percentage of population in rural areas
Percentage of population in rural areas	Restrictions on gatherings	*Happiness*
Average temperature	Average temperature	Average temperature
Workplace closing	Human Development Index	Population density
Restrictions on gatherings	*Happiness*	Human Development Index
Life expectancy	Workplace closing	Facial coverings
Happiness	Population aged between 10 and 19	Workplace closing
Pollution mortality rate	Out-of-pocket health expenditure	Restrictions on gatherings

Source: Authors' own calculations

Considering the results from reaching the 70, 80 and 90% thresholds, we notice recurring factors among the five most important factors. The factors are related to the vaccination policies, the COVID-19 policies to limit the spread of the virus, and country characteristics such as the percentage of the population residing in rural areas and the average temperature in the countries. This implies that regardless of the vaccination threshold goal, governments should focus on their vaccination policy, international travel controls, the percentage of the population in rural areas and the average temperature to achieve their maximum vaccination rates.

It's worth highlighting the significant role that subjective well-being measures play in attaining vaccination goals. To gain a 70% vaccination (all countries met this threshold except SA), happiness was among the top ten important factors at number nine (Fig. 10.9). If we increase our vaccination threshold to 80% (5 out of 10 countries met), happiness increases in importance and moves to the seventh place. However, to reach the vaccination threshold of 90% or more, we notice that people's happiness is again becoming increasingly important and reaches fourth place (Fig. 10.10). Therefore, regardless of the threshold level, happiness plays an important role, and the higher the vaccination threshold governments want to achieve, the more important it becomes.

If we only consider the lowest threshold of 70% vaccination (Fig. 10.9), most factors are objective and similar to the ones mentioned before. Although the share of the younger population also seems to be relatively significant. From our sample, we note that all except one country managed to reach the 70% threshold, and therefore, more attention should be paid to those factors from the 80% and 90% threshold models.

If we move to the 80% threshold model, we again find similar factors important—though restrictions on gatherings become important. Therefore, if governments want to reach the 80% threshold, they should consider the role

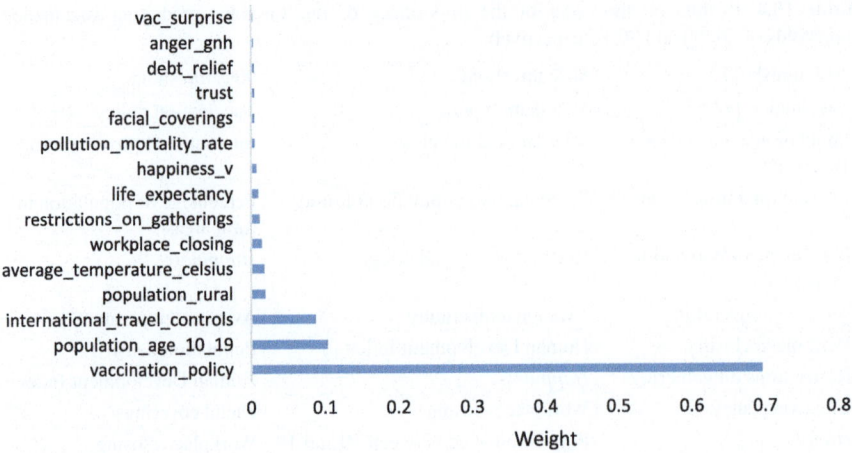

Source: Authors' calculations.

Fig. 10.9 Ranked variable importance—70% vaccination threshold. *Source*: Authors' calculations

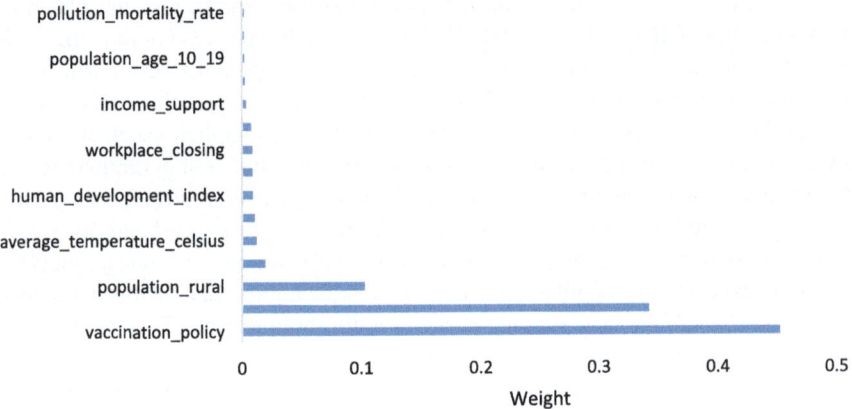

Source: Authors' calculations.

Fig. 10.10 Ranked variable importance—90% vaccination threshold. *Source*: Authors' calculations

COVID-19-related policy measures such as restrictions on gatherings play. We note that the association between restrictions on gatherings and vaccination rates can be positive or negative, and a trade-off is implied. If we allow a policy that does not restrict gatherings, higher vaccination rates become more important. However, implementing restrictions on gatherings decreases the possibility of spreading the disease. This implies that more stringent measures can limit the spread instead of vaccinations. However, this is not ideal, given the abundant evidence of the negative effect on well-being resulting from stringent measures such as lockdowns (Smith et al., 2021; Abadi et al., 2021).

10.7 Discussion on the Application

We will focus our discussion on the top 5 factors and use information from previous studies (see Sect. 10.3) to allude to the relationship with vaccination thresholds. Since we know from Plans-Rubió (2022) that more than 90% of a country's population would need to be vaccinated, given the infectiousness of the pathogen, to achieve herd immunity, our discussion will focus on achieving this "golden standard". Subsequent discussions will highlight where factors have significantly changed in ranking and discuss how happiness and collective emotions can increase vaccination rates. As far as we know, this is the first study that shows the importance of subjective well-being measures.

As noted in Sect. 10.6.3, regardless of the vaccination threshold goal, governments should focus on their vaccination policy, international travel controls, the percentage of the population in rural areas and the average temperature to achieve their maximum vaccination rates (see Figs. 10.9 and 10.10).

The vaccination policy implemented (groups that can access the COVID-19 vaccine) was shown in Sect. 9.4 that when more groups of people can access the vaccine, for example, all age groups compared to fewer groups, it is positively related to attitude towards the vaccine. This means more people will be vaccinated when more people can access the COVID-19 vaccine.

Regarding international travel controls, we know that, for example, in New Zealand (one of the countries with the most stringent lockdowns and highest number of lockdowns), people were told to get vaccinated if they wanted their freedoms back. The then Prime Minister, Jacinda Ardern, clearly stated, "If you want summer […] get vaccinated." If you don't, "there will be everyday things you will miss out on". It wasn't until September 2022 that New Zealand fully opened up their international borders, allowing visitors. Rossouw et al. (2021) found that international border controls acted as a dual shock, economic and social. Hospitality operators were impacted directly by the lack of international and domestic tourism and experienced a significant economic shock that negatively influenced their livelihoods. Furthermore, being unable to travel the world is a social shock, causing a decrease in happiness.

When it comes to the population percentage in rural areas, Barbieri et al. (2022) and Polašek et al. (2022) show that vaccine hesitancy is significantly higher in the rural than in the urban population. Additionally, De Boeck et al. (2020) and Oli et al. (2017) found that the complexity of the pipeline for vaccines from the regional depot to the facility level may create breaking points due to inadequate infrastructure and skills gap and that travelling to rural health facilities is more difficult than to urban health facilities. Rural populations, vulnerable and excluded people are among those for whom improved vaccination rates and access to care were urgently needed to prevent and treat COVID-19. Therefore, governments need to ensure that the rural populations receive targeted information related to the safety of vaccines and that the rural population's access to vaccines is not hampered by procurement and capacity issues.

This study is the first to show the importance of subjective well-being in achieving vaccination thresholds. Concerning the vaccination threshold of 90%, happiness ranks fourth (seventh in the 80% threshold model and ninth in the 70% model) and is therefore important for governments to address. Measuring happiness, thus a subjective measure that captures people's evaluative mood, is very important in any decision-making process. In an ideal world, people make rational choices. The rational choice theory states that when humans are presented with various options under the conditions of scarcity, they will choose the option that maximises their individual satisfaction. Alas, humans are not rational, and their emotions drive them, and therefore they make irrational decisions. Therefore, emotions and happiness levels also drive decision-making processes in considering whether to get vaccinated. Additionally, previous studies such as Kim et al. (2015) show that happier people make better health-related decisions since happier people are less inclined to engage in high-risk activities and take preventative action to mitigate risk. Also, happy people are not just self-centred or selfish; the literature suggests that happy individuals tend to be relatively more cooperative, prosocial, charitable, and "other-centred" (Kasser & Ryan, 1996; Williams & Shiaw, 1999).

Furthermore, Sarracino et al. (2023) showed that happiness and trust are positively correlated, meaning that as trust increases, so does happiness. Trust in others also promotes cooperation and solidarity with positive spillovers on compliance and well-being (Bargain & Aminjonov, 2020). The takeaway from trust and happiness is quite straightforward: the lower your vaccination rates, the more important people's levels of happiness and trust become. Happiness and trust are connected to compliance and doing something "for the greater good". Therefore, the more you want people to engage in a specific activity, such as getting vaccinated, the more important emotions and happiness levels become.

Average temperature ranks fifth important in all three of our threshold models. Jansson and Yamamoto (2022) studied five states in the US to determine the relationship between average temperature, the level of humidity and COVID-19 infection rates. The authors found that a higher-than-average temperature was consistently associated with a decreased relative risk of infection. Given that Fieselmann et al. (2022) found that one of the main reasons people do not get vaccinated is a perceived lower risk of infection, we can deduce that higher-than-average temperatures could lead to countries not meeting their maximum number of vaccine dosage uptake as a proportion of the population size of a country. Apart from the above, we know from studies conducted by Streefland et al. (1999a, b) that in developing countries, parents who do not adhere to vaccination schedules often do so because they are unable to go due to climatic conditions such as the weather being too hot, or roads being flooded from significant rainfall, or a crop needs to be to harvest before it withers in the heat. However, we note that the vaccine rollout was hampered in several European countries as well as the US as severe snowstorms and unusual cold fronts caused inoculation centres, including mega facilities capable of vaccinating up to 20,000 people a day, to close (The Guardian, 2021; CBC News, 2021; John Hopkins Healthcare, 2021).

Factors rated among the top 5 in our 80 and 70% threshold models that did not appear in the 90% threshold model are restrictions on gatherings and the population aged between 10 and 19.

Although not in the top 5 of the 90% threshold model, restrictions on gatherings play an important role in the 80% threshold model. When Americans began receiving the COVID-19 vaccine at the end of December 2020, people started fantasising about the first thing they would do when the pandemic ended: go back to work, visit family, and hug friends (Marcus, 2021). From Greyling and Rossouw (2022), we also know that compliance with restrictions is negatively related to attitudes against the COVID-19 vaccine. When people are reluctant to comply with orders such as staying at home, then those individuals would be more willing to receive the COVID-19 vaccine. A study by Wright et al. (2022) investigated the relationship between vaccinated individuals' willingness to comply and the implemented behavioural regulations. The entire premise of the study is that vaccinated individuals believe they are less at risk because of their vaccination status. People think that when vaccinated, they do not need to comply with, for example, mask-wearing, social distancing, etc., creating a more positive attitude towards vaccines. This finding is informative to policymakers as a message of "less strict regulations" after vaccination can increase vaccine uptake.

As the percentage of the population between 10 and 19 decreases, the population rate increases since they were last to be vaccinated. Therefore, if only a small proportion were this age, more people would be allowed, according to vaccine policy, to get vaccinated, and the vaccination rate would increase. For example, for all developed countries in the sample groups, between 10 and 19 were 12% or less of the population—whereas in South Africa, it was almost 18%. This indicates many things—also, Western countries' populations are getting older—thus, there is a higher need to vaccinate the larger older population.

10.8   Summary

In this chapter, we employed supervised machine learning to retrospectively evaluate the COVID-19 pandemic and determine the factors most important in increasing vaccine uptake. Therefore, we determined those factors associated with achieving herd immunity at the 70% vaccination threshold, estimated at the beginning of the COVID-19 pandemic and the 90% vaccination threshold, estimated later in the pandemic. By doing the aforementioned, we also determined those factors that differed between the 70% to 90% vaccination threshold, which were responsible for reaching the higher vaccination level. Throughout our analyses, we paid particular attention to the role of subjective well-being measures in achieving vaccine thresholds since we know that negative emotions, such as fear of the side effects of vaccines, influence peoples' attitudes towards receiving the vaccine and that happier people make better health-related decisions.

We trained our models on the merged data set of 6530 observations using an Extreme Gradient Boosting (XGBoost) algorithm and also used Random Forest and Decision Tree algorithms as robustness tests. After testing for precision, we found that the XGBoost model gave the best-fit measures and delivered the best results compared to the other two methods. Consequently, we discussed the results of the XGBoost model in determining the most important predicted factors that contribute to reaching different levels of herd immunity.

The above allowed us to make several contributions to existing literature. First, ours was the first study to conduct a post-COVID-19 cross-country analysis of the most important variables to reach different herd immunity levels. Second, we were also the first study to include subjective measures of well-being in our estimations. Third, we were the first study to differentiate between the most important factors to reach different herd immunity levels. Fourth, we were the first to accomplish the aforementioned using various machine learning algorithms to train our models and determine which algorithm gives us the best fit, i.e., the most reliable predictions. Subsequently, our XGBoost model can be used as a benchmark for future research related to the most important factors for reaching herd immunity levels. Furthermore, this study offered some actionable insights for policymakers on increasing vaccination rates to curb pandemics' health, economic and political effects.

Interestingly, our XGBoost model revealed similar important factors in predicting the 70% and 90% vaccination thresholds to reach different herd immunity levels. These included the vaccination policy implemented, international travel controls, the percentage of the population in rural areas and the average temperature. Of significance was happiness's role in attaining the 90% vaccine threshold. Whereas happiness had a lower importance level in achieving the 70% threshold, the importance of happiness in achieving the 90% vaccine threshold was clear. If governments want higher levels of compliance and vaccine uptake, subjective well-being measures such as mood and emotions must be prioritised. Addressing how people feel, in general, towards vaccines and governments is vitally important when policymakers want to push beyond the lower 70% vaccine threshold and achieve the "golden standard" of 90% fully vaccinated.

It would be negligent of us not to discuss our study's limitations. First, the sample of countries under investigation are primarily developed countries. It will be interesting to extend the sample to determine those policies, characteristics and subjective well-being measures deemed necessary to increase vaccination rates in developing countries and contrast those to the factors applicable to developed nations.

Second, although we know that lack of international support and cooperation played a significant role in procuring and disseminating vaccines in developing countries, we could not add variables reflecting international support or emergency investment in health care to our models due to high missingness. We acknowledge that these variables could have ranked among the most important variables and potentially have been included in the top five. The missingness of the observations of these variables is further proof of the failures of countries to prepare for pandemics and give international support. The missingness on international support was 67%, implying that international support was given infrequently. In the event where we added the amounts from the developed countries in our sample, it was still minimal. Furthermore, countries did not frequently invest in emergency health care. Of the observations in our dataset on this variable, 74% were missing. Note that these numbers are for developed countries; therefore, it is easy to imagine what the variable would reveal for developing countries. When we added these amounts, it was very little compared to the amounts spent on, for example, vaccines.

Supplementary Information A

To derive our time-series data, which captures sentiment and emotions, we construct variables using Big Data by extracting tweets from Twitter. In our analysis, we extracted two sets of tweets based on keywords, one related to COVID-19 vaccines and the other related to the government. The tweets containing these words amounted to 1,047,000 tweets. We extracted all tweets according to specific geographical areas (country).

For COVID-19 vaccines, we extract tweets using the keywords: *vaccinate, vacc, vaccine, Sputnik V, Sputnik, Sinopharm, Astrazeneca, Pfizer (if NEAR) vaccine, Pfizer-BioNTech, Johnson & Johnson,* and *Moderna.*

For the government, we extract tweets using the keywords: *government, parliament, ministry, minister, senator, MPs, legislator, political, politics, prime minister.*

The first step in our analysis is determining the tweets' language (we detected 64 different languages), and all non-English tweets were translated into English. After translation, we use NLP to extract the tweets' sentiment and underlying emotions. To test the robustness of coding the sentiment of the translated tweets, we use lexicons in the original language, if available, and repeat the process. We compare the coded sentiment of the translated and original text and find the results strongly correlated.

We make use of a suite of lexicons. Each differs slightly but primarily aims to determine the sentiment of unstructured text data. The two lexicons primarily used in our analysis are Sentiment140 and NRC (National Research Council of Canada Emotion Lexicon developed by Turney and Mohammad (2010)). The other lexicons are used for robustness purposes and are part of the Syuzhet package. The lexicons include Syuzhet, AFINN and Bing. The sentiment is determined by identifying the tweeter's attitude towards an event using variables such as context, tone, etc. It helps one form an entire opinion of the text. Depending on the lexicon used, the text (tweet) is coded. For example, if a tweet is positive, it is coded as 0; if neutral, 2; and if negative, 4.

We use the NRC lexicon to code the sentiment (as explained above) and analyse the underlying tweets' emotions. It distinguishes between eight basic emotions: anger, fear, anticipation, trust, surprise, sadness, joy and disgust (the so-called Plutchik (1980) wheel of emotions). NRC codes words with different values, ranging from 0 (low) to 8 (the highest score in our data), expressing the intensity of an emotion or sentiment.

To construct the time-series data, we use the coding of the tweets and derive daily averages. In this manner, we derive a positive sentiment, a negative sentiment and eight emotion time series. We derived the sentiment time series using different lexicons as a robustness test and compared these results using correlation analyses. We perform additional robustness tests, for example, determining whether the sampling frequency significantly influences the results.

To test the robustness of the *frequency,* we construct the relevant index (time series) per day (the norm); we repeat the exercise but construct the time series per hour. We find similar trends in our hourly and daily time series, indicating that the timescale at which sampling occurs does not significantly influence the observed trend.

To test whether the *volume* of tweets affects the derived time-series data, we extract random samples of differing sizes from the daily text corpus of tweets. The time series based on these smaller samples (50% and 80% of the daily extracted tweets) are highly correlated to the original time series.

Supplementary Information B

Full list of variables

Variable	Description	Scale	Coding	Source
Vaccination policy	Policies for vaccine delivery for different groups	Ordinal	0—No availability 1—Availability for ONE of following: key workers/ clinically vulnerable groups (non-elderly)/elderly groups 2—Availability for TWO of following: key workers/ clinically vulnerable groups (non-elderly) / elderly groups 3—Availability for ALL of following: key workers/ clinically vulnerable groups (non-elderly) / elderly groups 4—Availability for all three plus partial additional availability (select broad groups/ages) 5—Universal availability	Mathieu et al. (2021)
Workplace closing	Record closing of workplaces	Ordinal	0—no measures 1—recommend closing (or recommend work from home), or all businesses open with alterations resulting in significant differences compared to non-Covid-19 operations 2—require closing (or work from home) for some sectors or categories of workers 3—require closing (or work from home) for all-but-essential workplaces (e.g. grocery stores, doctors) Blank—no data	Mathieu et al. (2021)
Restrictions on gatherings	Record limits on gatherings	Ordinal	0—no restrictions 1—restrictions on very large gatherings (the limit is above 1000 people) 2—restrictions on gatherings between 101-1000 people 3—restrictions on gatherings between 11-100 people 4—restrictions on gatherings of 10 people or less Blank—no data	Mathieu et al. (2021)

Variable	Description	Scale	Coding	Source
International travel controls	Restrictions on international travel	Ordinal	0—no restrictions 1—screening arrivals 2—quarantine arrivals from some or all regions 3—ban arrivals from some regions 4—ban on all regions or total border closure Blank—no data	Mathieu et al. (2021)
Contact tracing	Record government policy on contact tracing after a positive diagnosis	Ordinal scale	0—no contact tracing	Mathieu et al. (2021)
Testing policy	Record government policy on who has access to testing Note: this records policies about testing for current infection (PCR tests), not testing for immunity (antibody test)	Ordinal scale	0—no testing policy 1—only those who both (a) have symptoms AND (b) meet specific criteria (e.g. key workers, admitted to hospital, came into contact with a known case, returned from overseas) 2—testing of anyone showing Covid-19 symptoms 3—open public testing (e.g. "drive through" testing available to asymptomatic people) Blank—no data	Mathieu et al. (2021)
Face coverings	Policies on the use of facial coverings outside the home	Ordinal	0—No policy 1 – Recommended 2—Required in some specified shared/public spaces outside the home with other people present or some situations when social distancing not possible 3—Required in all shared/public spaces outside the home with other people present or all situations when social distancing not possible 4—Required outside the home at all times regardless of location or presence of other people	Mathieu et al. (2021)

Variable	Description	Scale	Coding	Source
Income support	Record if the government provides direct cash payments to people who lose their jobs or cannot work Note: only includes payments to firms if explicitly linked to payroll/ salaries	Ordinal	0—no income support 1—government is replacing less than 50% of lost salary (or if a flat sum, it is less than 50% of median salary) 2—government is replacing 50% or more of lost salary (or if a flat sum, it is greater than 50% of median salary) Blank—no data	Mathieu et al. (2021)
Debt relief	Record if the government is freezing financial obligations for households (e.g. stopping loan repayments, preventing services like water from stopping, or banning evictions)	Ordinal	0—no debt/contract relief 1—narrow relief, specific to one kind of contract 2—broad debt/contract relief	Mathieu et al. (2021)
Public information campaigns		Ordinal	0 -No COVID-19 public information campaign 1—public officials urging caution about COVID-19 2—coordinated public information campaign (e.g. across traditional and social media) No data—blank	Mathieu et al. (2021)
Physicians per 1000		Continuous		Mathieu et al. (2021)
Nurses per 1000		Continuous		Mathieu et al. (2021)
Health expenditure (USD)		Continuous		World Bank (2023c)
Out-of-pocket health expenditure		Continuous		World Bank (2023c)
Population rural (Percentage of population in rural areas)	People living in rural areas as defined by national statistical offices. It is calculated as the difference between the total and urban populations	Percentage		World Bank staff estimates based on the United Nations Population Division's World Urbanization Prospects (2018)

Variable	Description	Scale	Coding	Source
Population density	People per square kilometre of land area			United Nations, Department of Economic and Social Affairs, Population Division (2022)
Infant mortality rate		Continuous		World Bank (2023c)
Population age 0–9		Continuous		World Bank (2023c)
Population age 10–19		Continuous		World Bank (2023c)
Population age 20–29		Continuous		World Bank (2023c)
Population age 30–39		Continuous		World Bank (2023c)
Population age 40–49		Continuous		World Bank (2023c)
Population age 50–59		Continuous		World Bank (2023c)
Population age 60–69		Continuous		World Bank (2023c)
Population age 70–79		Continuous		World Bank (2023)
Population age 80 and older		Continuous		World Bank (2023c)
Life expectancy	The average number of years a newborn would live if age-specific mortality rates in the current year were to stay the same throughout its life.	Years		United Nations, Department of Economic and Social Affairs, Population Division (2022)
Diabetes prevalence		Continuous		World Bank (2023c)
Comorbidity mortality rate		Continuous		Mathieu et al. (2021)
Smoking prevalence		Continuous		Mathieu et al. (2021)

Variable	Description	Scale	Coding	Source
Pollution mortality rate		Continuous		United Nations, Department of Economic and Social Affairs, Population Division (2022)
Average temperature		Celsius		World Bank (2023a)
Human capital index				World Bank (2018)
Human development index				Mathieu et al. (2021)
GDP (USD)		Continuous		World Bank (2023c)
GDP per capita (US$)		Continuous		World Bank (2023c)
GNH	General happiness	Continuous		Greyling et al. (2019)
Sadness GNH	The emotion general sadness	Continuous		Greyling et al. (2019)
Trust GNH	The emotion general trust	Continuous		Greyling et al. (2019)
Anticipation GNH	The emotion general anticipation	Continuous		Greyling et al. (2019)
Fear GNH	The emotion general fear	Continuous		Greyling et al. (2019)
Surprise GNH	The emotion general surprise	Continuous		Greyling et al. (2019)
Joy GNH	The emotion general joy	Continuous		Greyling et al. (2019)
Anger GNH	The emotion general anger	Continuous		Greyling et al. (2019)
Disgust GNH	The emotion general disgust	Continuous		Greyling et al. (2019)
GNH Gov	Happiness towards government	Continuous		Greyling et al. (2019)
Trust Gov	The emotion trust towards government	Continuous		Greyling et al. (2019)
Joy Gov	The emotion joy towards government	Continuous		Greyling et al. (2019)
Surprise Gov	The emotion surprise towards government	Continuous		Greyling et al. (2019)

Variable	Description	Scale	Coding	Source
Sadness Gov	The emotion sadness towards government	Continuous		Greyling et al. (2019)
Anticipation Gov	The emotion anticipation towards government	Continuous		Greyling et al. (2019)
Disgust Gov	The emotion disgust towards government	Continuous		Greyling et al. (2019)
Fear Gov	The emotion fear towards government	Continuous		Greyling et al. (2019)
Anger Gov	The emotion anger towards government	Continuous		Greyling et al. (2019)
VADER pos Gov	Positive sentiment towards the government	Continuous		Greyling et al. (2019)
VADER neg Gov	Negative sentiment towards the government	Continuous		Greyling et al. (2019)
VADER sent Vac	Sentiment towards the vaccine	Continuous		Greyling et al. (2019)
VADER neg Vac	Negative sentiment towards the vaccine	Continuous		Greyling et al. (2019)
VADER pos Vac	Positive sentiment towards the vaccine	Continuous		Greyling et al. (2019)
GNH Vac	Happiness towards the vaccine	Continuous		Greyling et al. (2019)
Surprise Vac	The emotion surprise towards vaccines	Continuous		Greyling et al. (2019)
Anticipation Vac	The emotion anticipation towards the vaccine	Continuous		Greyling et al. (2019)
Disgust Vac	The emotion disgust towards the vaccine	Continuous		Greyling et al. (2019)
Sadness Vac	The emotion sadness towards the vaccine	Continuous		Greyling et al. (2019)

Variable	Description	Scale	Coding	Source
Fear Vac	The emotion fear towards the vaccine	Continuous		Greyling et al. (2019)
Anger Vac	The emotion anger towards the vaccine	Continuous		Greyling et al. (2019)
Trust Vac	The emotion trust towards the vaccine	Continuous		Greyling et al. (2019)
Joy Vac	The emotion joy towards the vaccine	Continuous		Greyling et al. (2019)

Supplementary Information C

Importance of factors, XGBoost, Random Forest and Decision Tree—90 % threshold

XGBoost—90% threshold	Random Forest—90% threshold	Decision Tree—90% threshold
Vaccination policy	Vaccination policy	Vaccination policy
International travel controls	Restrictions on gatherings	Testing policy
Percentage of population in rural areas	International travel controls	Public information campaigns
Happiness	Debt relief	Contact tracing
Average temperature	Facial coverings	Facial coverings
Population density	Testing policy	International travel controls
Human Development Index	Income support	Income support
Facial coverings	Contact tracing	Restrictions on gatherings
Workplace closing	Comorbidity mortality rate	Population aged between 20-29
Restrictions on gatherings	Average temperature	Population aged between 0-9
Income support	Infant mortality rate	Population aged between 10-19
Life expectancy	Workplace closing	Human Development Index
Pollution mortality rate	Population aged 80 and older	Percentage of population in rural areas
Out-of-pocket health expenditure	GDP (USD)	Infant mortality rate
Debt relief	Public information campaigns	Out-of-pocket health expenditure
Trust (GNH)	Diabetes prevalence	Population aged between 30 and39
Human capital index	Out-of-pocket health expenditure	Population aged between 40 and 49
Diabetes prevalence	Population density	Health expenditure (USD)
Human Development Index	Smoking prevalence	GDP per capita (USD)
DDP per capita (USD)	Life expectancy	Human capital index
Sadness (GNH)—lack of happiness	Disgust (GNH)—lack of happiness	Population density
Sentiment towards vaccines	Human capital index	Smoking prevalence
Smoking prevalence	Anger (GNH)—lack of happiness	Anger (GNH)—lack of happiness

References

Abadi, D., Arnaldo, I., & Fischer, A. (2021). Anxious and angry: Emotional responses to the COVID-19 threat. *Frontiers in Psychology, 12*, 676116.

Abdurrahim, Y., Ali, A. D., Sena, K., & Huseyin, U. (2020). Comparison of deep learning and traditional machine learning techniques for classification of pap smear images. *arXiv*, 2009.06366v1.

Andrade, C., Gillen, M., Molina, J. A., & Wilmarth, M. J. (2022). The social and economic impact of Covid-19 on family functioning and wellbeing: Where do we go from here? *Journal of Family and Economic Issues, 43*(2), 205–212.

Anik, L., Aknin, L. B., Norton, M. I., & Dunn, E. W. (2009). Feeling good about giving: The benefits (and costs) of self-interested charitable behavior. Harvard Business School Marketing Unit Working No. 10–012.

Bajos, N., Spire, A., Silberzan, L., Sireyjol, A., Jusot, F., Meyer, L., et al. (2022). When Mistrust in the Government and Scientists Reinforce Social Inequalities in Vaccination against Covid-19. *Frontiers in Public Health, 10*, 908152.

Baldwin, R. (2020). Keeping the lights on: Economic medicine for a medical shock. VoxEU. Org. 2020.

Barbieri, V., Wiedermann, C. J., Lombardo, S., Ausserhofer, D., Plagg, B., Piccoliori, G., et al. (2022). Vaccine hesitancy in the second year of the coronavirus pandemic in South Tyrol, Italy: A representative cross-sectional survey. *Vaccine, 10*, 1584.

Bargain, O., & Aminjonov, U. (2020). Trust and compliance to public health policies in times of covid-19. *Journal of Public Economics, 192*, 104316.

Bartsch, S. M., Ferguson, M. C., McKinnell, J. A., O'Shea, K. J., Wedlock, P. T., Siegmund, S. S., et al. (2020). The Potential Health Care Costs and Resource Use Associated With COVID-19 In The United States. *Health Affairs, 39*(6), 927–935.

Bergmann, M., Bethmann, A., Hannemann, T.-V., & Schumacher, A. T. (2022). Who are the Unvaccinated? Determinants of SARS-CoV-2 Vaccinations among Older Adults Across Europe. *Easy Social Sciences, Mixed, 1*, 1–11.

Bíró-Nagy, A., & Szászi, A. J. (2022). The roots of COVID-19 vaccine hesitancy: Evidence from Hungary. *Journal of Behavioral Medicine*, 1–16.

Bloom, D. E., Cadarette, D., & Ferranna, M. (2021). The societal value of vaccination in the age of COVID-19. *American Journal of Public Health, 111*(6), 1049–1054.

Breiman, L. (2001). Random forests. *Machine Learning, 45*, 5–32.

CBC News. (2021). Canada's Pfizer vaccine shipment delayed by winter weather in the US. https://www.cbc.ca/news/politics/pfizer-delays-winter-weather-1.5915661. Accessed on 27.07.23.

Chen, T., & Guestrin, C. (2016). XGBoost: A scalable tree boosting system. In Proceedings of the 22nd ACM SIGKDD International Conference on knowledge discovery and data mining (KDD '16). Association for Computing Machinery, New York, NY, USA, pp. 785–794.

Cheong, Q., Quon, S., Concepcion, K., & Kong, J. D. (2021). Predictive modeling of vaccination uptake in US Counties: A machine learning–based approach. *Journal of Medical Internet Research, 23*(11).

Corcoran, K. E., Scheitle, C. P., & DiGregorio, B. D. (2021). Christian nationalism and COVID-19 vaccine hesitancy and uptake. *Vaccine, 39*(45), 6614–6621.

Czeisler, M. E., Rajaratnam, S. W. M., Howard, M. E., & Czeisler, C. A. (2021). COVID-19 vaccine intentions in the United States—December 2020 to March 2021. Working paper, MedRxiv.

De Boeck, K., Decouttere, C., & Vandaele, N. (2020). Vaccine distribution chains in low- and middle-income countries: a literature review. *Omega, 97*, 102097.

El-Mohandes, A., White, T. M., Wyka, K., Rauh, L., Rabin, K., Kimball, S. H., et al. (2021). COVID-19 vaccine acceptance among adults in four major US Metropolitan Areas and Nationwide. *Scientific Reports, 11*(1), 21844.

Fetzer, T. R., Witte, M., Hencel, L., Jachimowicz, J., Haushofer, J., Ivchenko, A., et al. (2020). Global behaviors and perceptions at the onset of the COVID-19 pandemic. National Bureau of Economic Research Working Paper No, 27082.

Fieselmann, J., Annac, K., Erdsiek, F., Yilmaz-Aslan, Y., & Brzoska, P. (2022). What are the reasons for refusing a COVID-19 vaccine? A qualitative analysis of social media in Germany. *BMC Public Health, 22*, 846.

Gatwood, J., McKnight, M., Fiscus, M., Hohmeier, K. C., & Chisholm-Burns, M. (2021). Factors influencing likelihood of COVID-19 vaccination: A survey of tennessee adults. *American Journal of Health-System Pharmacy, 78*(10), 879–889.

Geeks for Geeks. (2023). XGBoost. https://www.geeksforgeeks.org/xgboost/. Accessed on 21.07.23.

Goldblatt, D., Fiore-Gartland, A., Johnson, M., Hunt, A., Bengt, C., Zavadska, D., et al. (2022). Towards a population-based threshold of protection for COVID-19 vaccines. *Vaccine, 40*(2), 306–315.

Gomes, I. A., Soares, P., Rocha, J. V., Gama, A., Laires, P. A., Moniz, M., et al. (2022). Factors associated with COVID-19 vaccine hesitancy after implementation of a mass vaccination campaign. *Vaccine, 10*(2), 281.

Greyling, T., & Rossouw, S. (2022). Positive attitudes towards COVID-19 vaccines: A cross-country analysis. *PLoS One, 17*(3), 0264994.

Greyling, T., Rossouw, S., & Afstereo. (2019). *Gross National Happiness.today.* http://gnh.today. Accessed on 20.07.23.

Hapfelmeier, A., Hothorn, T., Ulm, K., & Strobl, C. (2014). A new variable importance measure for random forests with missing data. *Statistics and Computing, 24*, 21–34.

Jansson, M. K., & Yamamoto, S. (2022). The effect of temperature, humidity, precipitation and cloud coverage on the risk of COVID-19 infection in temperate regions of the USA—A case-crossover study. *PLoS One, 17*(9), e0273511.

John Hopkins Healthcare. (2021). Winter Storm Slows US COVID Vaccine Rollout. https://johnshopkinshealthcare.staywellsolutionsonline.com/RelatedItems/6,1650551452. Accessed on 25.07.23.

Kasser, T., & Ryan, R. M. (1996). Further examining the American dream: Differential correlates of intrinsic and extrinsic goals. *Personality and Social Psychology Bulletin, 22*, 280–287.

Kerr, J. R., Schneider, C. R., Recchia, G., Dryhurst, S., Sahlin, U., Dufouil, C., et al. (2021). Correlates of intended COVID-19 vaccine acceptance across time and countries: Results from a series of cross-sectional surveys. *BMJ Open, 11*(8), e048025.

Kim, E. S., Kubzansky, L. D., & Smith, J. (2015). Life satisfaction and use of preventive health care services. *Health Psychology, 34*(7), 779–782.

Latkin, C. A., Dayton, L., Yi, G., Konstantopoulos, A., & Boodram, B. (2021). Trust in a COVID-19 vaccine in the US: A social-ecological perspective. *Social Science and Medicine, 270*, 113684.

Liang, W., Luo, S., Zhao, G., & Wu, H. (2020). Predicting hard rock pillar stability using GBDT, XGBoost, and LightGBM algorithms. *Mathematics, 8*(5), 765.

Lincoln, T. M., Schlier, B., Strakeljahn, F., Gaudiano, B. A., So, S. H., Kingston, J., et al. (2022). Taking a machine learning approach to optimise prediction of vaccine hesitancy in high income countries. *Scientific Reports, 12*(1), 1–12.

Lindholt, M. F., Jørgensen, F., Bor, A., & Petersen, M. B. (2021). Public acceptance of COVID-19 vaccines: Cross-national evidence on levels and individual-level Predictors using observational data. *BMJ Open, 11*(6), e048172.

Lu, H., Nie, P., & Qian, L. (2020). Do quarantine experiences and attitudes towards COVID-19 affect the distribution of psychological outcomes in China? A quantile regression analysis. Global Labor Organization Discussion Paper No, 512.

Ludvigson, S. C., Ma, S., & Ng, S. (2020). Covid19 and the macroeconomic effects of costly disasters. National Bureau of Economic Research Working Paper No, 26987.

Lyubomirsky, S., Sheldon, K. M., & Schkade, D. (2005). Pursuing happiness: The architecture of sustainable change. *Review of General Psychology, 9*(2), 111–131.

Marcus, J. (2021). Vaccinated people are going to hug each other. *The Atlantic.* https://www.theatlantic.com/ideas/archive/2021/01/giving-people-more-freedom-whole-point-vaccines/617829/. Accessed on 22.07.23.

Mathieu, E., Ritchie, H., Roser, M., Hasell, J., Appel, C., & Giattino, C. (2021). A global database of COVID-19 vaccinations. *Nature Human Behaviour, 5*(7), 947–953.

Mental Health and Wellbeing Commission. (2023). COVID-19 and safety in the home. COVID-19 Impact Insights Paper Number 4. https://www.mhwc.govt.nz/assets/COVID-19-insights/Paper-4-COVID-and-safety-in-the-home/ENG_SafetyReport_Summary.pdf. Accessed on 21.07.23.

Nielsen, D. (2016). Tree boosting with XGBoost: Why does XGBoost win "every" machine learning competition? Norwegian University of Science and Technology. https://ntnuopen.ntnu.no/ntnu-xmlui/bitstream/handle/11250/2433761/16128_FULLTEXT.pdf. Accessed on 10.07.23.

Oli, A. N., Agu, R. U., Ihekwereme, C. P., & Esimone, C. O. (2017). An evaluation of the cold chain technology in South-East, Nigeria using Immunogenicity study on the measles vaccines. *Pan African Medical Journal, 27*, 1–5.

Osman, S. M. I., & Sabit, A. (2022). Predictors of COVID-19 vaccination rate in USA: A machine learning approach. *Machine Learning with Applications, 10*, 100408.

Paul, E., Steptoe, A., & Fancourt, D. (2021). Attitudes towards vaccines and intention to vaccinate against COVID-19: Implications for public health communications. *The Lancet Regional Health-Europe, 1*(100012), 1–10.

Plans-Rubió, P. (2022). Percentages of vaccination coverage required to establish herd immunity against SARS-CoV-2. *Vaccine, 10*(5), 736.

Polašek, O., Wazny, K., Adeloye, D., Song, P., Chan, K. Y., Bojude, D. A., et al. (2022). Research priorities to reduce the impact of COVID-19 in low- and middle-income countries. *Journal of Global Health, 12*, 09003.

Pronkina, E., & Rees, D. I. (2022). Predicting COVID-19 vaccine uptake. Institute of Labor Economics (IZA) Discussion Paper No. 15625.

Raciborski, F., Samel-Kowalik, P., Gujski, M., Pinkas, J., Arcimowicz, M., & Jankowski, M. (2021). Factors associated with a lack of willingness to vaccinate against COVID-19 in Poland: A 2021 nationwide cross-sectional survey. *Vaccine, 9*(9), 1000.

Randolph, H. E., & Barreiro, L. B. (2020). Herd immunity: Understanding COVID-19. *Immunity, 52*(5), 737–741.

Rossouw, S., Greyling, T., & Adhikari, T. (2021). The evolution of happiness pre and peri-COVID-19: A Markov switching dynamic regression model. *PLoS One, 16*(12), e0259579.

Rozek, L. S., Jones, P., Menon, A., Hicken, A., Apsley, S., & King, E. J. (2021). Understanding vaccine hesitancy in the context of COVID-19: The role of trust and confidence in a seventeen-country survey. *International Journal of Public Health, 66*, 636255.

Sallam, M. (2021). COVID-19 vaccine hesitancy worldwide: A systematic review of vaccine acceptance rates. *Vaccine, 9*(160), 1–14.

Sarracino, F., Greyling, T., O'Connor, K., Peroni, C. & Rossouw, S. (2023). A year of pandemic: Levels, changes and validity of well-being data from Twitter. Evidence from ten countries. *PLOS ONE, 18*(2), e0275028.

Shaham, A., Chodick, G., Shalev, V., & Yamin, D. (2020). Personal and social patterns predict influenza vaccination decisions. *BMC Public Health, 20*(222), 1–12.

Sheikh, A. B., Pal, S., Javed, N., & Shekhar, R. (2021). COVID-19 vaccination in developing nations: Challenges and opportunities for innovation. *Infectious Disease Report, 14*(2), 429–436.

Smith, L. E., Duffy, B., Moxham-Hall, V., Strang, L., Wessely, S., & Rubin, G. J. (2021). Anger and confrontation during the COVID-19 pandemic: a national cross-sectional survey in the UK. *Journal of the Royal Society of Medicine, 114*(2), 77–90.

Streefland, P. H., Chowdhury, A. M. R., & Ramos-Jimenez, P. (1999a). Patterns of vaccination acceptance. *Social Science and Medicine, 49*, 1705–1716.

Streefland, P. H., Chowdhury, A. M. R., & Ramos-Jimenez, P. (1999b). Quality of vaccination services and social demand for vaccinations in Africa and Asia. *Bulletin of the World Health Organization, 77*, 722–730.

Strobl, C., Boulesteix, A.-L., Kneib, T., Augustin, T., & Zeileis, A. (2008). Conditional variable importance for random forests. *BMC Bioinformatics, 9*(1), 1–11.

The Guardian. (2021). Severe snowstorm forces Greece to halt Covid vaccination drive. https://www.theguardian.com/world/2021/feb/16/severe-snowstorm-forces-greece-to-halt-covid-vaccination-drive. Accessed on 20.07.23.

United Nations, Department of Economic and Social Affairs, Population Division. (2022). *World Population Prospects 2022, Online Edition.* https://population.un.org/wpp/Download/Standard/MostUsed/. Accessed on 20.07.23.

Ward, J. K., Alleaume, C., & Peretti-Watel, P. (2020). The French public's attitudes to a future COVID-19 vaccine: The politicization of a public health issue. *Social Science and Medicine, 265*, 113414.

Williams, S., & Shiaw, W. T. (1999). Mood and organisational citizenship behavior: The effects of positive affect on employee organisational citizenship behavior intentions. *Journal of Psychology, 133*, 656–668.

Wollebæk, D., Fladmoe, A., Steen-Johnsen, K., & Ihlen, Ø. (2022). Right-wing ideological constraint and vaccine refusal: The case of the COVID-19 vaccine in Norway. *Scandinavian Political Studies, 45*(2), 253–278.

World Bank. (2018). *The Human Capital Project*. World Bank. https://data.worldbank.org/indicator/HD.HCI.OVRL.UB.MA?end=2020&start=2020&view=bar. Accessed on 20.07.23

World Bank. (2023a). Climate change knowledge portal. https://climateknowledgeportal.worldbank.org/. Accessed on 20.07.23.

World Bank. (2023b). Food and Agriculture Organization and World Bank population estimates. https://data.worldbank.org/indicator/EN.POP.DNST?view=chart. Accessed on 20.07.23.

World Bank. (2023c). World Bank Open Data 2023. https://data.worldbank.org/. Accessed on 20.07.23.

World Bank staff estimates based on the United Nations Population Division's World Urbanization Prospects: 2018 Revision. https://data.worldbank.org/indicator/SP.RUR.TOTL.ZS. Accessed on 20.07.23.

World Health Organization (WHO). (2023). WHO Coronavirus (COVID-19) Dashboard. https://covid19.who.int/. Accessed on 20.07.23.

Wright, L., Steptoe, A., Mak, H. W., & Fancourt, D. (2022). Do people reduce compliance with COVID-19 guidelines following vaccination? A longitudinal analysis of matched UK adults. *Journal of Epidemiology & Community Health, 76*, 109–115.

Chapter 11
The Effect of Non-vaccination on Health, Mental Health, Social Relationships, and the Economy

Abstract This chapter addresses the multifaceted consequences of negative attitudes and vaccine hesitancy toward COVID-19, emphasising its impact on health, mental well-being, social relationships, and the economy. Building on our Chaps. 7–10 results, we examine the potential ramifications if positive attitudes toward vaccination are not restored.

In assessing the effect of non-vaccination on health, we discuss the threat posed to achieving herd immunity, the increased risk of severe infections and fatalities among individuals and communities, and the global health security implications. Through a comprehensive review of studies and reports, including estimates of preventable deaths due to non-vaccination, we underscore the critical importance of widespread vaccination for mitigating the adverse health outcomes of the pandemic.

Furthermore, we explore the relationship between non-vaccination and mental health, drawing insights from studies highlighting the psychological distress experienced by vaccine-hesitant individuals and their communities. From improved mental health outcomes among vaccinated populations to heightened anxiety and depressive symptoms among the vaccine-hesitant, our analysis underscores the significant impact of vaccination decisions on mental well-being.

Turning to the effect of non-vaccination on social relationships, we highlight the divisive impact of vaccine hesitancy on interpersonal dynamics within families, communities, and social networks. Drawing from anecdotal evidence and media reports, we discuss how vaccine hesitancy increases trust deficits, deepens societal divides, and strains social cohesion, with implications extending beyond individual relationships to economic and political realms.

Finally, we examine the economic consequences of vaccine hesitancy, explaining its role in impeding economic recovery, increasing healthcare costs, reducing consumer confidence, and disrupting sectors such as tourism and hospitality. By analysing various studies and economic indicators, we underscore the importance of widespread vaccine acceptance to bolster economic resilience and foster global prosperity

Keywords Negative attitudes · Vaccine hesitancy · Health · Mental health · Social relationships · Economy

11.1   Introduction

This chapter addresses the consequences of negative attitudes or vaccine hesitancy toward the COVID-19 vaccine. Following our Chapters 7–10 results, we investigate what could happen should positive attitudes towards the COVID-19 vaccine not be restored. Therefore, negative attitudes and non-vaccination outcomes take centre stage in this chapter. To ensure we meet the aim of this chapter, we will recap the drivers of vaccine hesitancy (Chap. 10), the reasons discovered that made people hesitant to get vaccinated, and the effect of vaccine hesitancy on health, mental health, social relationships, and the economy.

Figure 11.1 indicates the effects of non-vaccination on health, mental health, social relationships and the economy. As can be seen, all these dimensions of well-being were negatively affected by the choice of non-vaccination. We elaborate on this in Sects. 11.3–11.6.

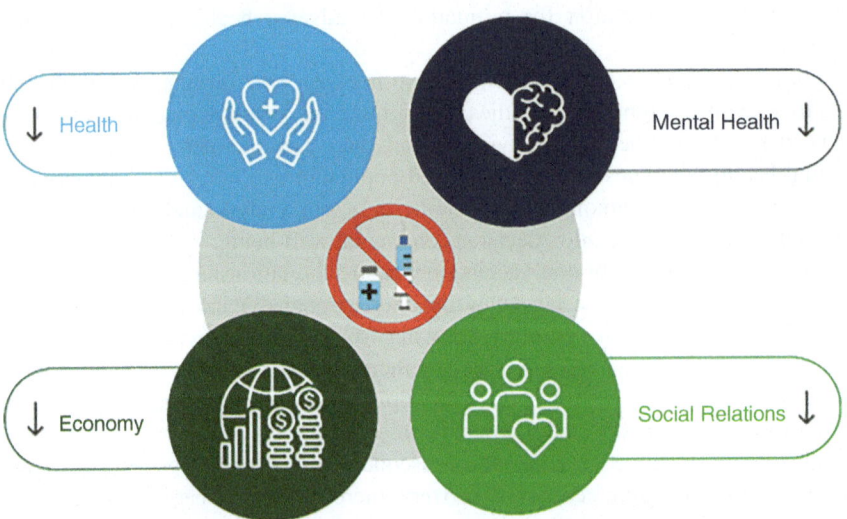

Source: Authors' own compilation of the non-vaccination effects on health, mental health, social relationships, and economics.

Fig. 11.1   shows the effects of non-vaccination on health, mental health, social relationships, and the economy. *Source*: Authors' own compilation of the non-vaccination effects on health, mental health, social relationships, and economics.

11.2   The Drivers of Vaccine Hesitancy

In this section, we briefly revisit the drivers of vaccine hesitancy, also discussed in Chap. 10 (Sects. 10.3.1 and 10.3.2), as it explains why people were vaccine-hesitant. We also consider studies that estimated the number of people who were reluctant to receive the vaccine.

In Chap. 10, we found the following factors were driving vaccine hesitancy globally: concern about the safety of vaccines, mistrust of the government and distrust of others, lower perceived seriousness of the COVID-19 pandemic, and right-wing political affiliation. Additionally, we see the following play a role: conservative religious beliefs, distrusting scientists, and pandemic conspiracy beliefs.

An interesting question is, how many people were found to be vaccine-hesitant? We do not have a specific number, though a few studies estimated the number of people within a country or a region. A study by Fieselmann et al. (2022) in Germany found that even though the vaccination against COVID-19 has been available in Germany since December 2020, about 30% of the population reported not wanting to be vaccinated. In this study, they analysed social media to determine the factors that drove vaccine hesitancy, and the reasons they found are similar to the causes we found in our research (Greyling & Rossouw, 2022). These reasons include low perceived benefits of getting vaccinated, a low perceived risk of being infected with COVID-19, concerns of potential adverse effects from the vaccine, poor health literacy, mistrust and spiritual and religious beliefs.

Other studies reporting similar ratios of people being vaccine-resistant are a study by Raut et al. (2023) for a region in Canada and Muhajarine et al. (2021) for a city in India.

These studies only report vaccine hesitancy in specific regions and countries. Therefore, it is not representative, and further study is needed to determine vaccine hesitancy globally as this can be a severe threat to stop the mitigation of pathogens in future pandemics.

11.3   The Effect of Non-vaccination on Health

In this section, we discuss the effects of non-vaccination on health, including the impact on herd immunity and the health of individuals, communities and the international community. We refer to announcements and publications of the World Health Organization (WHO) and Centres for Disease Control and Prevention (CDC) to inform us on these matters. We also discuss a study that estimated deaths due to non-vaccination to give an idea of the death costs of non-vaccination.

One of the significant effects of vaccination refusal is the threat of not achieving herd immunity. Herd immunity occurs when a high percentage of a population becomes immune to a disease through vaccination or previous infections (WHO, 2020). However, reaching herd immunity through vaccination is preferred as it limits severe sickness, hospitalisation, and loss of lives. Once herd immunity has been achieved, it constrains the spread of the disease. Thus, herd immunity protects vulnerable individuals and those who may not be able to receive vaccines, such as infants or people with medical conditions, from being infected (also refer to Sect. 10.2).

Some of the more apparent effects of non-vaccination are related to the health of individuals. Non-vaccination increases their risk of contracting and experiencing severe COVID-19 infections and even death. If individuals contract COVID-19, it could lead to hospitalisations and intensive care admissions, which raises private and public healthcare costs (CDC, 2023). The vaccine does not only protect against COVID-19 but also reduces the likelihood of new variants emerging, which safeguards populations from unknown variants and their effects (WHO, 2023).

Non-vaccination or vaccination refusal among vulnerable populations, including the elderly and those with comorbidities, had exacerbated effects on health. As these groups were already vulnerable, refusing to be vaccinated led to a higher probability of these groups suffering severe consequences, which could lead to acute health problems and, in some instances, death (WHO, 2023).

Vaccine hesitancy is not only a threat to an individual's health, but it also affects the health of a community. If an insufficient number of people get vaccinated and herd immunity is not reached, community members are still susceptible to contracting the disease with adverse effects on health.

Not being vaccinated can have far-reaching global effects, as diseases can easily cross borders in today's interconnected world. Therefore, vaccine hesitancy in one part of the world can affect global health security.

An interesting study related to vaccine hesitancy by Gupta et al. (2021) estimated how many deaths could have been averted by vaccination in the US among unvaccinated adults from 30 May 2021 to 3 September 2022. Their result showed that at least 232,000 deaths could have been prevented during the 15 months had they been vaccinated with at least a primary series of vaccines. However, they mention that more granular data are needed for an exact estimate. Future studies related to estimating the cost of vaccination should be conducted as it signals the importance of taking up vaccines.

In conclusion, we note that non-vaccination severely affects the health of individuals, communities, and the global community, threatening to achieve herd immunity, which can lead to prolonged pandemics and higher costs in life.

11.4   The Effect of Non-vaccination on Mental Health

We often read about the severe effects of COVID-19 on mental health, though the literature mainly refers to the effects of lockdowns, which increased loneliness, depression, and anxiety. The choice of being vaccinated or not and its relationship to mental health has received less attention. We turn to a selection of the literature published since the onslaught of COVID-19 to find insights into the complex relationships between vaccination and mental health.

In Chaudhuri and Howley's study (2022), vaccinated people experienced a significant improvement in mental health. Their results showed that the improvements in mental health were most pronounced among older and clinically vulnerable groups, thus those groups that had a higher risk of contracting COVID-19 and who were at risk of suffering severe outcomes. On the other hand, they found that those who refused vaccination suffered from increased anxiety related to contracting COVID-19, which negatively affected their mental health.

Penner et al. (2023) investigated the intricate relationship between COVID-19 vaccine hesitancy and parental mental health in the US. They found that COVID-19 vaccine hesitancy among parents, particularly when coupled with underlying medical conditions, was consistently associated with higher levels of depressive symptoms, anxiety, and acute stress symptoms related to COVID-19. Interestingly, individuals who had received at least one dose of the COVID-19 vaccine exhibited heightened levels of acute stress. However, this uptake in vaccination was not associated with higher depressive or anxiety symptoms. These results from the US contribute to our understanding that COVID-19 vaccine hesitancy is associated with higher levels of psychological distress.

A study by Kollamparambil et al. (2023) in South Africa highlights the relationship between mental distress, vaccine distrust, and vaccine hesitancy. They found that not trusting vaccines significantly predicts vaccine hesitancy and that mental anguish increases the likelihood of vaccine distrust. Thus, according to them, the relationship between vaccine hesitancy and mental health is not direct but mediated through vaccine trust. To put it differently, friendly individuals with a high risk of depression were more concerned about vaccine safety, which led to increased vaccine hesitancy.

In the study "Reluctance to Vaccination, Mental Health, and Quality of Life in Palestinians" by Veronese et al. (2023), the authors explore the effect of mental health in terms of depression, anxiety, stress, fear of COVID-19 and quality of life (QoL) on the reluctance to be vaccinated in a population of Palestinian adults living in occupied Palestinian territories and Israel. They found that mental health plays a role in vaccine reluctance in the West Bank and Gaza and that the failing Palestinian healthcare system increased the sense of dread among the population and made them less likely to get vaccinated. The opposite was found for those residing in Israel.

Smith et al. (2021) emphasise the need for targeted strategies to address vaccine hesitancy, especially among groups with mental health difficulties, including severe mental illness. Individuals with severe mental illness are at a higher risk of complications and mortality from COVID-19, making vaccination particularly important for this group. The study recommends specific discussions from mental health professionals, peer workers, vaccine education, and awareness tailored for those with severe mental illness.

In conclusion, these studies emphasise the critical relationship between COVID-19 vaccination, mental health, and vaccine hesitancy and agree that vaccine hesitancy is significantly related to mental health. Individuals with pre-existing mental health conditions may be particularly vulnerable to the mental health effects of non-vaccination. The added stress and anxiety related to the pandemic and the decision not to get vaccinated can increase mental health conditions. It is essential to recognise that mental health is a crucial component of overall well-being, and the decision to get vaccinated can have implications for an individual's mental state. Policymakers must be aware that interventions are needed to support mental health during pandemics. The interventions and policy measures should ensure that accurate information about vaccines is provided, and addressing concerns with empathy and understanding are essential steps in promoting a healthy and resilient community. Furthermore, there is a need for tailored interventions to address vaccine hesitancy and promote vaccination among people who suffer from mental health-related conditions.

11.5   The Effect of Non-vaccination on Social Relationships

The reluctance of individuals to get vaccinated during COVID-19 affected their social relationships with friends, family and within communities (Jagoo, 2021). However, there is a scarcity of research directly related to these matters. Research more often investigates the relationship between non-vaccination and health or economic consequences, which might indirectly affect social relationships. Some literature explores the drivers of vaccine hesitancy, of which social relationships are one. However, in this section, we explore the reverse relationship of how vaccine hesitancy itself affects social relationships. Due to the scarcity of academic literature, we draw insights from anecdotes, media reports and the shared experiences of people during COVID-19 times. The effect of non-vaccination on social relationships is essential and should be studied in future research to gauge the social capital costs associated with non-vaccination.

Our readings show that vaccine hesitancy or reluctance to be vaccinated leads to a breakdown in trust between different groups and significantly affects social relationships. For example, the media highlights strained relationships within families and marriages due to differing views on vaccination. For instance, headlines such as "The Divorce Diaries: I have split with my husband because he is an anti-vaxxer and I am a nurse" (O'Connell, 2022), "Vaccine wars, how the decision not to get the shot is tearing loved ones apart" (Abramson, 2021) underlines the divide caused by vaccine hesitancy. Furthermore, individuals who were pro-vaccination found it challenging to comprehend resistance to vaccines, which strained relationships with vaccine-hesitant individuals. Pro-vaxxers often distanced themselves from non-vaccinated individuals for fear of contracting the disease.

In a reported case, parents in New Zealand requested unvaccinated blood for their son. Instead, they lost guardianship of their child, emphasising the devastating consequences of vaccine-related decisions on social relationships between the public and the government (Corlett, 2022). Additionally, vaccine hesitancy increased social divides along racial, political, cultural, or religious lines. Misinformation about the COVID-19 vaccine within specific religious groups fostered beliefs that the vaccine is harmful and impacted by hostile forces. These beliefs further deepened the divides within communities. Such community divides limit open dialogue and cooperation and hamper collective efforts to combat the disease.

The spread of vaccine hesitancy within social networks and social media platforms such as Facebook, Twitter and Instagram influence individuals' beliefs and behaviours. Therefore, vaccine hesitancy, often driven by misinformation, spreads within these networks and spreads negative attitudes. This, in turn, contributes to widening social divides both in physical and virtual communities.

Considering these facts, vaccine hesitancy can have far-reaching effects on social relationships within families, among friends, in communities, and across social networks. These impacts extend beyond social relationships and spill over to economic and political spheres.

11.6   The Effect of Non-vaccination on the Economy

Vaccine hesitancy, the reluctance or refusal to be vaccinated despite the availability of vaccines, has significant consequences for countries' economies. We identified the following economic implications from the literature due to vaccine hesitancy. Please refer to Sect. 2.4 for our discussion on the macroeconomics of flu.

Vaccine hesitancy leads to slower economic recovery. In the paper "Economic Considerations in COVID-19 Vaccine Hesitancy and Refusal: A Survey of the Literature" by Rawlings et al. (2022), they refer to the WHO expressing concern that non-vaccination will have a lasting and profound impact on socioeconomic recovery (WHO, 2021). Furthermore, they mention that even in developed countries where the standard of healthcare is high, and supply is not an issue, a proportion of adults refuse to be vaccinated against COVID-19 or are hesitant to accept vaccination. The issue of vaccine hesitancy and refusal is critical, and the Organisation for Economic Cooperation and Development (OECD) issued the following warning: *"Many countries are observing increasing levels of distrust in government capacity to handle the crisis and implement coherent policies. This has resulted in declining compliance with public health-related rules and increasing scepticism about long-term economic recovery. More broadly, the pandemic has triggered widespread disinformation that has undermined both understanding and acceptance of science and public policy, and this extends to the issue of vaccine acceptance"* (OECD, 2021).

These statements by the WHO and the OECD indicate that vaccine hesitancy should be addressed and that high levels of vaccine hesitancy will prolong the COVID-19 pandemic by restricting the efforts to achieve herd immunity. This can lead to ongoing outbreaks, lockdowns, and restrictions, which in turn slows down economic recovery.

Vaccine hesitancy can lead to higher rates of COVID-19 cases, putting strain on healthcare systems and increasing healthcare costs. Vaccine hesitancy increases spending on hospitalisations, treatments, and long-term care for those affected by the virus. This increases private and public spending on healthcare. The higher spending on healthcare and decreased spending on other essential products and domains can lead to an economic downturn and hardships for people. Farrenkopf (2022) showed that in the US, between November and December 2021, over 692,000 preventable hospitalisations occurred in unvaccinated individuals, resulting in a cost of over $13.8 billion to the US economy. The increased health costs directly impacted the economy.

Persistent concerns about the virus due to vaccine hesitancy can reduce consumer confidence. This can result in decreased spending on non-essential goods and services, impacting businesses in various sectors. According to Leer (2021), the chief economist of Morning Consult's Global Economic Research found that even before being vaccinated, adults who planned on being vaccinated were more confident in the economy than those who did not plan on getting vaccinated or remained undecided. He further said that the future path of consumer confidence in the US depends on the speed of vaccine uptake, as it positively affects consumer confidence.

Vaccine hesitancy can have a severe effect on the tourism and hospitality industry. Travel restrictions and safety concerns can reduce travel, impacting hotels, airlines, restaurants, and related businesses. An analysis of the first phase of the pandemic by Lim et al. (2021) described widespread adverse effects from international border closures in Australia, affecting the tourism sectors and reducing migration. This significantly affected the labour market and negatively impacted domestic demand and consumption. The most severe effects were associated with accommodation and food services, transport, arts and recreation, and retail trade.

Due to vaccine hesitancy and ongoing health concerns, individuals are more cautious about returning to work. This affects the productivity of a country. Furthermore, Burdorf et al. (2021) found vaccine refusal was more prevalent among lower-skilled and lower socioeconomic-status individuals, often employed in at-risk occupations. This affects the production and mining industries with severe economic consequences (Burdorf et al., 2021). Although vaccine hesitancy is more prevalent among lower-skilled workers, it also affects higher-skilled workers. It reduces labour force participation across all industries, hurting economic activities and implying slower economic growth.

Vaccine hesitancy forces governments to allocate more resources towards public health campaigns, education, and outreach efforts to combat vaccine hesitancy, increasing government costs. They may also need to invest in additional healthcare capacity to manage outbreaks. Unforeseen and excessive government spending can lead to higher public debts and enormous budget deficits, negatively affecting economic growth.

Vaccine hesitancy is a global issue, and its effects are not confined to individual countries. In an interconnected world, the economic repercussions of vaccine hesitancy in one region can spill over to the global economy. Therefore, vaccine hesitancy in any country has a global economic effect.

From the literature reviewed, we surmise that vaccine acceptance is crucial for global economic recovery and sustained growth. Efforts to promote vaccine education, accessibility, and confidence can play a vital role in mitigating the economic impact of the pandemic and ensuring a return to normality and economic prosperity.

11.7 Summary

This chapter addressed the likely negative consequences of vaccine hesitancy or refusal. Reviewing the literature, we found that vaccine hesitancy significantly affected people's health and mental health.

Vaccine hesitancy has devastating effects on social capital as it drives relationships apart, with extended consequences that can spill over to economic and political spheres. It also has significant economic consequences, slowing economic recovery and growth.

Therefore, it is of utmost importance that health departments and policymakers employ strategies and policies to attain positive attitudes towards vaccines.

References

Abramson, A. (2021). Vaccine wars: how the decision not to get the shot is tearing loved ones apart. https://www.theguardian.com/us-news/2021/aug/28/vaccine-wars-decision-vaccine-tearing-loved-ones-apart. Accessed on 16.10.23.

Burdorf, A., Porru, F., & Rugulies, R. (2021). The COVID-19 pandemic: One year later–an occupational perspective. *Scandinavian Journal of Work, Environment & Health, 47*(4), 245–247.

Centres for Disease Control and Prevention (CDC). (2023). Benefits of getting a COVID-19 vaccine. https://www.cdc.gov/coronavirus/2019-ncov/vaccines/vaccine-benefits.html#:~:text=COVID%2D19%20Home-,Benefits%20of%20Getting%20Vaccinated,-Updated%20Sept.%2022. Accessed on 20.09.23.

Chaudhuri, K., & Howley, P. (2022). The impact of COVID-19 vaccination on mental well-being. *European Economic Review, 150*, 104293.

Corlett, E. (2022). Parents who refused 'vaccinated blood' transfusion speak out after court places Baby W in care. The Guardian. https://www.theguardian.com/world/2022/dec/08/parents-who-refused-baby-w-nz-vaccinated-blood-transfusion-speak-out-new-zealand. Accessed on 27.09.23.

Farrenkopf, P. M. (2022). Focus: Vaccines: The cost of ignoring vaccines. *The Yale Journal of Biology and Medicine, 95*(2), 265.

Fieselmann, J., Annac, K., Erdsiek, F., Yilmaz-Aslan, Y., & Brzoska, P. (2022). What are the reasons for refusing a COVID-19 vaccine? A qualitative analysis of social media in Germany. *BMC Public Health, 22*(1), 1–8.

Greyling, T., & Rossouw, S. (2022). Positive attitudes towards COVID-19 vaccines: A cross-country analysis. *PLoS One, 17*(3), e0264994.

Gupta, S., Cantor, J., Simon, K. I., Bento, A. I., Wing, C., & Whaley, C. M. (2021). Vaccinations against COVID-19 may have averted up to 140,000 deaths in the United States: Study examines role of COVID-19 vaccines and deaths averted in the United States. *Health Affairs, 40*(9), 1465–1472.

Jagoo, K. (2021). Differing opinions on the Covid 10 vaccine and our relationships. https://www.verywellmind.com/covid-19-vaccine-and-our-relationships-5201171. Accessed on 27.09.23.

Kollamparambil, U., Oyenubi, A., & Nwosu, C. (2023). Mental distress, COVID-19 vaccine distrust and vaccine hesitancy in South Africa: A causal mediation regression analysis. *PLoS One, 18*(3), e0278218.

Leer, J. (2021). Vaccines' Boost to Consumer Confidence Depends on Persuading Holdouts to Get Their Shots. Morning Consult Pro. https://pro.morningconsult.com/analysis/vaccine-consumer-confidence-holdouts. Accessed 02.11.23.

Lim, G., Nguyen, V., Robinson, T., Tsiaplias, S., & Wang, J. (2021). The Australian economy in 2020–21: The COVID-19 pandemic and prospects for economic recovery. *Australian Economic Review, 54*(1), 5–18.

Muhajarine, N., Adeyinka, D. A., McCutcheon, J., Green, K. L., Fahlman, M., & Kallio, N. (2021). COVID-19 vaccine hesitancy and refusal and associated factors in an adult population in Saskatchewan, Canada: Evidence from predictive modelling. *PLoS One, 16*(11), e0259513.

O'Connell, A. (2022). The divorce diaries: "I've split with my husband because He's An Anti-Vaxxer—And I'm a Nurse". https://capsulenz.com/be/divorce-diaries-antivaxxer/ Accessed on 28.09.23.

Organisation for Economic Cooperation and Development (OECD). (2021). Enhancing public trust in COVID-19 vaccination. https://www.oecd.org/coronavirus/policy-responses/enhancing-public-trust-in-covid-19-vaccination-the-role-of-governments-eae0ec5a/. Accessed on 28.09.23.

Penner, F., Contreras, H. T., Elzaki, Y., Santos, R. P., & Sarver, D. E. (2023). COVID-19 vaccine hesitancy, vaccination, and mental health: A national study among US parents. *Current Psychology*, 1–11.

Raut, A., Samad, A., Verma, J., & Kshirsagar, P. (2023). Acceptance, hesitancy and refusal towards COVID-19 vaccination. *Clinical Epidemiology and Global Health, 21*, 101283.

Rawlings, L., Looi, J. C., & Robson, S. J. (2022). Economic considerations in COVID-19 vaccine hesitancy and refusal: A survey of the literature. *Economic Record, 98*(321), 214–229.

Smith, K., Lambe, S., Freeman, D., & Cipriani, A. (2021). COVID-19 vaccines, hesitancy and mental health. *BMJ Mental Health, 24*(2), 47–48.

Veronese, G., Mahamid, F., El-Khoudary, B., Bdier, D., Ismail, A., & Diab, M. (2023). Quality of life is associated with vaccine reluctance via mental health and fear of COVID-19: An exploratory investigation on a Palestinian sample. *Psychology, Health & Medicine, 28*(9), 2647–2659.

World Health Organization (WHO). (2020). Coronavirus disease (COVID-19): Herd immunity, lockdowns and COVID-19. https://www.who.int/news-room/questions-and-answers/item/herd-immunity-lockdowns-and-covid-19. Accessed on 05.10.23.

World Health Organization (WHO). (2021). Vaccine inequity undermining global economic recovery. https://www.who.int/news/item/22-07-2021-vaccine-inequity-undermining-global-economic-recovery. Accessed on 05.10.23.

World Health Organization (WHO). (2023). COVID-19 advice for the public: Getting vaccinated. https://www.who.int/emergencies/diseases/novel-coronavirus-2019/covid-19-vaccines/advice#:~:text=Safe%20and%20effective%20vaccines%20help,you%20by%20your%20health%20authority. Accessed on 04.08.23.

Part III
Policy Perspective and Future Preparedness

The concluding trio of chapters are focused on practical policy advice to combat vaccine hesitancy and mitigate the impact of future global pandemics. We begin by discussing the policy lessons we have learned from previous pandemics, introduced in Chap. 2, and how these can be seen as a prologue for the future.

Following this, we analyse the various policies implemented during COVID-19, initially presented in Chaps. 3 through 5. Some of these policies decreased trust in institutions and ensured millions of people remained out of reach of effective prevention and treatment approaches. Part III concludes by providing best-case practices and sound government policy, building upon the findings from Part II, aimed at addressing COVID-19 vaccine hesitancy and preparing for future pandemics.

Chapter 12
Policy Lessons from Past Pandemics: The Past Presents a Prologue for the Future

Abstract This chapter extends our discussion from Sects 2.2–2.3. It draws on the lessons we can learn from previous pandemics, recognising that history serves as a prologue for the future in pandemic preparedness and response. Drawing from the experiences of previous pandemics since the 1900s (summarised in Table 2.1 in Sect. 2.2), including the more recent COVID-19 outbreak (Chap. 13), we examine the strategies and policies that have effectively mitigated the impact of these global health crises.

Historically, pandemics have posed significant threats to human societies, resulting in widespread illness, death, and socioeconomic disruption. By studying the policies implemented during past pandemics, we gain valuable insights into curbing the spread of infectious diseases and minimising their socioeconomic impacts. Notably, we highlight the success of simultaneous technological, social, and legislative approaches, alongside efforts to strengthen health infrastructure and protect healthcare workers in limiting the spread of viruses and treating the infected.

Effective policy responses to past pandemics have included early identification of infected individuals, testing, isolation, contact tracing, and quarantine measures. Information campaigns emphasising preventive measures such as social distancing, mask-wearing, and hand hygiene have also played a crucial role. Additionally, the development and deployment of vaccines, informed by research on vaccines used in previous pandemics, have been instrumental in building immunity against new pathogens.

However, we also acknowledge that policy effectiveness can be hindered by delays in implementation, inadequate health infrastructure, unclear communication, and public non-compliance with preventive measures. International collaboration and coordination are crucial in combating global health crises, necessitating knowledge sharing, resource sharing, and expertise exchange.

Therefore, this chapter underscores the importance of learning from past pandemics to inform future policy responses. While successful policy measures have been identified, their effectiveness depends on specific circumstances, timing, implementation, and institutional trust. By applying the lessons learned from past

© The Author(s), under exclusive license to Springer Nature Switzerland AG 2024
S. Rossouw, T. Greyling, *Resistance to COVID-19 Vaccination*, Human Well-Being Research and Policy Making,
https://doi.org/10.1007/978-3-031-56529-8_12

pandemics, policymakers can better prepare for and respond to future health emergencies, safeguarding public health and minimising socioeconomic disruption.

Keywords Policy · Spanish flu · Asian flu · Hong Kong flu · SARS · Swine flu · HIV/AIDS

I had a little bird.
    And its name was Enza.
    I opened the window.
    And in-flew-Enza.

12.1 Introduction

This chapter extends our discussion from Sects. 2.2–2.3 and draws on the lessons we can learn from previous pandemics and how the past presents a prologue for the future. Pandemics have historically posed significant threats to human societies, leading to widespread illness, death, and socioeconomic disruption. Each pandemic suffered by the human race has been unique as each new virus is spread differently, causing different symptoms with varying mortality rates. However, by studying the policies and building on the experiences during previous pandemics, we gain valuable insights to curb the spread and limit the socioeconomic impacts of future pandemics. Pandemics that have historically threatened human lives since the 1900s are summarised in Table 2.1 in Sect. 2.2; however, we also add COVID-19, which started in 2020, to this list[1] (Munnoli et al., 2020). Therefore, Chap. 12 considers the strategies and policies that effectively mitigated the impact of these pandemics.[2]

The majority of the pandemics in the 1900s, excluding SARS, Ebola and HIV, were flu pandemics and were outbreaks of a new Influenza A virus, which infected people effectively and sustainably, as the population did not have immunity against these new viruses (Centres for Disease Control and Prevention, 2020). SARS and Ebola were caused by positive-sense RNA viruses belonging to the Coronaviridae family, similar to COVID-19. Interestingly, SARS-CoV (SARS) shares almost 90 per cent of the genome with SARS-CoV-2 (COVID-19) (Chan et al., 2020).

---

[1] COVID-19 is discussed in Chap. 13.

[2] Note that we exclude Ebola due to its uniqueness and difference from other pandemics. The Ebolavirus causes the disease. It appeared mostly in West Africa, and it caused approximately 11,310 deaths. To learn more about the policies implemented during Ebola, consult the World Health Organization (https://www.who.int/) and Centres for Disease Control and Prevention (https://www.cdc.gov/).

12.2 Measures Introduced to Curb the Spread of Pandemics

Public health care policies and measures are introduced to curb the spread of the virus during a pandemic. We can distinguish between outbreak control and prevention measures.

Outbreak control refers to the measures and actions taken to control an ongoing disease outbreak and limit the spread in a region. The primary goal when an outbreak occurs is to identify and control the spread of the disease rapidly. The key strategies include rapid response to curb the outbreak by mobilising resources and staff, identifying and isolating infected cases, tracing individuals that had contact with infected individuals, monitoring them for symptoms, testing, and quarantine. Providing medical care to those infected reduces the severity of the illness and limits complications. Information campaigns (communicating) and education about the transmission and prevention strategies are essential. Disseminating accurate information to the public and healthcare workers and sharing information with international organisations about disease outbreaks, new cases, and pathogens-related information is necessary for transparency.

Prevention refers to measures to stop the disease's initial spread and reduce the risk of future outbreaks. Prevention strategies are implemented before an outbreak occurs, aiming to minimise the disease's transmission. Before developing a vaccine, the key measures include encouraging personal protection, such as hand washing, wearing masks, and maintaining physical distance. Health campaigns should be run to educate people about the transmission of the disease and methods to avoid these risks. Implementing sanitation and hygiene practices in public places minimises the spread, for example, by limiting the number of people in a closed or open environment. Once a vaccine has been developed, measures should be taken to encourage people to get vaccinated in order to develop immunity against the disease.

Therefore, the main difference is that outbreak control focuses on managing and containing an ongoing disease outbreak, whereas prevention aims to minimise the disease's initial spread and prevent outbreaks. However, both approaches are crucial in effectively managing infectious diseases (Vora et al., 2023).

The policy measures introduced during pandemics can be divided into public healthcare measures, which include limiting the spread of the virus and protection against the virus; healthcare infrastructure, public healthcare campaigns (education); international communication and cooperation; distribution of medicines, research and development and data collection.

In Table 12.1, we summarise the factors related to the previous pandemics, including the name of the pandemic, the countries or regions most affected, the pathogen, the estimated number of deaths, and the policy measures introduced to mitigate the impact of the pandemic. For example, the Spanish flu occurred from 1918 to 1919; the regions most affected were Europe, Australia, Africa and North America. The pathogen was H1N1 Influenza A. It is estimated that between 20 million and 50 million people died during the pandemic. At that time, there was no vaccine, and public healthcare measures and policies were essential to prevent the spread of the disease and save human lives (Barry, 2020). Scientists actively worked on developing a vaccine, but before it could be launched, the Spanish flu disappeared in the 1919s (Tambolkar et al., 2022). Also, refer to our discussion in Sect. 2.2.1. The other pandemics are summarised similarly in Table 12.1. It is important to note that the list of policies mentioned in Table 12.1 is extensive; however, these policies vary from country to country and within regions.

The policy measures implemented during the previous pandemics include early identification of cases through surveillance, voluntary and enforced quarantine or isolation, social distancing, avoiding public gatherings, preventing overcrowding of carriages, and school closure. Implementation of sanitation laws included restaurants and bars having to sterilise their plates and cups, prohibiting roller towels and

Table 12.1 Global pandemics since the 1900s, countries affected, pathogen and severity, and policy measures

Pandemic/ years	Countries	Pathogen / Deaths	Policy measures
Spanish flu 1918–1919	Europe, Australia, Africa and North America	H1N1 Influenza A virus 20–50 million deaths	**Public Health Care** *Outbreak control* Early identification of cases through surveillance Voluntary and enforced quarantine or isolation Social distancing Avoid public gatherings Overcrowding prevention is also on tramways and railway carriages School closure *Sanitation laws* Restaurants and bars had to sterilise their plates and cups Prohibit roller towels and everyday drinking glasses in public restrooms *Education and Campaigns* Newspaper and leaflet information on the therapeutic benefits of water A health teaching campaign was also held involving schoolteachers, postal workers, and Boy Scouts *Border crossings and travel* Limiting travel Closing borders Medical staff at border crossings *Prevention* Wearing masks Hand washing Using a disinfectant mouthwash to safeguard the oropharynx Prohibiting spitting in the street Care for health care workers, nurses and doctors. *Interventions by local health departments* Provide free soap and clean water as needed Services for the removal of human waste *Health infrastructure* New spaces were opened up for the sufferers of the disease *Vaccinations* It was unavailable during the Spanish flu, but existing vaccination serums were used to immunise people

Table 12.1 (continued)

Pandemic/ years	Countries	Pathogen / Deaths	Policy measures
Asian flu 1956–1958	China, Singapore, Hong Kong and the US	H2N2 Influenza A virus Two million deaths	**Public Health Care** *Outbreak Control* Disease surveillance and reporting Early detection and response to outbreaks Quarantine of people exposed to the virus Isolation of infected individuals *Travel restriction* Screening measures and quarantine of travellers coming from affected areas *Prevention* Education and campaigns Education about the symptoms *Methods of transmission and prevention of the disease* Hygiene, washing hands, respiratory etiquette (covering nose and mouth when sneezing) Vaccination campaigns *Vaccinations* Efforts for early development of a vaccine By August 1957, a vaccine was developed and distributed Vaccination programmes prioritise health workers and vulnerable populations to reduce the severity and spread of the pandemic
Asian flu 1956–1958	China, Singapore, Hong Kong and the US	H2N2 Influenza A virus TWO million deaths	**Public Health Care** *Outbreak Control* Disease surveillance and reporting Early detection and response to outbreaks Quarantine of people exposed to the virus Isolation of infected individuals *Travel restriction* Screening measures and quarantine of travellers coming from affected areas *Prevention* Education and campaigns: Education about the symptoms *Methods of transmission and prevention of the disease* Hygiene, washing hands, respiratory etiquette (covering nose and mouth when sneezing) Vaccination campaigns *Vaccinations* Efforts for early development of a vaccine By August 1957, a vaccine was developed and distributed Vaccination programmes prioritise health workers and vulnerable populations to reduce theseverity and spread of the pandemic

(continued)

Table 12.1 (continued)

Pandemic/ years	Countries	Pathogen / Deaths	Policy measures
Hong Kong Flu 1968	Hong Kong, Singapore, Vietnam/ Philippines, India, Australia, Europe and the US	H3N2 Influenza A virus one million deaths	**Public Health Care** Detection of the pathogen Care for health care workers, nurses, and doctors *Health Infrastructure* Increase healthcare infrastructure Increasing hospital beds and setting up temporary medical facilities Management of capacity and the influx of patients *Outbreak Control* *Contact tracing and quarantine and the use of quarantine centres* Isolation of the infected Identifying high-risk areas *Travel and border control* Screening measures Quarantine of people coming from affected areas *Prevention* Education and campaigns about the symptoms Transmission and prevention Promoting personal hygiene, such as handwashing, respiratory etiquette, and staying home when sick Wearing masks *Community* *Social distancing* *International Communication Cooperation* Sharing information with international health organisations *Vaccinations* Although a vaccine was developed against the virus, it became available only after the pandemic had peaked in many countries
SARS 2002–2003	China, Hong Kong, Taiwan, Singapore, Canada	SARS-CoV virus, which is a type of coronavirus 774 deaths	**Public Health Care** *Outbreak control* Strict infection control Isolation Contact tracing Quarantine measures *Border crossings and travel* Travel restrictions *Prevention* Education and Campaigns Implemented extensive public health campaigns to raise awareness: symptoms, preventive measures, hygiene practices, seeking medical attention and vaccination *International Collaboration* Governments and international health organisations, such as the World Health Organization (WHO), collaborated and shared information. They coordinated response efforts and guided affected countries *Vaccinations* The SARS outbreak was contained by 2004 Due to the rapid containment, the development of a SARS vaccine was deprioritised, and no licensed vaccine was produced for SARS-CoV The knowledge gained and research efforts from the SARS outbreak contributed to developing COVID-19 vaccines; some have been authorised and administered to combat the ongoing COVID-19 pandemic

Table 12.1   (continued)

Pandemic/ years	Countries	Pathogen / Deaths	Policy measures
Swine Flu 2009	The US, Mexico, Canada, Europe (UK, Spain, France, Germany and others), Asia (Japan, China, South Korea and more), Australia and New Zealand	H1N1 Influenza A virus 100,000 deaths	**Public Health Care** *Outbreak control* Enhanced surveillance systems to track the spread of the virus School and workplace intervention—encouraging remote work, flexible leave and social distancing in educational and workplace settings *Border crossings and travel* Travel advisories and restrictions, especially for regions heavily affected by the virus Screening checks at airports and other points of entry to identify potential cases *Prevention* Education and Campaigns Implemented extensive public health campaigns to raise awareness: symptoms, preventive measures, hygiene practices, seeking medical attention and vaccination *International Collaboration* Governments and international health organisations, such as the World Health Organization (WHO), collaborated and shared information. They coordinated response efforts and guided affected countries *Vaccinations* Vaccine development was prioritised Once the vaccine was approved, governments initiated mass vaccination campaigns to administer the vaccine to populations
HIV/AIDS pandemic 2005–2012	Africa, globally 131 countries	HIV/AIDS 36 million deaths	**Public Health care** *Prevention* No heterogeneous sex Use of condoms Personal hygiene Testing Treatment *Education and Campaigns* Bringing awareness De-stigmatisation of HIV/AIDS Care and support programs *Vaccinations* No vaccine is available

Source: Authors' summaries are based on various sources (Barry, 2020; CDC, 2020; Chan et al., 2020; Munnoli et al., 2020; Piret & Boivin, 2021; Vora et al., 2023)

everyday drinking glasses in public restrooms, as well as washing hands and wearing face masks. Education campaigns included informing the public about the pathogen's spread and the measures taken to limit infections. Steps were also taken to limit travel and border crossings. Lastly, the development of vaccines and the policies related to the distribution of vaccines and encouraging vaccine uptake were implemented.

12.3   Measures Introduced to Mitigate the Economic Effects of Pandemics

Although we do not discuss the specific economic policies introduced during each pandemic in Table 12.1, we recognise that apart from the significant health effects (morbidity and mortality), pandemics also cause substantial economic losses. Therefore, we briefly mention examples of economic policies introduced to mitigate the economic effects of pandemics (also refer to Sect. 2.4, where we discuss the macroeconomics of flu).

During pandemics, governments have introduced fiscal stimulus packages to support affected sectors, promote recovery, and mitigate the economic impact of the pandemic. These measures could include tax incentives, subsidies, and infrastructure spending to support industries most affected by the pandemic (tourism). Furthermore, the policies could provide financial assistance, loan guarantees, or subsidies to help businesses cope with economic pressures and minimise unemployment.

Other policies may include rent relief programs, eviction moratoriums, or emergency housing assistance to prevent homelessness and ensure housing stability for those affected by the pandemic. Transfers payments to those who lost their work or could not earn an income during the pandemic to alleviate the economic pressures. These policy measures differed between countries and regions (OECD, 2020).

12.4   Successful Policy Responses to Mitigate the Spread of Pandemics

From the measures taken during previous pandemics to limit the spread of the virus, it seems that the simultaneous implementation of technological, social and legislative approaches, as well as the strengthening of the health infrastructure and the protection of healthcare workers, proved to be successful in limiting the spread of the virus and treating the infected during the early days of the pandemics (Munnoli et al., 2020). For example, early identification of the infected persons, testing, isolation of the infected, contact tracing, and quarantine proved effective. Information campaigns on the precautions that need to be taken, including social distancing, mask-wearing, avoiding public gatherings and washing hands regularly, were also influential. Methods of transmission to inform people to limit exposure to the virus, transborder controls, international communication and sharing information on the pathogen helped during previous pandemics.

Historically, considering the pandemics we reviewed, vaccines were not available at the time of outbreaks. Still, except for the Spanish flu, vaccines were rapidly developed after the outbreak of a new pathogen and populations were vaccinated to build immunity against the virus. Research on vaccines used during previous pandemics, such as polio, H1N1, measles, SARS and other viral diseases, has contributed to the early development of vaccines.

12.5   Unsuccessful Policy Responses

Policy responses per se are not unsuccessful. However, the effectiveness of policy measures during pandemics varies depending on the specific circumstances, the timing, implementation and the trust in the institutions that implement the measures.

Policies can be less effective if there are delays in implementing measures, for example, travel restrictions, isolation or quarantine. Additionally, if the health infrastructure, including the healthcare facilities, diagnostic capabilities, and surveillance systems, is insufficient, it can contribute to the rapid spread of the disease.

Furthermore, communication is essential. If communication is not clear, consistent and accurate, it can lead to confusion, misinformation, and non-compliance with preventive measures. There is also a need for public compliance with preventative measures, such as wearing masks, practising good hand hygiene, and maintaining social distancing to increase containment efforts.

As pandemics are global health crises, international collaboration and coordination, such as knowledge sharing, sharing of resources, and expertise, are essential to combat the pandemic.

12.6   Summary

In this chapter, we discussed the policies implemented during previous pandemics to learn from the past as a prologue for the future. We discussed the policy measures implemented to curb the spread of historic pandemics, such as the Spanish flu of 1918 (H1N1), the Asian flu (H2N2) of 1957, the Hong Kong flu (H3N2) of 1968, Human Immunodeficiency Virus (HIV)/Acquired Immunodeficiency Syndrome (AIDS) (HIV is the virus that causes AIDS) epidemic from 1981 to the present, Severe Acute Respiratory Syndrome (SARS) in 2002 and 2003, Swine flu (H1N1) from 2009 to 2010.

From the measures taken to limit the spread of the virus during previous pandemics, it seems that the simultaneous implementation of technological, social and legislative approaches, strengthening of the health infrastructure and the protection of healthcare workers proved to be successful in mitigating the effects of the pandemics.

The measures implemented historically to limit the spread of pandemics are successful. However, the effectiveness varies depending on the specific circumstances, the timing and implementation, and the trust in the institutions that implement the measures.

References

Barry, J. M. (2020). *The great influenza: The story of the deadliest pandemic in history*. Penguin UK.

Centres for Disease Control and Prevention (CDC). (2020). Pandemic Influenza. https://www.cdc.gov/flu/pandemic-resources/index.htm#:~:text=A%20flu%20pandemic%20is%20a,population%20do%20not%20have%20immunity. Accessed on 18.07.23.

Chan, J. F. W., Kok, K. H., Zhu, Z., Chu, H., To, K. K. W, Yuan, S., et al. (2020). Genomic characterisation of the 2019 novel human-pathogenic coronavirus isolated from a patient with atypical pneumonia after visiting Wuhan. *Emerging Microbes & Infections, 9*(1), 221–236.

Munnoli, P. M., Nabapure, S., & Yeshavanth, G. (2020). Post-COVID-19 precautions based on lessons learned from past pandemics: a review. *Journal of Public Health*, 1–9.

Organisation for Economic Cooperation and Development (OECD). (2020). Tax and Fiscal Policy in Response to the Coronavirus Crisis: Strengthening Confidence and Resilience. https://read.oecd-ilibrary.org/view/?ref=128_128575-o6raktc0aa&title=Tax-and-Fiscal-Policy-in-Response-to-the-Coronavirus-Crisis. Accessed on 18.07.23.

Piret, J., & Boivin, G. (2021). Pandemics throughout history. *Frontiers in Microbiology, 11*, 631736.

Tambolkar, S., Pustake, M., Giri, P., & Tambolkar, I. (2022). Comparison of public health measures taken during Spanish flu and COVID-19 pandemics: A Narrative Review. *Journal of Family Medicine and Primary Care, 11*(5), 1642.

Vora, N. M., Hannah, L., Walzer, C., Vale, M. M., Lieberman, S., Emerson, A., & Epstein, J. H. (2023). Interventions to Reduce Risk for Pathogen Spillover and Early Disease Spread to Prevent Outbreaks, Epidemics, and Pandemics. *Emerging Infectious Diseases, 29*(3), 1–9.

Chapter 13
Policy Responses to COVID-19

Abstract This chapter explores the diverse policy responses implemented during the COVID-19 pandemic, drawing insights from both successful measures and notable failures. Building upon the policy lessons discussed in previous chapters, we examine how various countries responded to the unprecedented challenges posed by the pandemic.

Firstly, we highlight successful policy measures adopted by countries such as Vietnam, Taiwan, and South Korea, which swiftly contained the spread of COVID-19 through proactive measures and efficient healthcare systems. Additionally, European countries like Germany and Austria capitalised on their robust healthcare infrastructure to implement effective containment measures. In contrast, Nordic countries, except for Sweden, employed strategies that resulted in lower infection rates while minimising economic disruptions.

However, alongside these successes, we also analyse national and international failures in addressing the pandemic. Drawing on insights from the Lancet Commission report, we discuss systemic issues such as procurement challenges, corruption, and the proliferation of vaccine hesitancy. Moreover, we delve into the implications of controversial policies like mandatory vaccination, the use of COVID-19 passports and the perceived lack of stringency in vaccine development.

Ultimately, many of these failures could have been mitigated through increased trust in governmental and scientific institutions, transparent communication, enhanced cooperation to address capacity constraints, and improved emergency preparedness plans. International collaboration is critical in navigating future health crises, underscoring the importance of collective action and global solidarity in combating pandemics.

Keywords Policy · COVID-19 · Government failure · Rollout of vaccines · Mandatory vaccinations · COVID-19 passports · Vaccine hesitancy

© The Author(s), under exclusive license to Springer Nature Switzerland AG 2024
S. Rossouw, T. Greyling, *Resistance to COVID-19 Vaccination*, Human Well-Being Research and Policy Making,
https://doi.org/10.1007/978-3-031-56529-8_13

13.1   Introduction

This chapter builds on the policy measures implemented in previous pandemics to mitigate the spread of the disease reviewed in Chap. 12 by discussing different policy responses introduced during the COVID-19 pandemic. We first consider successful policy measures implemented by various countries to contain the spread of the virus and mitigate the effects of COVID-19 (refer to Chap. 14 for policies specific to increasing COVID-19 vaccine uptake). Second, we consider government failures in implementing COVID-19 policies and the rollout of vaccines. Vaccine failures include procurement issues, mandatory vaccination using COVID-19 passports, and increased vaccine hesitancy.

13.2   Successful Policy Responses to COVID-19

During the COVID-19 pandemic, countries and regions implemented different policy responses to mitigate the impact of COVID-19 before the development and roll-out of vaccines. The success rates differed from country to country. In this section, we first refer to the measures implemented as advised by the World Health Organization (WHO) and the Organisation for Economic Cooperation and Development (OECD). Secondly, we discuss a selection of countries recognised in the news and academic journals as having success stories.

13.2.1   WHO and OECD Recommended Measures

Which policy interventions were expected to be implemented to limit the spread of COVID-19? Considering the recommendation of the WHO (2020), the countries' primary goal was to control the pandemic by slowing down the transmission and reducing the mortality rate. The WHO's (2020) global objectives to reach these goals included a collection of actions: to mobilise all, control cases, suppress community transmissions, reduce mortality, and develop vaccines and therapeutics.

According to the OECD, while there were no effective vaccines that could protect people against the COVID-19 virus, it was essential to have containment and mitigation policies in place (OECD, 2020). Containment strategies aim to minimise the risk of transmission from infected to non-infected individuals to stop the outbreak, including early detection and tracing of infected individual's contacts or the confinement of affected persons.

Mitigation strategies are designed to curb the transmission of the disease, reduce the demand for healthcare resources, and include measures such as social distancing, lockdowns, and improved personal and environmental hygiene. Both containment and mitigation strategies operate in tandem to curb the transmission of the

Fig. 13.1 Successful mitigation and containment strategies implemented by countries. *Source*: Shutterstock (n.d.) *COVID-19 response* (https://www.shutterstock.com/search/covid-19-response)

virus by suppressing outbreaks and slowing down the disease. Figure 13.1 shows images related to the containment and mitigation policies implemented. The most widely used COVID-19 measures included school and workplace closures, cancellations of public events and restrictions on public gatherings, stay-at-home orders, restrictions on travel, testing and contact tracing, and general information campaigns (Ritchie et al., 2020). We will refer to these measures below when we discuss our country examples.

13.2.2 Country Success Stories

Here, we discuss countries recognised in the news and academic journals as examples of different levels of success in implementing COVID-19 policies, including Vietnam, Taiwan, and South Korea, which showed early advances in combatting COVID-19 (Boccia et al., 2020). We also discuss Germany and Austria as affluent countries in Europe. Finland, Denmark, and Iceland are conventional Nordic cases with lower death rates than most European countries. At the same time, Sweden deviated with a soft strategy, attempting to build herd immunity without too many other disruptions. New Zealand is one of the most widely discussed countries regarding successful government intervention.

Vietnam's reactions to COVID-19 were remarkable, seeing that its neighbour was China, the epicentre of COVID-19 (Jones, 2020). Vietnam managed to limit the number of cases and deaths. They proactively embraced an early preventive containment strategy, initiating preparations for the impending pandemic as early as January 2020, even before they confirmed any cases. After the first confirmed case, its emergency plan was in place and swung into action. This encompassed travel restrictions, closing the border with China and increasing health checks at borders and other strategic places. Additionally, schools were closed and remained so for several months. Simultaneously, an extensive and labour-intensive contact tracing initiative was launched. By mid-March 2020, people who entered the country or had contact with a confirmed case were mandated to enter quarantine facilities and stay there for 14 days. People were generally willing to comply with coronavirus restrictions.

Taiwan reacted efficiently and proactively, relying on the knowledge it gained from the SARS outbreak. This proactive stance led to the formation of a National

Health Command Centre (NHCC) and additional units dedicated to public health emergencies (Su et al., 2017). Taiwan's initiatives commenced with inspecting plane passengers arriving from Wuhan (the city from which COVID-19 originated) and a blanket entry ban for Wuhan residents. Using new data and technology, Taiwan's measures included case identification, quarantine protocols for suspicious cases and a proactive approach to finding positive cases. The government facilitated access to affordable facemasks. They proactively identified patients with severe respiratory symptoms using National Health Insurance database information. The government established a hotline number that citizens were asked to use to report suspicious symptoms or cases, which enabled authorities to trace and map infected individuals. Educating the public about the coronavirus and taking precautionary measures contributed to their success (HealthManagement.org, 2020; Duff-Brown, 2020; Wang et al., 2020).

South Korea acted swiftly and followed the 3T strategy (Trace, Test, Treat) (Kim, 2021). Their approach relied on active, accessible, and massive screening for symptomatic individuals, contacts, and travellers. Schools were closed, working remotely was encouraged, and large gatherings were banned. Notably, there were no lockdowns or restrictions to movement. South Korea relied on open health informatics, including real-time information on COVID-19 disseminated by the government through dedicated websites, mass media, phone messages and mobile applications (Reynolds & Baeck, 2020). By 19 March 2020, approximately 85 drive-through testing stations were established, facilitating the testing of nearly 20,000 people daily. People under mandatory self-quarantine were monitored through a government and police-operated app, with strict penalties for violators (HealthManagement. org, 2020; Moon, 2020; Kim, 2021).

Germany and Austria adopted aggressive and early control strategies. As a result, their death toll was lower than many other European countries, such as Italy, France, and Spain (Gibney, 2020). Protecting risk groups and the well-functioning healthcare system have contributed to the success. Austria took several restrictive actions in March, which appeared to be successful. It presented Europe's first crisis exit plan in April 2020 (Robinet-Borgomano, 2020). Their actions speak of a balanced approach.

Iceland had an effective containment strategy, which required testing and tracing infected individuals as well as their contacts. Iceland followed WHO's recommendations in its strict test, trace, and isolate policy. Besides this, Iceland's strategy emphasised cooperation and coordination (Hsieh & Child, 2020) and leveraged health informatics and the latest technology, including a government-supported automated tracing app (Johnson, 2020).

Denmark and Finland followed a typical Nordic approach, emphasising civic responsibilities while simultaneously imposing reasonable restrictions. Denmark adopted social distancing, lockdown, and screening of people with mild symptoms. In mid-April 2020, they eased the rules and focused on widespread testing. They were the first to re-open daycare and primary schools in Europe. They followed policies to limit the spread of the virus but also ensured that the epidemic did not threaten the functioning of the welfare state (Marin, 2020). Finland followed similar policies. They called it a hybrid strategy, protecting people from the spread of the virus through targeted mitigation and suppression measures. Finland was initially slow to implement travel restrictions. However, after the government realised the challenges in controlling widespread transmissions, they declared an emergency and publicised a comprehensive set of 19 strategic measures to tackle the coronavirus epidemic. One of the government's principles was to focus on implementing non-pharmaceutical measures in the least harmful way to society. Finland followed the textbook-style "test, trace, isolate and treat" but did it flexibly (Finnish Government, 2020).

Sweden was the only country in Europe that uniquely adopted a strategy rooted in the concept of herd immunity. Their approach aimed to maintain normalcy and minimise the pandemic's impact on the economy and everyday life. Diverging from more stringent measures seen in other countries, Sweden instead relied on the collective responsibility of its population to create a socially generated mitigation effect. For example, it kept shops and cafes open. It is noteworthy that by Nordic standards, Sweden experienced a higher number of confirmed infections and death toll. However, the effects on its economy and education were limited (Marin, 2020).

New Zealand announced that it eliminated COVID-19 on 8 June 2020. It lifted social distancing and business restrictions but closed its borders with mandatory isolation and quarantine (Baker & Wilson, 2020). New Zealand's achievement can be explained by it being a remote island with a relatively low population density. When New Zealand had only 100 confirmed cases and no deaths, it closed its borders to foreign travellers and applied a 14-day quarantine rule to people returning from abroad. Ten days later, it introduced total lockdown measures, which were strict by international standards. The duration of the restrictions extended over a month before the New Zealand government started a gradual easing process. Another critical factor was the effective communication of regulations and new rules, facilitating people's understanding and acceptance of the exceptional measures. Moreover, the New Zealand government adhered to the precise guidelines for handling the virus. Their strategy involved identifying, testing, isolating and caring for every case while tracing and quarantining every contact. Lastly, another beneficial move was ramping up testing capacity (Matthews, 2020). Although measures such as lockdowns successfully contained the virus, they devastated the economy, caused immense mental harm to individuals and families, and strained social relationships (refer to Sect. 5.2.2).

If we consider the actions within regions, the European Union demonstrated cooperation in procuring and distributing medical supplies, sharing information, and coordinating response efforts across borders, which increased the successful implementation of COVID-19 measures in the region. This serves as an example of what should be achieved globally.

In conclusion, agile-adaptive approaches, transparency in communicating COVID-19 measures and risks, and citizens' voluntary cooperation were critical to successfully implementing COVID-19 policies. Furthermore, the healthcare system's capacity and the countries' preparedness level were crucial in successfully mitigating the pandemic.

13.3   Unsuccessful Policy Responses Regarding the COVID-19 Policy and the Vaccine Uptake

In this section, we discuss the unsuccessful policy responses that led to the global failure of handling the COVID-19 pandemic. Second, we investigate and discuss the failures related to the vaccine rollout, and lastly, we acknowledge the controversies surrounding vaccine development and the likely adverse effects of vaccines.

In the words of the Lancet Commission on lessons for the future from the COVID-19 pandemic, *"As of 31 May 2022, there were 6.9 million reported deaths and 17.2 million estimated deaths from COVID-19, as reported by the Institute for Health Metrics and Evaluation (IHME; throughout the report, we rely on IHME estimates of infections and fatalities; note that the IHME gives an estimated range, and we refer to the mean estimate). This staggering death toll is both a profound tragedy and a massive global failure at multiple levels. Too many governments have failed to adhere to basic norms of institutional rationality and transparency, too many people—often influenced by misinformation—have disrespected and pro-tested against basic public health precautions, and the world's major powers have failed to collaborate to control the pandemic* (Sachs et al., 2022).

As is evident from the report and Fig. 13.2, the COVID-19 response was a global failure at many levels. Figure 13.2 shows that COVID-19 adversely affected peo-ple's health and countries' economies, directly affecting individuals' consumer spending and secondary and tertiary services. It had a severe impact on social rela-tionships and increased mental health issues.

We summarise the main points of the report below (Sachs et al., 2022):

(i) The report criticises the WHO. It mentions that they reacted too slowly and cautiously in responding to the COVID-19 pandemic. The delays include warnings about human virus transmission, declaring a Global Health Emergency, considering travel protocols, and supporting face masks.

COVID-19 RESPONSE: A MASSIVE GLOBAL FAILURE

Widespread failures at multiple levels worldwide have led to millions of preventable deaths and a reversal in progress towards sustainable development for many countries.

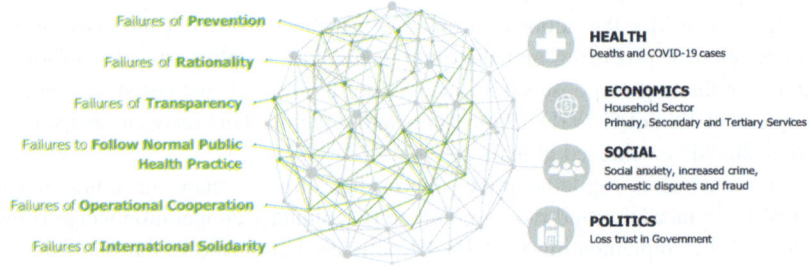

Fig. 13.2   COVID-19 response: A massive failure. *Source*: Authors own figure

(ii) Furthermore, many governments were slow to react to the severity of the pandemic and did not have existing plans to contain it. This lack of planning extended to travel protocols, testing strategies, public health policies, data collecting standards, and communication about the virus.

(iii) The public resisted the health measures introduced to limit the spread of the disease, such as wearing face masks and getting vaccinated. The resistance seems to be due to a lack of social trust, low confidence in government, limited health literacy, insufficient, and misinformation on social media.

(iv) The report emphasised that public policies did not consider behavioural and social sciences that could have explained people's behaviour (refer to Chap. 14 for more details). Understanding how people make decisions and react to health measures could have built trust and improved the implementation.

(v) Additionally, the report highlights the failure of public policies to address the unequal burden the COVID-19 measures and pandemic placed on essential health workers, children, women, those in special care facilities, and individuals with chronic conditions or disabilities.

(vi) There were also inequalities regarding the success of addressing COVID-19. High-income countries with robust health systems were better equipped to handle the pandemic, while low-income and middle-income countries faced challenges due to a lack of funding and strong health systems.

(vii) Vaccines were developed rapidly, with many controversies on the development protocol and the efficacy and likely side effects coming to light. Nonetheless, the vaccines were developed in record time. However, there was a lack of coordinated global approaches to manage the vaccine distribution, with poorer countries unable to access sufficient doses.

(viii) The COVID measures, such as lockdowns, had an immense adverse effect on economies, and the recovery of these economies depends on effective fiscal and monetary policies, which are often lacking in poorer countries (Brodeur et al., 2021; Greyling et al., 2021).

(ix) During Covid-times emergency, global financing would have contributed to limiting the global effect of the virus. However, financial flows from high-income to low-income regions were minimal, which means the devastating impact of the virus on the health of populations and struggling economies was severe.

In addition to the global failures mentioned in the Lancet Commission report (Sachs et al., 2022), there were also failures regarding the procurement and rollout of vaccines, vaccine-mandated policies, and various failures coming to light regarding the COVID-19 vaccine.

The procurement and distribution of the vaccines presented risks of corruption. The corruption risks were related to the theft of vaccines within the distribution systems, leakages in emergency funding designated for developing and distributing vaccines, nepotism, favouritism, and corrupted procurement systems (UNODC, n.d.). Many of these risks have become a reality, and there are ongoing investigations into these matters. Often, we also found evidence of political interference in the procurement and distribution of vaccines and a lack of coordination between public health sectors and significant role players. These actions slowed down the distribution of the vaccines (Moss et al., 2022).

Certain countries are also making accusations of being overcharged for vaccines. South Africa has revealed that companies that supplied COVID-19 vaccines overcharged them. For example, Johnson & Johnson (J&J) charged South Africa 15 per cent more per dose of its COVID-19 vaccine than it charged the European Union. In contrast, Pfizer-BioNTech charged South Africa nearly 33% more than it reportedly charged the African Union. This was revealed after the vaccine contracts were opened for scrutinisation. However, the companies still need to respond to these accusations (Ismail, 2023). Administrative bottlenecks, paperwork, and complex eligibility criteria slowed the vaccination process, frustrating healthcare workers and the sick as it limited the supply of vaccines (Tichy, n.d.). In certain countries, this slowed down the distribution of vaccines considerably.

The policies that encouraged or mandated people to be vaccinated, such as vaccine passports, were questionable and negatively impacted vaccine acceptance (refer to Chaps. 4, 5 and 9). Additionally, government responses to mandate the vaccine caused harm to both social relationships and the economy. Mandatory vaccine policies caused more societal harm than good, as people's vaccination status determined their access to work, education, public transport, and social life. This impinged on human rights, promoted stigma and social polarisation, and hurt the health and well-being of populations. The vaccine passports also increased mistrust in the government (Bardosh et al., 2022).

In 2023, various failures regarding the development and efficacy of the Pfizer vaccine came to light (refer also to Sect. 3.6). The efficacy of the COVID-19 vaccine was questioned with the emergence of new COVID-19 variants. The initial vaccines gave coverage to the Omicron variant, though the efficacy of the vaccines decreased against new variants. This raised the question of whether people should be vaccinated if the vaccine only offered low coverage. The COVID-19 vaccine has been exposed to suffering from side effects. Some side effects have been revealed and publicised since 2020, but many might only be shown over time. In 2021, the US Food and Drug Administration warned that the Pfizer and Moderna coronavirus vaccines could cause mild cases of heart inflammation seen in some teens and young adults following vaccination, though the incidence rate is low. In Chap. 11, Sect. 11.3, we also discussed the negative effect of vaccines on mental health. A few studies showed that vaccines negatively affected the mental health of the vaccinated.

In 2023, an alleged scandal came to light regarding Pfizer vaccines: Pfizer did not test the vaccine to prevent transmission of COVID-19 before it was made available to the public. However, the message people received was that it was safe to get vaccinated and that being vaccinated would protect others (Fullfact.org, 2022). Furthermore, allegations against Pfizer were made stating they considered (i) mutating the virus to create effective vaccines in advance (illegal gain-of-function research), (ii) declaring COVID-19 a "cash cow" for years, and (iii) claiming that US federal regulators went 'easy' on Pfizer in hopes of getting jobs later (Daily Wire News, 2023).

Lastly, as mentioned in previous chapters (Chap. 10 and Sect. 11.2), vaccine hesitancy is one of the adverse outcomes of the COVID-19 drive to increase vaccination uptake. Vaccine hesitancy was mainly driven by a lack of clear communication about the importance of being vaccinated, the safety of the vaccines, distrust in governments, and misinformation related to vaccines that was mainly spread using social media. Future uptake of vaccines can be at risk due to the actions taken by governments during COVID-19.

To conclude, we revealed the global failure of COVID-19 responses nationally and internationally. Furthermore, we showed evidence of failure related to COVID-19 policy measures and various discrepancies and trust issues associated with COVID-19 vaccines.

13.4   Summary

In this chapter, we discussed the successful policy measures implemented by countries that swiftly mitigated and contained the spread of COVID-19, such as Vietnam, Taiwan and South Korea. We also discussed European countries fortunate enough to have adequate healthcare systems that increased the efficiency of measures taken to curb the spread of the disease, such as Germany and Austria. Finally, we considered the strategies followed in Nordic countries, where the infection rates were lower than in other European countries, except for Sweden. Sweden had less severe restrictions, trying to maintain normal conditions to minimise the adverse effects on their economy.

Secondly, we considered national and international failures in addressing the COVID-19 pandemic. We discussed the report of the Lancet Commission on lessons for the future from the COVID-19 pandemic. Furthermore, we described the vaccine failures, including procurement issues, corruption, mandatory vaccination using COVID-19 passports, increased vaccine hesitancy and the lack of stringency related to vaccine development.

Many of these failures could have been avoided if there had been increased trust in the government's and scientists' capabilities, honesty, cooperation in dealing with capacity constraints, improved emergency plans and international collaboration.

References

Baker, M., & Wilson, N. (2020). *New Zealand hits zero active coronavirus cases. Here are five measures to keep it that way.* The Conversation. https://theconversation.com/new-zealand-hits-zero-active-coronavirus-cases-here-are-5-measures-to-keep-it-that-way-139862. Accessed on 03.11.23.

Bardosh, K., De Figueiredo, A., Gur-Arie, R., Jamrozik, E., Doidge, J., Lemmens, T., et al. (2022). The unintended consequences of COVID-19 vaccine policy: Why mandates, passports and restrictions may cause more harm than good. *BMJ Global Health, 7*(5), e008684.

Boccia, S., Ricciardi, W., & Ioannidis, J. P. (2020). What other countries can learn from Italy during the COVID-19 pandemic? *JAMA Internal Medicine, 180*(7), 927–928.

Brodeur, A., Clark, A. E., Fleche, S., & Powdthavee, N. (2021). COVID-19, lockdowns and Well-being: Evidence from Google trends. *Journal of Public Economics, 193*, 104346.

Daily Wire News. (2023). Project Veritas Video: Pfizer Official Says Firm Considering Ways To 'Mutate' Virus Via 'Directed Evolution'. https://www.dailywire.com/news/project-veritas-video-pfizer-official-says-firm-considering-ways-to-mutate-virus-via-directed-evolution. Accessed on 18.08.23.

Duff-Brown, B. (2020). *How Taiwan used big data, transparency and a central command to protect its people from coronavirus.* Stanford University. https://fsi.stanford.edu/news/how-taiwan-used-big-data-transparency-central-command-protect-its-people-coronavirus. Accessed on 19.08.23.

Finnish Government. (2020). Government decides on plan for hybrid strategy to manage coronavirus crisis and for gradual lifting of restrictions. Government Communications Department, Press release. https://valtioneuvosto.fi/en/-//10616/hallitus-linjasi-suunnitelmasta-koronakriisin-hallinnan-hybridistrategiaksi-ja-rajoitusten-vaiheittaisesta-purkamisesta. Accessed on 20.08.23.

Fullfact.org. (2022). Claims that Pfizer vaccine wasn't tested on preventing transmission need context. https://fullfact.org/health/coronavirus-vaccine-pfizer-transmission-test/. Accessed 19.11.23.

Gibney, E. (2020). Whose coronavirus strategy worked best? Scientists hunt most effective policies. *Nature, 581*(7806), 15–17.

Greyling, T., Rossouw, S., & Adhikari, T. (2021). The good, the bad and the ugly of lockdowns during Covid-19. *PLoS One, 16*(1), e0245546.

HealthManagement.org. (2020). Where are the most effective anti-COVID-19 strategies? https://healthmanagement.org/c/hospital/news/where-are-the-most-effective-anti-covid-19-strategies. Accessed on 19.11.23.

Hsieh, L., & Child, J. (2020). What coronavirus success of Taiwan and Iceland have in common. The Conversation. https://theconversation.com/what-coronavirus-success-of-taiwan-and-iceland-has-in-common-140455. Accessed on 12.11.23.

Ismail, S. (2023). South Africa 'held to ransom' by big pharma, overcharged for COVID vaccines. Aljazeera. https://www.aljazeera.com/news/2023/9/6/south-africa-held-to-ransom-by-big-pharma-overcharged-for-covid-vaccines. Accessed on 19.11.23.

Johnson, B. (2020). Nearly 40% of Icelanders are using a covid app—and it hasn't helped much. MIT Technology Review. https://www.technologyreview.com/2020/05/11/1001541/iceland-rakning-c19-covid-contact-tracing/#:~:text=Policy-,Nearly%2040%25%20of%20Icelanders%20are%20using%20a%20covid%20app%E2%80%94and,'%20t%20a%20game%20changer.%E2%80%9D&text=When%20Iceland%20got%20its%20first,entire%20apparatus%20sprang%20into%20action. Accessed on 19.11.23.

Jones, A. (2020). Coronavirus: How 'overreaction' made Vietnam a virus success. BBC News. https://www.bbc.com/news/world-asia-52628283. Accessed on 12.11.23.

Kim, P. S. (2021). South Korea's fast response to coronavirus disease: Implications on public policy and public management theory. *Public Management Review, 23*(12), 1736–1747.

Marin, C. (2020). Europe versus coronavirus—putting the Danish model to the test. Institut Montaigne. https://www.institutmontaigne.org/en/expressions/europe-versus-coronavirus-putting-danish-model-test#:~:text=Governed%20by%20a%20left%2Dwing,borders%20early%20in%20the%20crisis. Accessed on 13.11.23.

Matthews, A. (2020). Coronavirus: 5 things New Zealand got right. DW, Science. https://corporate.dw.com/en/jacinda-ardern-leadership-in-coronavirus-response/a-53733397. Accessed on 12.11.23.

Moon, M. J. (2020). Fighting COVID-19 with agility, transparency, and participation: Wicked policy problems and new governance challenges. *Public Administration Review, 80*(4), 651–656.

Moss, E., Patterson, N. A., & Seals, B. F. (2022). An examination of US COVID-19 vaccine distribution in New Jersey, Pennsylvania, and New York. *International Journal of Environmental Research and Public Health, 19*(23), 15629.

Organisation of Economic Cooperation and Development (OECD). (2020). OECD Policy Responses to Coronavirus (COVID-19) Flattening the COVID-19 peak: Containment and mitigation policies. https://www.oecd.org/coronavirus/policy-responses/flattening-the-covid-19-peak-containment-and-mitigation-policies-e96a4226/. Accessed on 2.11.23.

Reynolds, S., & Baeck, P. (2020). Smart cities during COVID-19: How cities are turning to collective intelligence to enable smarter approaches to COVID-19. Digital Leaders. https://digileaders.com/smart-cities-during-covid-19-how-cities-are-turning-to-collective-intelligence-to-enable-smarter-approaches-to-covid-19/. Accessed on 05.11.23.

Ritchie, H., Mathieu, E., Rodés-Guirao, L., Appel, C., Giattino, C., Ortiz-Ospina, E., et al. (2020). COVID-19: School and workplace closures. Our World in Data. https://ourworldindata.org/covid-school-workplace-closures. Accessed on 06.11.23.

Robinet-Borgomano, A. (2020). Europe versus coronavirus-Germany, a resilient model. Institut Montaigne–Blog. https://www.institutmontaigne.org/en/expressions/europe-versus-coronavirus-austria-and-road-new-normal. Accessed on 09.11.23.

Sachs, J. D., Karim, S. S. A., Aknin, L., Allen, J., Brosbøl, K., Colombo, F., et al. (2022). The lancet commission on lessons for the future from the COVID-19 pandemic. *The Lancet, 400*(10359), 1224–1280.

Shutterstock. (n.d.). COVID-19 response. https://www.shutterstock.com/search/covid-19-response. Accessed 20.11.23.

Su, Y. F., Wu, C. H., & Lee, T. F. (2017). Public health emergency response in Taiwan. *Health Security, 15*(2), 137–143.

Tichy, E. (n.d.). Breaking down supply chain bottlenecks in vaccine distribution. Fourkites. https://www.fourkites.com/blogs/breaking-down-bottlenecks-in-vaccine-distribution/. Accessed on 20.11.23.

UNODC. (n.d.). COVID-19 vaccines and corruption risks: preventing corruption in the manufacture, allocation and distribution of vaccines. https://www.unodc.org/documents/corruption/COVID-19/Policy_paper_on_COVID-19_vaccines_and_corruption_risks.pdf. Accessed on 20.11.23.

Wang, C. J., Ng, C. Y., & Brook, R. H. (2020). Response to COVID-19 in Taiwan: Big data analytics, new technology, and proactive testing. *JAMA, 323*(14), 1341–1342.

World Health Organization (WHO). (2020). Key messages and actions for COVID-19 prevention and control in schools. https://www.who.int/docs/default-source/coronaviruse/key-messages-and-actions-for-covid-19-prevention-and-control-in-schools-march-2020.pdf. Accessed on 19.11.23.

Chapter 14
Policy for Future Pandemics: Creating a Positive Attitude Towards Vaccines

Abstract This chapter ties all our findings related to vaccine uptake, positive attitudes towards vaccines, and real-time data to gauge the mood and emotions of nations towards vaccines. The chapter begins by discussing successful policies to create favourable perceptions of vaccines and exploring effective messaging strategies leveraging social media platforms. Furthermore, it discusses the important role of data-driven insights derived from the sentiments and emotions expressed by individuals online in informing policymakers' decision-making processes in real time.

The chapter explains the significance of harnessing real-time social media sentiment data (RTSocMed) to gauge the prevailing mood of nations and guide proactive policy interventions. By employing advanced Natural Language Processing (NLP) techniques, policymakers gain invaluable insights into public sentiments and emotions, enabling them to swiftly anticipate and address emerging concerns. Moreover, integrating geo-tagged social media data facilitates geographically targeted policy responses, enhancing their efficacy and relevance.

An essential aspect highlighted is the role of live dashboards in visualising RTSocMed sentiment data, providing decision-makers with dynamic, easily interpretable insights. These dashboards facilitate the monitoring of evolving public sentiments and enable timely adjustments to policy implementations. Additionally, they empower decision-makers with predictive capabilities, allowing for proactive planning and resource allocation based on anticipated shifts in public mood.

The chapter concludes by emphasising the transformative potential of RTSocMed sentiment data and live dashboards in augmenting policymakers' understanding of population behaviour and reactions to events. It advocates for integrating these innovative data sources into official statistical analyses, thereby effectively enhancing the responsiveness of policymaking processes in addressing societal needs.

Keywords Positive attitudes · Vaccination · Natural language processing ·
Real-time data · Mood · Emotions · Twitter · Dashboards · Statistical offices

© The Author(s), under exclusive license to Springer Nature
Switzerland AG 2024
S. Rossouw, T. Greyling, *Resistance to COVID-19 Vaccination*, Human
Well-Being Research and Policy Making,
https://doi.org/10.1007/978-3-031-56529-8_14

Fig. 14.1 Social media icons. *Source*: Authors' own compilation of icons

14.1 Introduction

This chapter ties all our findings related to vaccine uptake, positive attitudes towards vaccines, and real-time data to gauge the mood and emotions of nations towards vaccines.

First, we will mention successful policies in increasing positive attitudes towards vaccines. Second, we discuss proper messaging to build positive attitudes using social media. Third, we describe how decision-making by policymakers can be enhanced through data-driven information related to the sentiments and emotions of people. Lastly, we describe future developments and recommendations for statistical offices and policymakers on the use of real-time social media data on people's sentiments and emotions. This data deepens the understanding of people's behaviour and reactions to events.

To explain the benefits of real-time emotion and sentiment data, we use our unique Twitter datasets. Note that the use of Twitter as a social media platform for research purposes was abruptly cut short in February 2023.[1] Therefore, our research and development are testing other social media platforms, such as Facebook, Instagram, TikTok, Reddit, LinkedIn, and web search engines, such as Google Trends, to derive new indices of happiness and emotions. Furthermore, we are refining our methods to construct more representative datasets and using advanced sentiment and emotion analysis techniques. Figure 14.1 shows well-known icons of social media platforms. Note that Twitter is no longer available for academic research.

14.2 Policies to Increase Positive Attitudes Towards Vaccines

This section considers the policies from our research that can increase positive attitudes towards vaccines. Our main findings show that increasing trust in vaccines and trust in governments in conducting the vaccine rollout, handling procurement and capacity issues can positively affect vaccine attitudes (refer to Sect. 9.4).

---

[1] A note on Twitter: All academic research projects were discontinued in February 2023 since the take-over of Twitter (2023)—a decision of X, the new name of the Twitter Company. X aims to monetise the service, and researchers cannot afford to pay for access to the API, which amounts to $42,000 a month or more for an enterprise account. This means the end of an era of research projects which contributed a wealth of knowledge on the behaviour of populations driven by sentiment and emotions. This is a significant loss of understanding of populations' collective actions and behaviours.

Elaborating on the measures that could increase vaccine trust, we found that policymakers and health officials should disseminate vaccine information transparently and in layman's terms. This will allow people to comprehend the risks and benefits easily. They can also emphasise the stringent safety and efficacy standards of the COVID-19 vaccine development process.

Governments should use multiple communication strategies and platforms to reach large audiences and give regular updates to inform the public about the latest developments, vaccine availability, and safety updates.

Furthermore, policymakers should be cognisant of people's fears, anger, and other negative emotions related to vaccines, which they can follow using data related to the sentiment and emotions of populations towards vaccines.

Additional measures that can increase positive attitudes towards vaccines are positive vaccination messages delivered by expert scientists and medical professionals and messages by community members explaining their positive experiences regarding vaccine uptake (Salali & Uysal, 2021).

Policymakers can also enhance positive attitudes towards vaccines by focusing on people's sense of collective responsibility. Thereby activating positive emotions such as altruism and hope as part of vaccine education endeavours.

Health department officials and policymakers must raise awareness of emotional manipulations by anti-vaccine disinformation efforts and misinformation spread across social media to influence attitudes towards vaccines negatively.

Increasing the trust in governments in order to increase vaccine uptake successfully includes a combination of actions such as transparent communication, making public practical policy implementations to improve vaccine rollouts, and steps taken to increase community engagement.

From the explained vaccination policy to increase positivity towards vaccine uptake, it is apparent that proper policy measures can contribute to positive attitudes towards vaccines.

14.3   Proper Messaging to Build Positive Attitudes Using Social Media

Policymakers should use suitable messaging strategies to convey positive messages to the public that will increase positive sentiment and positive emotions.

We need to know our target audience before we communicate vaccine messages via social media platforms. The demographic characteristics of different social media platforms differ; therefore, the message should be tailored to the specific audience. For example, users of LinkedIn might have higher levels of education and be older and more sophisticated than users of Instagram. Therefore, the message can be more mature. Instagram users' profiles are primarily teenagers and young adults, likely with lower levels of education than LinkedIn users. The message should be lively and visually attractive to attract the target market.

The message should be positive and empathetic, notwithstanding the target audience, using words that convey positive emotions and encourage positive attitudes (CMG et al., n.d.). For example, messages should not only focus on the side effects of vaccines but should also include additional information on the benefits of vaccination. The side effects should disclose the true nature of the impact and emphasise that post-vaccine symptoms are mild and that the vaccine effectively mitigates severe illness, hospitalisation, and death. It is essential to be transparent and honest to build trust. Any misconceptions should be addressed, and the audience should be referred to reputable sources they can research.

Common concerns about the vaccine, such as safety, side effects, and trust in the vaccines, should be addressed in the messages. Here, it is important to provide information to counter the concerns. Be prepared to answer questions, approaching the audience with understanding and empathy.

Personal stories emphasising the perceived and experienced benefits of vaccination uptake can be powerful and persuasive—for example, sharing individuals' narratives on positive experiences after vaccination.

Any facts related to the vaccines should be clear and accurate, using layman's terms. The message should be easily understood. The message should be in the home language or the official language of the audience.

Furthermore, the messages should include the importance of social responsibility and altruism. We can emphasise that vaccination protects individuals and the greater society, including those who cannot be vaccinated, such as infants, older people and those with health risks.

Using visuals, such as appealing graphics or videos, is important to reach younger audiences and contributes to conveying clear, eye-catching messages with better cognitive retention. Infographics, which portray data and statistics, are more efficient for sharing critical facts. See Fig. 14.2 for the trend in the different negative emotions experienced during the first COVID-19 lockdown. Here, we can clearly see how anger was the first emotion that responded to the lockdown.

We also illustrate the type of messaging that health workers and policymakers should use to attain positive attitudes. Furthermore, we show how statistical offices can adopt our social media real-time data constructed using sentiment and emotion analyses (Natural Language Processing (NLP)) and live dashboards to enhance decision-making.

The finding that the use of animation and humour in messaging positively influences people's moods is interesting. It also increases positive attitudes towards a topic. See Fig. 14.3, which portrays how immune systems develop memory (Donohew et al., 1988).

Another way to portray positive messages about vaccines is to include messages from Influencers and Community Leaders that are respected and have a significant following. The endorsement can increase the message's credibility and reach a wider audience.

Hashtags (#vaccine) have become a popular method to focus attention on a specific topic. Therefore, vaccine awareness hashtags can help gain visibility and become part of a broader conversation.

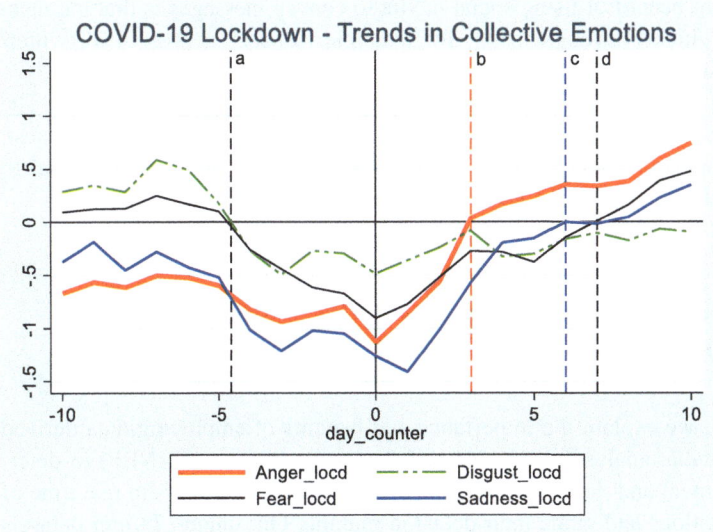

Source: From Collective emotions and macro-level shocks: COVID-19 vs the Ukrainian war. GLO Discussion Paper Series 1210, by R. Rossouw & T. Greyling, 2022.

Fig. 14.2 Infographics to visualise data related to COVID-19 vaccine uptake. *Source*: From Collective emotions and macro-level shocks: COVID-19 vs the Ukrainian war. GLO Discussion Paper Series 1210, by Rossouw and Greyling (2022)

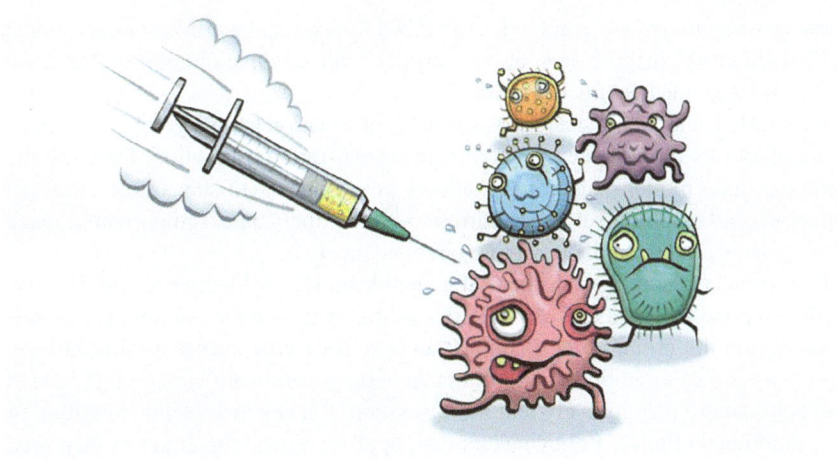

Fig. 14.3 An example of using animation to explain how vaccines help our immune system develop memory. *Source*: From Big Picture Education (2016) (http://bigpictureeducation.com/animation-developing-immunological-memory). In the public domain

A significant benefit of using social media to convey messages is that the message spreads quickly through using, for example, "share" a post of a Twitter/Facebook message (Anne, n.d.).

To conclude, positive communication should consider the target audience. The messages should be in a language easily understood, be informative, with honest, correct information to build trust. Building trust and understanding is crucial to encourage vaccine uptake using social media.

14.4   Decision-Making by Analysing the Sentiment and Emotions of People's Posts on Social Media

In this section, we explain the importance and benefits of employing data derived from social media, analysed using Natural Language Processing (NLP) to determine the sentiment and the emotions of text to inform policymakers in real time of the mood of nations and guide their decision-making. Our unique Twitter datasets from the *Gross National Happiness (GNH).today* website are examples of such data (https://www.gnh.today/) (Greyling et al., 2019). Our research and development aim to construct datasets using various social media platforms like Facebook, Instagram, and TikTok and search engines like Google.

Real-time data constructed from social media posts analysed employing NLP (we refer to this type of data as real-time social media sentiment data (RTSocMed sentiment data)) has various benefits to policymakers. As mentioned, this type of high-frequency time-series data is available from our *GNH.today Happiness Project* (https://www.gnh.today/). It includes the GNH Index and eight different emotions: joy, sadness, trust, disgust, fear, anger, surprise, and anticipation indices. Next, we discuss some of the benefits of RTSocMed.

RTSocMed sentiment data presents timely information to policymakers as social media platforms provide a constant stream of real-time information. Deriving the sentiment and emotions of the data allows policymakers to stay informed about sentiments and emotions related to current events. Timely data is important to make relevant decisions in rapidly changing circumstances.

Policymakers using the information gained from RTSocMed sentiment data can rapidly respond to crises and emergencies as this type of data monitors the moods of nations on the ground. For example, suppose a vaccine intervention negatively impacts a country's emotions (mood). In that case, governments can use RTSocMed sentiment data to preemptively halt the formation of a negative identity, culture, or toxic emotional climate. Policymakers can rapidly mitigate the effect of increased negative emotions by nurturing positive emotions. These can foster trust and effective coping, thereby creating a more positive and amiable disposition that encourages positive decision-making.

A significant benefit is that policymakers can also receive responses via social media opinions on the actions taken. Thus, social media can serve as a platform for social discourse. Policymakers can collect feedback on policy measures they intend to implement before the due date. An example is the use of vaccine passports to mandate vaccination, which was heavily opposed by the public. This signalled negative sentiment and assisted policymakers in redesigning the policy measures to create positive attitudes towards a topic such as vaccines.

The feedback received from social media posts can also be used to evaluate intended or implemented policy. Sentiment analysis discussions related to policies can provide insights into the effectiveness and public reception of those policies. Policymakers can use this information to assess whether an approach achieves its intended goals and make necessary adjustments.

RTSocMed sentiment data can act as an early warning system as it swiftly detects changes in public sentiment and emotions before they become widespread and lead to detrimental actions such as riots. Therefore, policymakers can proactively access the necessary information to avoid crises and disasters.

Geo-tagged social media posts allow us to use data to determine a specific region's dissatisfaction or concerns. This information allows for a more geographically direct approach to address issues and meet the needs of specific communities.

Although using RTSocMed sentiment data has many benefits, we must remember that the data attained this way does not necessarily represent the broader population. However, validation of the data indicated that the data is apt for robust analyses. Additionally, sentiment analysis algorithms may have limitations in accurately capturing the sentiment and emotions of languages and need to be frequently tested for accurate analyses. We advise policymakers to use RTSocMed sentiment data as part of a broader strategy for gathering insights and combining it with other forms of data.

14.5 Dashboards for Statistical Offices and Policymakers

Statistical offices, other government departments, and policymakers can benefit from using our datasets derived from the GNH.today project that tracks real-time changes in people's moods and emotions. Furthermore, using live dashboards to visualise data increases our ability to observe changes, allowing decision-makers to act swiftly. Next, we discuss a few benefits of using RTSocMed sentiment data and live dashboards.

Statistical offices can enhance their ability to capture and interpret the evolving mood of the population by incorporating sentiment analysis into their data collection and analysis toolkit. RTSocMed sentiment and traditional data provide more nuanced and timely insights for informed decision-making.

An additional benefit is that policymakers and decision-makers can track the impact of their decisions in almost real-time. The data indicates acceptance of new policy measures and interventions. Having real-time information, policymakers can make timely adjustments to their policy implementations to improve attitudes.

The use of high-frequency time-series data also gives us the ability to do predictive analysis or nowcasting. We can predict future trends using machine learning algorithms to analyse historical sentiment data. This can help statistical offices anticipate shifts in public mood and proactively plan for potential social, political or economic changes. For example, if negative emotions are predicted to increase continuously, it serves as an early warning system to policymakers of the probability of violent unrest.

As mentioned, RTSocMed sentiment data (all data) can be displayed on live dashboards, which enhances the swift observation of changes in the data series. Any emotions and sentiment related to an event can be displayed in real-time on a live dashboard. The events include sports events, implementing policies (lockdowns), elections, riots, natural disasters and acts of terrorism. The dashboards are dynamic; we can create various boards with different visuals.

We give an example of a dashboard portraying the emotions and sentiment of countries participating in the FIFA Soccer World Cup in 2022 (see Fig. 14.4). We use this example to illustrate the broad application possibilities of the sentiment and emotion data derived from a project such as the *Today Happiness Project*. Figure 14.4 shows the best and worst performing countries' happiness in the FIFA World Cup, depicted on bar charts. It also reflects the happiness of the different countries on a world map. Lastly, it displays all countries' happiness on an area chart in descending order. With a click of a button, this visualisation can change to show the emotion and sentient data per country or to capture all events on a specific day.

Other benefits of dashboards are that they enhance the accessibility and comprehension of data and grant broader access to well-being trends. They assist in transforming intricate data into easily understandable visualisations, making them accessible to a broader audience.

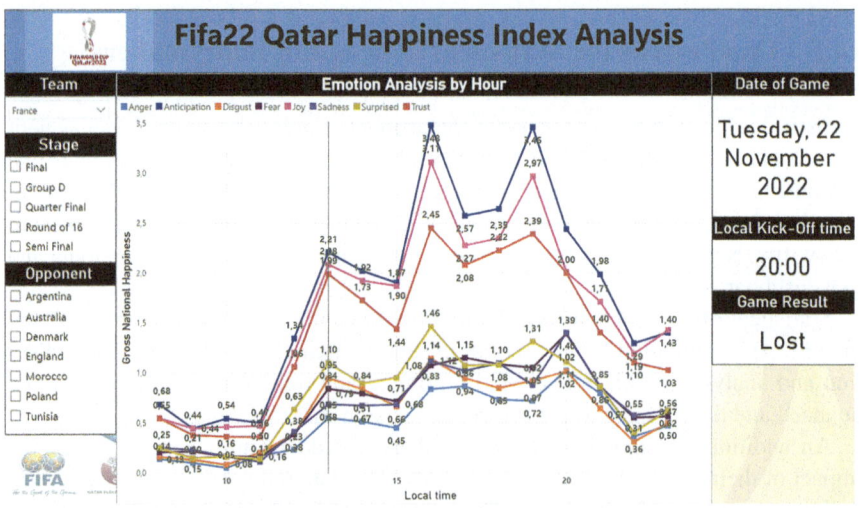

Fig. 14.4 An example of a dashboard giving nuanced information about a specific topic. *Source*: Authors' own Figure using the GNH.today dataset (https://www.gnh.today/) on countries participating in the FIFA Soccer World Cup 2022

The dashboards empower decision-makers with data-driven insights. It empowers them to make timely, informed choices aligned with their objectives. This, in turn, enhances the efficiency of resource allocation, ensuring the needs of the people are met.

In conclusion, RTSocMed sentiment data, such as the time series data derived from the *GNH.today Happiness Project* can enhance decision-makers' insights into the behaviour of populations, and data displayed on live dynamic dashboards leads to swift observations of changes and allows policymakers to take affirmative actions.

14.6   Summary

In this chapter, we brought together our findings related to vaccine uptake, positive attitudes towards vaccines, and using real-time data to gauge the mood and emotions of nations towards vaccines. We reviewed successful policies to change the sentiment towards vaccines to increase vaccine uptake. We examined proper messaging to build positive attitudes using social media.

Next, we described how decision-making by policymakers can be enriched through data-driven information related to the sentiments and emotions of people and the use of state-of-the-art dashboards to visualise data.

Lastly, we described future developments and recommendations for statistical offices and policymakers on using real-time data derived from social media on people's sentiments and emotions. This data deepens the understanding of people's behaviour and reactions to events. We used our unique Twitter datasets as an example of real-time data derived from social media using sentiment and emotion analysis. We recommend that policymakers introduce data derived from sentiment and emotions to their official data and use live dashboards to increase the swift observation of data and changes in data to increase policymakers' response time.

References

Anne. (n.d.). *Five positive uses of social media and how it has changed the world for the better.* We Do Stories. https://www.wedostories.com/content-marketing/five-positive-uses-of-social-media-and-how-its-changed-the-world-for-the-better/. Accessed on 12.10.23.

Big Picture Education. (2016). *Animation developing immunological memory.* http://bigpicture-education.com/animation-developing-immunological-memory. Accessed on 12.10.23.

CMG Health Marketing. (n.d.). Why positive social media messages work right now. https://www.cmghealthmarketing.com/news/why-positive-social-media-messages-work-right-now. Accessed on 13.10.23.

Donohew, L., Sypher, H. E., & Higgins, E. T. (Eds.). (1988). *Communication, social cognition, and affect.* Psychology Press.

Greyling, T., Rossouw, S., & Afstereo. (2019). Gross National Happiness Index. http://gnh.today. Accessed on 5.11.23.

Rossouw, S., & Greyling, T. (2022). *Collective emotions and macro-level shocks: COVID-19 vs the Ukrainian war. GLO Discussion Paper Series 1210*. Global Labor Organization (GLO).

Salali, G. D., & Uysal, M. S. (2021). Effective incentives for increasing COVID-19 vaccine uptake. *Psychological Medicine*, 1–3.

Chapter 15
Conclusion

Abstract The concluding chapter of this book reflects on key insights and lessons learned from the COVID-19 pandemic and vaccination campaigns. It emphasises the importance of vaccines in pandemic control and achieving herd immunity while acknowledging that they are not the sole solution. Antiviral medications serve as complementary tools to prevent severe outcomes in future outbreaks. The chapter underscores the profound impact of vaccine hesitancy on health, mental well-being, social dynamics, and the economy, urging proactive measures to address misinformation and rebuild trust. Critically, it highlights missed opportunities in transparent communication and effective vaccine rollout strategies, suggesting that governments and pharmaceutical companies must regain public confidence to ensure successful vaccination campaigns. Moreover, it critiques the collateral damage caused by non-pharmaceutical interventions like lockdowns, advocating for more targeted approaches in future crises. Vaccine mandates are scrutinised for their infringements on personal liberties and potential to exacerbate hesitancy, offering information campaigns and collective responsibility for future-focused strategies instead. The chapter advocates integrating subjective well-being measures into policymaking and leveraging Big Data analytics to monitor public sentiment and guide swift responses. It concludes by emphasising the importance of global collaboration and resilience in navigating health challenges, echoing Sherlock Holmes' maxim to seek truth amidst complexity.

Keywords Lockdown · Mental harm · Antiviral medications · Vaccine hesitancy · Subjective Well-being · Big Data

So, what are the takeaways from this book? Several things come to mind.

First, whether you love or hate the COVID-19 vaccine, it is here to stay as it is the most effective method to combat a pandemic and achieve herd immunity. However, the vaccine alone does not constitute the sole defence against pandemics, as illustrated by the human immune system's resilience during the 1918 influenza outbreak. Additionally, antiviral medications are supplementary pharmaceutical

S. Rossouw, T. Greyling, *Resistance to COVID-19 Vaccination*, Human
Well-Being Research and Policy Making,
https://doi.org/10.1007/978-3-031-56529-8_15

tools at our disposal that can help individuals avoid hospitalisation in future outbreaks.

Second, vaccine hesitancy negatively affects health, mental health, social relationships and the economy. Non-vaccination increases the risk of individuals contracting and experiencing severe COVID-19 infections and even death and affects the health of a local and global community. Additionally, people who refuse to be vaccinated suffer from increased anxiety related to contracting COVID-19, which negatively affects their mental health. Furthermore, the reluctance of individuals to get vaccinated negatively affected social relationships with friends, family, and others within communities. Vaccine hesitancy strains healthcare systems and increases healthcare costs, reduces consumer confidence, severely affects the tourism and hospitality industry and affects the productivity of a country, thereby leading to a slower economic recovery.

Third, much of the COVID-19 vaccine hesitancy people displayed (and still display) could have been mitigated. If governments had more openly disseminated information regarding the vaccine in layman's terms and acknowledged people's fears, anger, and other negative emotions, there could have been a more positive attitude towards the vaccine. Additionally, governments could have fostered our trust in them if they successfully handled procurement and capacity issues and their vaccine rollouts by delivering what they promised when they promised it. In parallel, pharmaceutical companies did not help people overcome their hesitancy to get vaccinated. The rapid development and approval, transparency surrounding the efficacy, and excess deaths undermined the public's trust in vaccination initiatives. Controversial allegations such as gain-for-function research, whether true or not, have seriously damaged future vaccination campaigns. Governments and pharmaceutical companies have some serious work to do if they want to persuade individuals to take booster shots to prevent new outbreaks. If they fail, future vaccination campaigns may be a lost cause.

Fourth, non-pharmaceutical policy measures such as lockdowns, intended to slow the spread of the virus and save lives before the option of vaccination, directly led to the immense mental harm done to individuals and families, disproportionately affected disabled persons, severely impacted businesses and caused a global economic recession. Weighing up the benefits of locking down entire populations against the cost to societies, this policy should not be contemplated at the same scale and length in the future. Governments must practice forward-thinking and ensure that health expenditure is directed towards ensuring health sectors are resourced sufficiently. Ensuring supply-side factors can cope with increased demand will enable governments to use lockdown only as a last resort for specific cohorts (vulnerable and elderly communities) and short time periods. Additionally, suppose governments succeed in decreasing vaccine hesitancy. In that case, large-scale lockdowns will not be necessary, which is crucial since the harm done by locking people down will most likely have long-lasting effects.

Fifth, the policy of vaccine mandates, while aiming to protect, took away people's liberty and autonomy over their bodies, damaged social relationships, caused higher unemployment, and, most importantly, contributed to vaccine hesitancy. In the future, governments should instead focus on information campaigns to address vaccine hesitancy and highlight the benefits of protecting loved ones and vulnerable communities to increase people's sense of collective responsibility, ultimately steering their decision-making. Moreover, if governments want higher vaccine uptake levels, subjective well-being measures such as mood and emotions must be prioritised going forward. Addressing how people feel, in general, towards vaccines and governments is vitally important when policymakers want to achieve higher vaccination rates.

Sixth, using subjective measures, such as the sentiment and emotions of people, is vitally important to reveal trends and monitor tension or dissatisfaction related to policy choices, which cannot be observed using traditional measures. Furthermore, measuring people's sentiment and emotions allows us to empirically predict real-world behaviours, enabling policymakers to take affirmative action to create positive sentiments and emotions. These data are particularly beneficial and relevant to governments during pandemics when there is a need to monitor societal developments and changes related to an event.

Lastly, Big Data and Big Data analytics used to derive the sentiments and emotions of populations in almost real-time are undoubtedly the most powerful tools to understand the intricacies within the vast amount of data generated from various sources during the COVID-19 pandemic. Undoubtedly, Big Data assisted policymakers in mitigating and managing the impact of the pandemic. In a time when almost real-time data was needed, no other data sources could be engaged to fulfil the real-time needs of knowledge related to COVID-19 regulations and attitudes towards vaccines. Unfortunately, engagement with Big Data is still low, and several governments and statistical offices have not utilised the full potential of Big Data. We have shown how Big Data analytics can be (and should be) used beyond the scope of the pandemic. We strongly recommend that policymakers introduce data derived from sentiment and emotions to their official data and use live dashboards to increase the swift observation of data changes to increase policymakers' response time.

Ultimately, learning from both the successes and failures related to non-pharmaceutical and pharmaceutical interventions of countries, governments and non-government agencies can be used to work towards a more resilient and prepared global response to health challenges, reinforcing trust and promoting vaccine acceptance.

"How often have I told you that when you have eliminated the impossible, whatever remains, however improbable, must be the truth?"
– Sherlock Holmes

GPSR Compliance

The European Union's (EU) General Product Safety Regulation (GPSR) is a set of rules that requires consumer products to be safe and our obligations to ensure this.

If you have any concerns about our products, you can contact us on ProductSafety@springernature.com

In case Publisher is established outside the EU, the EU authorized representative is:

Springer Nature Customer Service Center GmbH
Europaplatz 3
69115 Heidelberg, Germany

The manufacturer's authorised representative in the EU is Springer
Nature Customer Service Centre GmbH, Europaplatz 3, 69115 Heidelberg,
Germany. If you have any concerns regarding our products, please
contact ProductSafety@springernature.com

Printed and bound by CPI Group (UK) Ltd, Croydon, CR0 4YY
24/04/2026
02096316-0004